Reading 2 59 58 60 Marlow

LONDON

3

Southampton Portsmouth

1

N
W ⬡ E
S

St Malo

Mont St Michel 7

BRITTANY

4 5-6

7

Fougères 8

NORMANDY

9

10

CHEMIN DES PLANTAGENETS

LOIRE 11

12 Chinon

ANJOU 13 14 Richelieu

15

Poitiers

16

Saintes 19 18

17 Chalus
Chabrol

20 CHARENTE

SCAY

CHEMIN DE TOURS

Blaye 21

AQUITAINE

antander

Bordeaux 22

CAMINO
DEL NORTE 23

24

25 26

St Jean Pied de Port

IA

NAVARRE 28 27 PYRENEES

32 30 Pamplona

ango 31 29

RIOJA Puente la Reina

'A vivid, beautifully written and often moving book, skilfully dovetailing memoir, history, art and a cycling pilgrimage across Europe into a unique and uplifting whole. If you think you know who Timmy Mallett is, you're in for a rewarding surprise!'
Professor Brian Cox

'This is a journey brimming with love and laughter that's also deeply moving. Timmy's glass isn't just half full, it's positively overflowing!'
Lorraine Kelly

'There are not many people who would put themselves through this much to achieve their dream. Timmy has always aimed for the summit and, most importantly, always remembers to smile and take time to reflect along the way.'
Chris Evans

'A beautiful, life-affirming book. It shows Timmy in a new light and demonstrates his talents and astonishing versatility.'
Wendy Craig

'Timmy Mallett, I still have my WAC PAC and all its contents! You're the kind of hero who has probably influenced me more than I realise. What a lovely man!'
Keith Lemon

'Funny, fascinating and insightful, just like Timmy himself. A must read for anyone who likes an adventure.'
Yvette Fielding

'The world is a dark and confusing place to be right now, but there are still times that make a person glad to be in it. Timmy's journey throughout this book is one of them.'
The Secret Footballer

'I loved this book. It's absolutely delightful. An adventure told in a uniquely Timmy way, full of humour and charm.'
Michaela Strachan, from the Foreword

Timmy Mallett is a popular English TV presenter, broadcaster, entertainer, artist and cyclist. Curiosity and wonder at the world are his inspiration.

The illustrations throughout this book are all by Timmy. The pen-and-ink line drawings reflect the places, people and issues covered in each chapter. Paintings include watercolour and acrylic pieces he produced on location throughout the cycling Camino and oil paintings completed in the Mallett studio from sketches and images made along the journey.

You can see more of his artwork and purchase prints at <www.mallettspallette.co.uk> or follow the art links from <www.timmymallett.co.uk>.

This Camino is a personal adventure inspired by Timmy's older Down's syndrome brother, Martin. Each day was marked with Martin Mallett name tags as a reminder of his example to reach your potential, and their location is revealed in the maps on the endpapers. Use the key on pages ix–xii to find every secret place.

There are more photos from Timmy's Camino at <www.timmymallett.co.uk/camino>. If you find one of Martin's name tags, please leave it there and tell Timmy!

Twitter @TimmyMallett
Facebook @TheTimmyMallett
Instagram @Timmy.Mallett
Strava @ Timmy Mallett

TIMMY MALLETT

Utterly Brilliant!

spck

First published in Great Britain in 2020

Society for Promoting Christian Knowledge
36 Causton Street
London SW1P 4ST
www.spck.org.uk

Copyright acknowledgements can be found on pp. 321–2.

British Library Cataloguing-in-Publication Data
A catalogue record for this book is available from the British Library

ISBN 978–0–281–08387–9
eBook ISBN 978–0–281–08320–6

1 3 5 7 9 10 8 6 4 2

Typeset in 13/16½ pt Minion Pro by Falcon Oast Graphic Art Ltd
Printed in Great Britain by TJ International

eBook by Falcon Oast Graphic Art Ltd

Produced on paper from sustainable forests

Contents

Key to the map

The map locations are listed in the table on the following pages. Each place has its GPS and what3words link.

If you ever come across one of the Martin Mallett name tags I left at each of these locations, I'd love to know (please leave it there!). what3words is the simplest way to talk about location. Every three-metre square in the world has been given a three-word address. Now you can refer to any precise location using just three dictionary words. For example, in Chapter 6 I left a name tag in the castle gate at Angers, which can be found at the three-word address, ///itself.tickets.removed.

Use the free what3words app to search for the other three-word addresses I encountered along my journey. Simply download the free app via the QR code below or use <what 3words.com> to get started.

Key to the map

Location number	Description	GPS co-ordinates	what3words address
1	Broken chain on Blackamoor lane, Maidenhead	51.529287, -0.714604	///wage.coins.cover
2	War memorial @ Axford	51.1855000, -1.1283056	///improvise.stutter.broad
3	Bishop's Palace @ Winchester	51.058851, -1.310727	///replayed.belly.hikes
4	St Malo fence post	48.6842500, -1.9637222	///finely.mature.confident
5	In town wall *Maison du pèlerin* @ Mont St Michel	48.6366944, -1.5104722	///errands.whereas.watched
6	Under statue Église Saint-Pierre @ Mont St Michel	48.6361667, -1.5100833	///shipyards.scraped.damaging
7	Chapel, Église Notre-Dame @ Pontorson	48.5546389, -1.5104444	///grouchy.economy.awaken
8	Churchyard Église @ Montautour	48.2044167, -1.1474722	///albatross.oxidation.supplemental
9	Le Rideau Mine B & B @ Lion d'Angers	47.640610, -0.688628	///scuffled.incidentally.forget
10	Église Saint-Martin @ Grez-Neuville	47.6030000, -0.6876389	///incarnation.reworking.infancy
11	Castle gate @ Angers	47.4703889, -0.5590833	///itself.tickets.removed
12	Rock @ Béhuard	47.379963, -0.643676	///customs.untimely.hogwash
13	Vineyard @ Grézillé	47.3189444, -0.3374722	///bleach.fondest.sightsee
14	Next to Eleanor @ Fontevraud Abbey	47.1815000, 0.0518333	///decreasing.flunked.reinstate
15	Waymarker @ Signy	46.7517222, 0.3277222	///harden.programmers.monitored
16	Église Saint-André @ St Benoit	46.549427, 0.341123	///storage.punk.clash
17	Grosbot @ Champagne-Mouton	46.008435, 0.405134	///behinds.luncheon.earphones
18	St Hilaire Church @ Melle	46.2199722, -0.1496111	///tidiness.misused.eradicate
19	St Eutrope Church crypt @ Saintes	45.7434722, -0.6413333	///signal.guardian.park
20	Pilgrim shelter @ St Léger	45.6169444, -0.5758333	///bendable.screeched.hugely

Location number	Description	GPS co-ordinates	what3words address
21	Vineyard on Rue Sainte-Luce @ Blaye	45.1153611, -0.6488889	///defiance. scorecards.easiest
22	St James statue, Basilique Saint-Seurin @ Bordeaux	44.8432500, -0.5856944	///progress.land.daisy
23	Pilgrim statue outside @ old church Moustey	44.3599722, -0.7612778	///declares.swooshed.scoped
24	Pilgrim auberge @ Lesperon	43.9693611, -1.0930278	///chimpanzee. cranky.storming
25	Route de Cazordite @ Cagnotte	43.6177500, -1.0685833	///bedrock. monarchies.defer
26	Croix de Galcetabaru @ D933 Gamarthe	43.210855, -1.137330	///pumping.huskily.pitches
27	Ermita de San Salvador @ top of the pass Roncesvalles	43.0202222, -1.3241944	///minty.aboriginal.pieced
28	Side altar, Church of St Nicholas @ Pamplona	42.815706, -1.644814	///runways.salt.incomes
29	Memorial post, statues @ Alto del Perdon	42.735762, -1.742681	///director.coldly.crisp
30	Wine fountain @ Monastery Santa Maria de Irache	42.650871, -2.043526	///contestants.poach.lisping
31	Behind altarpiece, Church of La Asunción @ Navarrete	42.4296389, -2.5612500	///turkey.unhook.purchases
32	Ruin of church of Valdefuentes @ Villafranca opposite rest area on N120	42.364183, -3.369738	///medicines. comforter.rusted
33	Choir stalls @ Burgos Cathedral	42.3408056, -3.7043889	///tiling.toast.blur
34	Wall opposite Albergue Juan de Yepes @ Hontanas	42.312761, -4.042950	///packets.billowing.garlics
35	Under St James statue, Church of St Martin @ Frómista	42.2666944, -4.4069167	///lawyers.resurface.sags
36	Arch of San Benito @ Sahagún	42.3710000, -5.0335833	///deliveries.radical.repute
37	Bridge wall @ Hospital de Órbigo	42.4640556, -5.8786111	///point.homily.ribcage
38	Tree by cross of Santo Toribio @ Astorga	42.454099, -5.999821	///cocktail.scuttle.quota
39	Rood screen gap @ Astorga Cathedral	42.4578889, -6.0568889	///beanpole.plop.giraffe
40	Iron cross	42.4888333, -6.3614167	///hesitation.ample.inked

Key to the map

Location number	Description	GPS co-ordinates	what3words address
41	Bench on the Camino de Invierno above river Sil reservoir	42.4143333, -6.8351111	///murmured.thrill.granite
42	Fountain on LU617 near O Eivedo	42.5485000, -7.5856944	///beefed.flinching.trivia
43	Round bellrope of Church of San Salvador @ Vilasante	42.5825833, -7.6316111	///overall.coffeehouse.decode
44	Wayside stone memorial @ Chantada	42.6160556, -7.7788611	///shuts.quells.restless
45	Santiago Cathedral @ left of grille before tomb of St James	42.880642, -8.544311	///jingles.vision.refrain
46	Lighthouse Finisterre opposite iron boot	42.881772, -9.271963	///contraband.horseback.foots
47	In wall in front of Muxia Chapel	43.112094, -9.219960	///amaze.blipped.stardust
48	Cypress trees @ pilgrim statues Mont Gosso, Santiago	42.8846667, -8.4943056	///spanner.hefty.supermarkets
49	Tree by Chapel of Carmen @ Melide	42.9137222, -8.0188333	///mastery.examples.sieving
50	Tree by the Chapel of San Román de Retorta	42.9555000, -7.7376111	///whiling.pies.spoof
51	Lintel of workman's hut @ stream by water trough, Fonsagrada	43.158818, -6.991575	///overpay.lovable.custodial
52	On the lookout @ dam	43.236403, -6.843092	///glittering.direct.butting
53	Bike puncture on the AS14 on the way to Montefurado, Asturias	43.260423, -6.707127	///conceive.ammonia.nimbly
54	Oviedo Cathedral @ gold side altarpiece	43.3626111, -5.8431667	///supreme.pots.upstairs
55	Bend on AS331 @ Camino sign in wall	43.4040278, -5.6274444	///boats.oppose.walking
56	Chapel of Cantu on Camino @ Colombres	43.374647, -4.530864	///explode.instance.dilutes
57	Fountain @ Santander Cathedral	43.4613611, -3.8074167	///wrong.bikers.mute
58	Barton's Mill @ Old Basing	51.272946, -1.053359	///vision.oiled.stored
59	Pilgrim Chapel, St James Church @ Reading	51.457040, -0.965355	///broom.dating.lamps
60	Behind lectern @ Holy Trinity Church Cookham	51.561370, -0.707223	///phones.fleet.tight

Foreword

Full of warmth and wit, facts and fun, thought provoking and thoughtful, entertaining and a tad eccentric . . . am I talking about the book or about Timmy? Well, both actually.

Timmy and I have known each other since 1986, when I joined the presenting team of the Saturday morning kids' programme, the *Wide Awake Club*. We instantly clicked. I loved his sense of humour, his passionate interest in everything, his unique talent as an entertainer and his enviable gift as an artist. He was fiercely determined, always up for a challenge and ever so slightly bonkers! So when Timmy told me he was planning to cycle the Camino de Santiago from his home in Berkshire – an extraordinary 3,500-kilometre journey there and back – on his own, and painting along the way, I wasn't too surprised. The last time I did a bike ride with Timmy was in 1987; we filmed the *Wide Awake Club* team doing the London to Brighton cycle ride, a mere 89 km. Timmy's Camino is only, well, 28 times that distance and Timmy is at least 32 years older! Could he really complete the challenge?

I never doubted it.

Once Timmy makes a plan, he sees it through to the end, no matter what the obstacles. He made it to Santiago de Compostela and this fantastic book tells the tale of his adventure. *Utterly Brilliant: My life's journey* is a feel-good read. It cleverly interweaves Timmy's challenging two-month cycle ride with the history of the Camino, told in his unique and captivating way. It includes hugely enjoyable anecdotes from Timmy's past; the inspiration for and the intriguing stories behind his numerous paintings; and the heart-warming reason why 'reaching your potential' means so much to him.

Timmy, what a journey your life has been. And what an undertaking the Camino turned out to be. I laughed at the stories I thought I knew, but clearly didn't know fully. I cried at the endearing way you talk about your brother Martin, and I pondered the lessons we can all learn from making the most of each journey and not just heading blindly to our destination.

I loved this book. It's absolutely delightful. An adventure told in a uniquely Timmy way, full of humour and charm. I hope you enjoy it as much as I did.

Michaela Strachan, friend and TV presenter

Prologue

Once upon a time, something went missing . . .

It's a warm Friday evening at the beginning of August, and the world has gone away on holiday. Those friends of mine who are still here are heading to the pub after five-a-side football. 'Join us at the pub for a beer, Timmy, and tell us about your Camino . . .'

The light is fading as I cycle over the causeway through the village. I may spend the night on the trampoline in the garden tonight and fall asleep watching the satellites and shooting stars.

It's really quiet at the pub, hardly a soul around. A couple of cars in the car park. Nobody at the bar. We head into the garden with our pints and it's a great hour or so putting the world to rights, talking nonsense till they want to close up. The football season starts tomorrow – son Billy is going to Barnsley v Oxford away, and there's Gateshead at home for Maidenhead. I look around at my friends and count myself lucky to have such great pals. Friends are really special. They laugh at your jokes, they share your adventures, they rejoice at your successes and commiserate with you in your disappointments. They encourage you, they give you a sense of perspective, occasionally they even buy you a beer. We call to each other as we head to the car park. 'See you over the weekend, tennis next week, have a good holiday, enjoy the night on the trampoline . . .'

My bike isn't there. A very nice Giant Explore 1, black with green trims, Timmeee E-bike with disc brakes, pannier racks, stand, blue saddle, battery and serial number EACA2631, with around 4,700 kilometres on the clock, has gone.

I chained it up by the wall in the well-lit parking area. Has someone moved it? Anyone seen something . . .? There's only one way into the car park under the single arch. My friends head off in different directions looking for the bike, or a suspicious vehicle.

My heart sinks. I can't believe it. You know that moment when you feel it's just a dream? Hope it's just a dream, or a bad joke gone wrong? But deep down, don't go there, because you know something you love really has been taken. Why do we have such ownership of things? Why does it feel like a bereavement? I know – it's just a bike.

Just a bike that for some reason has become my very best friend and reliable, dependable companion on the adventure of a lifetime. Cycling the Camino de Santiago, a thousand-year-old ancient pilgrimage route across Europe, from home – alone.

I've done plenty of big things. Really big things. I've been number one in the charts around the world with a million seller, 'Itsy Bitsy Teeny Weeny Yellow Polka Dot Bikini'; I've had hit TV programmes that are loved by generations, like the *Wide Awake Club* and *Wacaday*; I've got the biggest, funniest, most recognised prop ever – the giant foam Mallett's Mallet; I've hosted the loudest, fastest pop radio shows – *Timmy on the Tranny*; I've headlined packed, sell-out pantomime and theatre dates, run my own Brilliant TV production company, performed in stadiums and at the Royal Variety Performance, met stars and royalty; and I'm a collected fine artist with paintings on show across the world. And yet the biggest thing I've ever done I did for personal reasons, solo across Europe, inspired by someone very dear, to reach my potential, on a bicycle – the bicycle that has been nicked from my local pub while I laughed and chatted with my friends.

1

An ominous beginning

It's a grey, damp, drizzly day with a cold wind, in the middle of an emotionally unsettling March, and Mrs Mallett wakes up, turns to me and says, 'All right, Malley, this is it. How are you feeling?'

A big long sigh and I rub my tummy, something I seem to do to comfort myself, and roll out of that lovely warm bed, thinking, *It's going to be the middle of May before I enjoy these sheets again.*

I don't have to do it.

It's my choice.

I put my things out on the chair last night. I like the feeling of preparation; it means I haven't got to worry this morning about what to wear. Anyway, it's not as if there's a lot of options ... Over the next two months I'm cycling with a couple of changes of clothes and some extra layers for the freezing cold days – like today. It promises to get up to an almost balmy 9 or 10 degrees Celsius, so I'm wearing padded longs, knee-length shorts with lots of pockets, merino undershirt, green lycra vest, two pairs of socks (warm, thin, knee-length socks and over the top a pair of clashing coloured ankle socks in case I get cold); I've got my neck buff, cycle jumper and the high-vis, map-of-Europe top last worn on my TV show *Wacaday* in 1990 and found in the collection of 'Wow! I wonder when I'll ever wear that again?' tops. I love it, it looks great, and with a map on my chest there's a chance I might not get lost. I've also got on a Christchurch College Oxford tie, gifted to me by the porters in the lodge when I met the Bishop of Oxford for a 'Good luck – you are going to need it' blessing last month. The blessing was in the stunning surroundings of Christchurch quad, and worked as far as the city boundary. When I reached Oxford United football ground I got a puncture. Hmmm. United's press officer, Chris Williams, was delighted and laughed. 'It's always exciting when you plan something, Timmy!'

That Christchurch tie is going to get heavier and heavier as I pin badges to it all along the way. I've made a typically nutty Timmy decision to wear it every day. Cyclists don't wear ties; and I haven't worn one since the last funeral I went to. Oh, hang on, that was two days ago, over 500 miles away, in Aberdeen: my older brother Martin, who with Down's syndrome and language and learning difficulties had lived 64 filled years, died last week. 'Ma bubba' Martin has always been the inspiration for my Camino – to reach my potential, as he did, with all the challenges he faced every day. Now it feels even more important.

I can't let him down. I'm carrying my brother's memory and his courage, and I'm determined to live each day with his example in my heart. Martin always wore a tie and was the best-dressed Mallett in all our family. I've decided to follow his example and dress for the occasion.

The occasion is to cycle alone, from home, across three European countries to Santiago de Compostela in north-west Spain and back again, painting the adventure as I go.

I've always made a Mallett statement through the things I've worn. Colour has always been key in my fashion sense. One Thursday night I saw Trevor Horn of the Buggles on *Top of the Pops* singing 'Video Killed the Radio Star'. He was wearing bright red glasses and I was immediately struck by them. I've worn specs since the age of seven and when I saw Trevor's on TV I went straight into town and had my own pair made. The optician understood what I wanted from the photo I showed him and his lab created them – the first in my collection of fabulous glasses. I began with that blood-red pair, then had bright blue, followed by a pink fluorescent pair that came from the optician's chuck-out drawer, where they keep frames they can't get rid of until Mallett walks in. During *Wacaday* I came across a company in London that manufactured custom designs, and so began the great collection of several hundred pairs I have today. The only downside is that my prescription has changed over the years and trying to read through lenses that are three decades old can be a little tricky.

Next up after the red specs was the multicoloured hair. Red, emerald, yellow and purple. 'He's quite safe really,' Mum explained to the neighbours when I visited. On *Wacaday* I made my dress sense part of the uniform for Wideawakers. One leg of your shorts rolled up; two caps – twin peaks; odd socks.

Let's make a statement. One day I may even get around to

having the colours match. At least I'll be seen on the bike and that's got to be a good thing, surely?

I linger over my favourite breakfast – a poached egg, baked beans and mushrooms, and toast thick with my homemade Mallett marmalade – contemplating what is about to unfold.

Son Billy the Gardener is working nearby. 'Are you sure you don't want to change your mind? Oxford are at home to Peterborough on Saturday and Maidenhead are playing Barrow. How can you miss all those matches? What if we make the playoffs?'

'I've got the notebook packed for predictions,' I tell him. There are 28 of us each week that predict the scores for every match in Oxford United's league and Maidenhead United's game. Winner at the end of the season gets glory. Billy gives me a withering, compassionate smile that says: 'You won't be able to keep that up every week.' Just you wait.

Friends turn up to watch me pack the bike. Terry, in lycra, to pedal the first couple of miles or so, and Andy, in his suit, on the way to work.

'Hi, Andy. What was number one on the day you got married?' I greet him the same way every time and we both know the answer.

'You were, Timmy, with "Itsy Bitsy"! And what was number one when you Malletts were married?'

'I was, Andy, with "Itsy Bitsy"!'

All great adventures begin with a single footstep, or a push on the pedals and a turn of the wheels on my Giant Timmeee Explore 1 touring E-bike. It's quite a sight to see how the bike is loaded each day. I'm methodical and try to close my ears to any passing comments as I attach the two red waterproof panniers on either side of the rack with their sewn-on fluorescent painted scallop shells.

'Spectacles, testicles, phone and Mallett!' I say every morning as I pack up all I need. 'Have you got a puncture repair kit? Will you remember which side of the road to cycle on?' Then the waterproof dry bag with A3-size artboards and my bag of essential acrylic colours and brushes goes over the top, with a backpack that will act as my day bag, including watercolour pads and paints and the wet weather poncho on top of that. It's all held in place by a bungee cargo net. On the handlebars is a bar bag in which I keep my sketchbook, diary, maps, spare phone, pilgrim passport and snacks, as well as my stone from home, good luck letters and sunglasses. (Wonder if I'll get to wear them anytime?) And a roll of the all-important Martin Mallett name tags, that I don't know yet will come to mark my journey.

I've also got a medical emergency kit with plasters and paracetamol under the saddle.

The panniers weigh nine kilos, the painting things another seven kilos, charger and day bag add another five; and then there's me. That's a total of over 90 kilos on this bicycle. Ride safely, Mr Mallett. Don't come home dead.

We get out Mrs Mallett's bike and our little group sets off through the village to Holy Trinity Church, where I'm surprised to find ten people waiting in the drizzle to send me on my way and looking forward to getting a cuppa after I've left (so make it quick, Timmy). Nick the Vic wants to say a little prayer for me. 'I can do better than the bishop!' he begins. 'Be your guide at the crossroads, strength in your weariness, defence against dangers, shelter on the way, a comforter in discouragements and firmness in your intentions.' Nothing about being a help with any bike issues. I go off singing 'It's a long way to Santiago . . .', detour around people on the path past the yew trees and swing out through the gravestones.

There are four of us for the first mile: Mrs Mallett, Terry (videoing us), Stevie my companion for three days, to make sure I get safely to France, and me at the front with the wind in my face as we cross the wild and lovely common and ride along to Boulter's Lock on the River Thames in Maidenhead. Everyone knows how I like to stop at every opportunity and here's a chance to see the new footbridge, the swans and the instructions in English, Polish and Romanian: 'Please don't jump in the river'. Stevie has a little gift for me, a hip flask engraved 'Timmy – Home to Santiago 2018 *Buen Viaje*'. We've been friends for 30 years, since he was my cameraman on *Wacaday* at TV-am. You can imagine the sort of wacky nonsense he is used to seeing. Originally from the sparkling city of Dundee, Stevie's married to Lorraine Kelly on the telly, we play five-a-side football together with the Wanderers and we are part of a group of bike pals who like to go exploring on two wheels. 'I'll come with you for the first few days and keep an eye on you,' he says. Half a mile later my chain snaps. Fat lot of good, that blessing from the vicar! Both bishop and priest's blessings lasted only as far as the parish boundary.

Statistics say that you are most likely to have an accident within five miles of home. The drizzle is coming down and I've done barely a mile of my adventure. I'm standing by the bike with a broken chain, not quite sure what to do. Mrs Mallett offers to go home and get the car and bike rack, just in case. Terry helpfully takes photos as I stand forlorn on the roadside and make a call to Paul at Flat Harry's Cyclery.

'How are you getting on?' he asks.

I tell him.

Howls of laughter down the phone. 'OK, give me a few minutes.' And God bless him, he's my Good Samaritan and drives out to fit a new link in the chain.

Ian the photographer from the paper turns up too, grinning delightedly. What a scoop! Mallett looking pathetic with a broken chain and going nowhere. Tony Prince, radio's Royal Ruler, likewise says, 'What a great story for my show!'

I'm not a lot of help here. I had a very good lesson on how to fix a chain only last week from mobile bike man Rich. But embarrassingly I keep quiet and watch as someone else puts it together with ease. 'That should do you,' says Paul, which doesn't really sound as reassuring as it might do.

'What do you mean – should?' Oh no, that's something else to worry about. I've been given stern words by my family. 'Keep off main roads. Don't do anything foolish, look after yourself and be aware of your surroundings . . .'

I've recently been filming a fun segment for *Ant and Dec's Saturday Night Takeaway* and there were a bunch of household names gathered to do their part. Over lunch in the green room, the subject of my cycling the Camino cropped up. Gloria Hunniford, Alan Shearer, Noel Edmonds, Chris Moyles, Gareth Malone, Judy Murray . . . they looked at me in amazement and offered genuine messages of support and encouragement. The idea of raising awareness on reaching your potential started to resonate. A couple of people suggested my adventure would make a great TV series, but I'm not disappointed that there aren't TV cameras following me. This is a personal journey to be shared only with those who choose to follow it. Right now, I know TV would have loved it. Talk about a dramatic start.

Messages have come from lots of friends. Like Professor Brian Cox, one of my original Timmy helpers on the radio, whom I've known since he was 17. His happy smiling support is very welcome. Bear Grylls, the adventurer, knows what it takes to look after yourself; actress Wendy Craig is aware of the importance of being prepared to have a go, and offers to come along and sit on the panniers! My great friend, Michaela Strachan, reminds me how we rode the London to Brighton cycle ride over 30 years ago and that this will be tougher. Hmmm, I remember that day and how I was knocked off my bike and got a buckled wheel. She also offers this advice: 'Go with a smile on your face and love in your heart . . .' Nothing about a poncho for the rain, and a spare chain.

We've arranged to say farewell to home at the local paper next to the football ground, and an hour or so later than expected, they give us a cup of tea and wave me off. Mrs Mallett and I have a rather public kiss goodbye – the sort all long-married couples would recognise. Lips crushed, bodies turning already halfway ready to head to the shops – or Santiago. We plan to meet in France in ten days' time. The day is rushing away and there are nearly 40 miles to ride to Basingstoke.

Stevie and I still manage to find some funny photo opportunities, at the old ford and on the flooded shortcut that is really just a muddy track leading to an even muddier lake. And we get a shot outside El Camino's restaurant in Crowthorne – a fitting name for my Camino adventure.

I'm new to following the dotted-line route on my GPS, but I know the route . . . I think. Just in case, I've brought my trusty old Ordnance Survey map of the area. But I don't expect to find the Roman road under water, deluged by the Beast from the East, which has brought widespread snow and blizzards, heavy rain, floods and unusually utterly low temperatures across Britain and northern Europe. This means a diversion. And the map isn't quite up to date, so I ditch it with disdain. The young woman in the garden centre café runs out to hand it to me. 'No thanks, I don't really need it.' Mistake, Mallett. Should have kept hold of the thing . . .

It ought to be an easy ride, but it's an absolute stinker. My sense of direction seems to have evaporated; I don't trust my technology, I haven't got a map, and I can't picture where we are and how to find a nice safe cycle track. Somehow we get ourselves stuck on the fast and furious A30, after taking a turn the wrong way down a one-way road and rightly getting honked at. I've already broken my promise to friends and family not to ride on any main roads. My route on the Strava app looks as though we have no idea where we are going. Er, we don't. We take a detour through the woods along a footpath that quickly sinks into ankle-deep mud. By late afternoon I'm feeling anxious and annoyed. This isn't supposed to be such a difficult day. I planned a simple easy ride and I'm beginning to think the whole trip is madness. Maybe I'm affected by the enormity of what I'm trying to do; maybe the weight of expectation; maybe the grief. As Stevie reassuringly points out, 'Good job I'm with you; you are all over the place . . .' Perhaps it will be better tomorrow? I don't know. I'm sure I'm overloaded, and the saddle is uncomfortable. Why on earth am I attempting this? Surely it would make more sense to call it off now and go home?

Then I remember . . .

This is not a jolly jaunt.

It's not a holiday.

It's a pilgrimage with a purpose.

To reach my potential.

To make the most of every day.

To smile.

I'm staying the night with my cousin, Katy Cuz, and her lovely noisy family. 'It's Timmy in the toilet!' they cry. 'Bring the bike in, Cuz. Ah! No, don't. Where have you been? It's covered in mud. You're covered in mud. You're just a muddy mess!' I hose the bike, and thick clumps of glutinous cack swirl around my feet. I need a bath, and afterwards hand wash my things – something I will do every night for the next two months.

They all look at me in delighted horror. Mud, mess, Mallett. They seem to go together. It's been an eventful first day. Like most beginnings when you think you're prepared but really you aren't.

Some days are memorable. Like the first day at school. Shirt and tie that Mum tied, which ended up around the back of my neck. Shorts, long grey socks and a blazer that had been big brother Paul's, so it was far too large. The three silver buttons looked brilliant and with my hands in the pockets I looked taller. Best of all, with the blazer open I could flick the jacket out from side to side and it made me look as if I was running faster. I whizzed around the playground and ran into my best friend Jeremy, because I was looking behind at the blazer to see how fast I was going. I fell over and started crying. The teacher came over to see what had happened. 'I didn't do anything!' said my best friend. I got a sticking plaster and it looked good. At three o'clock the infants came out and I had to wait 15 minutes for Paul and the juniors to finish so we could walk home together. Some big boys came out and said, 'You're too small to go to school. Bet you're only three!'

'I'm five, blockhead!'

Paul arrived and we met Mum. 'How was school?' she asked.

'Jeremy blobbed me, I fell over and got a plaster and I told the big boys I was five, blockhead!' It was a good first school day.

I'm glad the olden days have gone. They might make a nice story about growing up, but it's a whole lot better now. And there's colour too . . .

'Are you sure about this, Cuz? It's not like a *Wacaday* trip,' says Katy.

TV *Wacaday* trips are usually good fun – stressful, a bit, for the director: 'Have we got all the shots? Have we been fair and funny?' My job is to carry a range of colourful clothes that clash, lots of different shaped bright specs and the big Mallett's Mallet in its special bag marked 'Top Secret', and think of as many fun gags as we can stick into each story. The hardest part is long days in the minibus, wondering if I'll be accepted by the locals when I start dressing up and acting like Timmy Mallett. This Camino is not the same sort of trip . . . I think.

The pizza this evening is the best ever. We talk quietly about Martin, and how this journey really started in the far north-east of Scotland at his funeral a couple of days ago. Earlier, in the eulogy, we heard how Martin would unusually bless the parish priest. Mostly, we ask other people for encouragement. How often do we offer it? Brother Martin had some impressive gifts.

There had been the little task of boxing up his belongings: photo albums, CDs, cufflinks – things that we keep to remind ourselves of who we are and where we fit into our families and friends. I was glad that big brother Paul had sorted through Martin's clothes – his collection of smart ties and shirt-sleeve holders; the suits and braces. There was a bundle of Martin Mallett name tags, the things that Mum sews into your clothes so you don't lose them at school. 'Do you want these?' asked Paul and an idea started forming. I put them in my things to take on the Camino. I wondered if I could use them somehow to record the journey.

Katy and I put a name tag on the star in the little collection of memories on her kitchen shelf. It's a handy reminder of why on earth I am attempting such a trip.

2

Hand me a reason for this madness

Now here's a question. What's the connection between a mid-week dinner party 2,000 years ago, the unusual wedding gift presented to William the Conqueror's granddaughter, a Prime Minister on her day off from trying to juggle Brexit, and a cycling artist on a mission to pedal halfway across Europe, during a winter that never seemed to end, leaving brotherly name tags along the way?

There has to be a reason for getting on your bike and heading off into the unknown like this . . .

The Thursday night dinner party is one of the most famous supper gatherings in history.

The charismatic speaker, with 12 of his friends, met in an upstairs room in Jerusalem for the Last Supper. Two brothers (James and John) sat either side of the big man and the conversation was strange and full of instructions about how to share a meal. They passed around a glass of wine to the others and shortly afterwards one of those friends betrayed their leader. For a little while, in the following months, James headed up the fledgling Christian movement.

His letter in the Bible is one of the first instruction manuals to the early Church in the early years after the crucifixion, and it's got a couple of good points that resonate with me: be nice to people you meet along the way and don't gossip too much.

I'm not sure you could call James the greatest of preachers. On his missionary trip to Spain he came back with barely a handful of converts; he landed at the wrong place at the wrong time and promptly had his head cut off. That's not a great CV entry.

It all looked to be over very quickly.

James and his severed head were sailed back to Spain (rumour has it on a stone boat, which would have made it rather a tricky journey – I presume it's an analogy for 'this was not a jolly'), and came ashore in Galicia surrounded by scallop shells. The scallop shell became a symbol of St James, and you see it everywhere. He was buried in a delightful spot in a starlit field, and they poetically named it Santiago de Compostela – Saint James in the field of stars. James then quietly disappeared from the story and was forgotten for about 700 years until . . .

Locals needed a hero to lead them in revolt against the occupying Muslims. James appeared at just the right time, on a white horse with a sword, and, as in all good stories, the legend says he delivered Spain from captivity. A very good reason to make him patron saint of the country.

And with that dramatic victory began a never-ending tradition of pilgrimage to his tomb in Santiago's magnificent cathedral. The numbers grew and grew, especially when the Crusades put the Holy Land out of reach and a papal schism made Rome less attractive. Arguments, gossiping, falling out with people. Ho hum. Thus has it been since Adam was a young lad in short trousers.

For more than a thousand years pilgrims, carrying their badge of the scallop shell, have come from all across Europe to Santiago. Forget backpacking around Southeast Asia, this is a gap-year trip that anyone and everyone has made. In 1212 St Francis of Assisi walked there and back, talking to the birds and the animals, no doubt. (Well, they wouldn't gossip, would they?)

It was a high-water mark of medieval pilgrimage. All these people coming to see a silver tomb supposedly containing the remains of one of the 12 Apostles. (I wonder where the other 11 are. And can you name them?) Except for one slightly awkward fact. Not quite all James's remains were there . . .

In the depths of a cold winter in January 1114, the 12-year-old granddaughter of William the Conqueror, Matilda, married the Holy Roman Emperor at a glittering spectacular ceremony at Mainz in Germany. For her wedding present she was given a massive crown and the left hand of St James the Apostle. (Nowadays, she would probably have preferred some make-up, a new mobile phone or a 'Keep calm I'm nearly a teenager' T-shirt.)

When her husband succumbed to cancer shortly afterwards, Matilda headed home to her dad, King Henry I of England, taking with her the crown ('That'll look good in London') and the Hand of St James. Daddy was delighted and put the hand in pride of place in his new abbey in the Thames Valley in Reading. As he predicted, the hand was a massive hit among pilgrims, and for 400 years was a huge tourist attraction. There was even a secret viewing platform for the money monks, who checked to see how big a donation was left by each pilgrim.

But all things must pass, and when King Henry VIII needed a divorce from his first wife, Catherine of Aragon, and the Pope (her nephew's prisoner) wouldn't oblige, Henry made himself head of the Church of England. The next step was monastic reform, and for that he went the whole hog and closed all the monasteries and abbeys, and seized their assets. This was the biggest, most spectacular land grab in English history.

That's when the bailiffs went along to Reading Abbey and did an inventory: 'gold crucifix, candlesticks, treasures, Hand of St James . . . etc.'. The abbot, Hugh of Faringdon, tried to stop them, saying, 'I'm a friend of the king.' It didn't work. To show they meant business, the bailiffs took him outside and hanged him from the entrance gate. Dear Hugh was 80 years old.

'We'll be back tomorrow with the wagons . . .'

So with a gasp and gulp and 'We'd better not end up like the abbot . . .', that night the terrified monks hid the Hand of St James in a secret hole in the abbey walls, where it remained for the next 250 years.

I love these stories. They last for ever!

In October 1786 when the ruins of Reading Abbey were being cleared to make way for a brand-new public building – Reading gaol – workmen discovered a box in the wall in which was a mummified left hand. You can imagine their reaction: 'What do we do with this? Chuck it on the fire, give it to the police, or what?' The simplest answer was to give it to Reading Museum to deal with, and in a time of austerity (they always come around at convenient moments) the museum sold it to a collector for the grand sum of £30. Remember that scoundrel Judas, who betrayed his pal for 30 pieces of silver? Spooky.

The collector put the hand on show in his chapel at Danesfield Manor on the River Thames (where film star George Clooney celebrated his wedding). When Danesfield didn't want it any more – hotels don't tend to be keen on having such things in the dining room – the Hand of St James was gifted to the new Catholic church of St Peter's being built by Pugin (the architect responsible for the Houses of Parliament) in Marlow, and that's where the hand is today. (Around the corner from where Mary Shelley wrote *Frankenstein*. Weird.) Just a few miles from my house and right on the edge of the constituency of a Prime Minister overloaded with Brexit negotiations, but interested in meeting a constituent with an unusual story to share.

So here I am, cycling to Santiago de Compostela and the tomb of St James, where most of his remains are, when I could just go on a morning cycle ride across the bridge to Marlow and see his hand. Is this significant? I don't know.

Let's see if day two can be any easier than day one. Sometimes you need a nine-year-old to show you how the world works. At Cousin Katy's this morning, I can't empty the wash basin – the plug is stuck, and I think I've broken something. Logan looks at me with pity as he presses the plug side and it swivels and empties. Youngsters have their uses.

Katy is making egg-in-the-hole this morning. 'What's that?'

Now all three boys look at me in amazement. 'It's the breakfast of champions, and you need it!'

This calls for a slice of bread, a circle cutter, an egg, a frying pan. Bread in the pan, egg in the hole, fry one side, flip it over, fry the other side, put the circle of toast on top of the egg and pretend it's not there. Smother in ketchup – food of the gods! I've discovered so much on a family overnight stay.

We walk to school so Jed can proudly show me off to his

teacher, a surprised Wideawaker. 'This is my cousin Timmy Mallett. He had egg-in-the-hole this morning and now he's riding his bike to France and Spain.'

Terry is joining Stevie and me as far as Winchester. I was whingeing yesterday and worried about comfort, so he's brought me two spare saddles, and a discussion ensues.

'Which is the saddle you usually prefer?'

'The one I've got on the bike.'

'Well, then it's psychological. You're worrying about it because your mind is in worrying mode. You'll be fine with it. Don't give it another thought.' He's right. Then an even better piece of advice: 'Take a drink every 20 minutes whether you need it or not. You need to keep hydrated.' Good comment. All day every day I will hear that little instruction and chuckle at my friend's voice. It certainly makes me pee more, but then I know the advice is working.

The proud Basingstoke locals call it 'Amazinstoke', and Basingstoke's colourful parks are covered in crocuses as we follow cycle route 23 up to the delightfully named Farleigh Wallop and through happy Hampshire lanes of trimmed hedges and celandines. This is special, the three of us pedalling, sunshine and thatched villages and hardly a soul about. I love England. Country lanes, clouds, happy days. At the village of Axford, we stop to admire the daffodils and I slide a Martin Mallett name tag into the cracks of the wooden beams of the war memorial. There's a quiet nod of approval from my friends, and at the village phone box, now turned into a second-hand book share, I leave my Cycling Artist card in the window. A little different from other postcards you find in phone boxes . . .

Red telephone boxes are part of the street furniture we love. In Parliament Square, tourists queue up to have their photo taken beside them, and one of my Mallett paintings I most enjoyed is that of the row of seven iconic phone boxes in Preston at night and a figure walking past in the rain – on her mobile!

TV personality Esther Rantzen got in touch. Would I paint a fibreglass phone box in aid of Childline? It was delivered to my home and over the next few weeks I portrayed members of the royal family on each side – the Queen on the phone, the Duchess of Cambridge on her mobile, Prince Harry doing his Usain Bolt pose, all draped in a Union Jack with the royal standard over the roof. The project evolved as I included as many little touches as I could. 'Itsy Bitsy' polka dots because that was one of Catherine's first favourite records; Pinky Punky because William and Harry would watch *Wacaday* with their mother, Princess Diana. I added the Queen's favourite corgi dog at her feet and my signature is down at the bottom there too, so that as you look for it, you bow your head to Her Majesty. Meghan, Duchess of Sussex, is wrapped in the Union Jack to symbolise embracing her new country. The box has been on public display at the Royal Albert Hall, the O2 Arena, in Windsor opposite the castle, in Bristol by the suspension bridge and at Blackpool Pleasure Beach. Many have tried to get inside, but the door doesn't open, so you have to do your selfies outside, next to your favourite side, and share them with #RingARoyal.

Have you ever compared screensavers on your friends' phones? I was intrigued to discover that Chris Evans's Jewish agent, Michael Cohen, collects cathedral images, ever since his family took him as a child around the medieval stone masterpieces of England. Winchester has a brilliant cathedral, with monuments to two great women I admire: Joan of Arc, whose career lasted a matter of months (and who will pop up again on my Camino), and Jane Austen, whose books are among the finest in the English language, and whose memorial is delightfully modest and can easily be missed.

22

William the Conqueror headed to Winchester before taking London, in order to get his hands on the royal mint. His son Henry dashed here on the evening of 2 August 1100, just hours after the 'unfortunate' death of his brother, King William II, in a hunting accident in the New Forest. Henry was after the dosh too. I can imagine the impact he would have made, banging on the door surrounded by heavily armed followers and demanding the custodian hand over the valuables. Fortune favours the brave, the loudest and most threatening. Henry was a man in a hurry, and he had the crown on his head in Westminster Abbey just three days later. In Winchester Castle is the Round Table that Edward III had made to recreate King Arthur's court. I like the idea of kings playing at being kings. It's a sort of real-life *Game of Thrones*.

I knock on a different Winchester door and am surprised when Bishops' House is opened by Bishop Tim Dakin himself, who admires my tie. 'Hello, Timmy. Are you a Christchurch alumni then?' I had envisaged a few minutes together having my bike pannier and pilgrim passport signed, and a photo taken, before Stevie and I go on our way. Instead we're greeted with tea and biscuits and a discussion in the bishop's office about his role in the church, including the importance of recognising changing attitudes to sexuality. It's a refreshing conversation and I wonder where the Hand of St James and relics fit into today's spirituality, if indeed they have any relevance at all.

What are the catalysts for faith? That's a little tricky to answer. Think I'll leave it as a query in the in tray . . . We lay one of Martin's name tags by the daffodils on the altar of Tim's private chapel and I ask for a proper bishop's blessing with crook in hand. Now, this looks the business. Martin's presence, the bishop's crook . . . It's a powerful way to use grief to remind me to reach my potential. The bishop's chaplain, Mat Phipps, is a real bonus. Mat lived in Spain, speaks fluent Spanish, and has walked part of the Camino. I'm delighted and encouraged when he produces the letter of Spanish introduction he's written to Archbishop Julian of Santiago. It isn't his last help either in smoothing the way to an unexpected and climactic meeting in six weeks' time.

On the cycle route out of Winchester, at the start of a long, surprisingly warm afternoon, I admire the skeletal winter trees, the verges thick with daffodils and celandines, the village ponds overhung with mossy boughs. We laugh at the *Dad's Army* signpost in the village of Upham – 'They don't like it Upham', you know! There's a strange altercation with teenage travellers on horseback outside a village store. My greeting to them, 'That looks fun!', is misinterpreted and I get a mouthful of colourful, threatening abuse. How we are perceived in the world is not always obvious. We ride down to Gosport and take the passenger ferry across Portsmouth Harbour.

Portsmouth has a connection to our family. It was here that Eisenhower made his fateful decision to launch the second front during the Second World War – D-Day. In spring 1944 my mum received a telegram: 'Corporal Foster [her maiden name] report immediately to Supreme Headquarters Allied Expeditionary Force. Repeat Immediately.' Mum became secretary to Group Captain James Stagg, responsible for the D-Day weather forecasts. Every morning she would pin up the forecasts for the Normandy landing beaches and General Eisenhower would come into the map room and greet her, saying, 'Ah, Corporal. The weather . . .' She was one of very few who knew where the landings were to take place on the Normandy beaches, and the proposed date in early June. As the day grew nearer, the weather deteriorated. Low pressure, rain and storms dominated the English Channel, and with thousands of troops in place on their ships, things looked increasingly bleak. 'Put these headphones on, Corporal,' said her boss, 'and you will hear the advice of the forecasters.' It was one of those early conference calls on scrambled, encoded top-secret lines. The military advisors all said that the weather made it too risky to proceed, until a junior forecaster pointed out a small ridge of high pressure rising over the Azores. 'It may, perhaps, bring twelve hours of calmer weather . . .' Eisenhower asked his generals what they thought and few were willing to commit. Finally, he took a breath, paused and said, 'Gentlemen, we'll go.' Mum noted the sigh of relief as the decision was taken. She removed the headphones, knowing she had heard history being made, and cycled home, alone, thinking of all the men and boats in the Channel heading off to their date with destiny. The prayer for the week was 'God give us grace to make a right judgement in all things . . .' and she wondered what German Christians might be praying that night.

I'm wondering what part the weather will play in my Camino.

Brittany Ferries have kindly arranged berths for us on their overnight *Pont-Aven* flagship ferry to St Malo, and as we sit down to dinner we consider the first two days and our dash to the coast. England has been wet, muddy, sunny and spring-like. The temperate climate that we like to bemoan is really benign and the familiarity of colourful little villages, abundant gardens and small meadows is very appealing. What will the weather be like in France? Nothing is predictable.

3

Brexit and the Camino

'Why don't you invite the Archbishop of Santiago to come and visit?'

It's February, the day after I got the Timmeee E-bike, when I head to Christchurch College to meet the Bishop of Oxford and have my adventure blessed. A bright blue sky, a bitterly cold winter's day, and in the porter's lodge we warm up with a chat about a favourite subject – Oxford United. When the team does well, the town does well. Faith and football can be intertwined.

Bishop Steven signs my pannier and my pilgrim passport, and gives me and the bike a great blessing – twice, cos the first time the video doesn't work. He has a few minutes before taking a service, so I show him the photos and tell him the tale of the mummified Hand of St James, which has been in the Thames Valley for 900 years. 'I've never heard of this story. That's amazing. In that case the Oxford diocese and Santiago are connected. Invite Archbishop Julian to come over and see it, and us.'

There's no such thing as a free lunch, or a free bishop's blessing. His good luck message comes with a task and to make it a little easier Steven has written a letter of introduction to Julian Barrio Barrio for me. (I love the repeated surname – just to make sure.)

'It is good to take every opportunity in these times to reinforce bonds of Christian love and friendship between our two countries and our churches. I am glad to support Timmy Mallett's endeavours and I hope you enjoy meeting with him . . .'

How do you get to meet an archbishop? How do you get to meet anyone? You start by asking politely, so I've written to him. Sent my letter by email, and by hard copy in the post. So far I've also written and had responses from Prince William, President Macron of France, Archbishop of York John Sentamu, and the Bishops of Winchester and Portsmouth.

In the olden days you couldn't go on pilgrimage without the permission of your parish priest and Lord of the Manor. Often, you'd be heading off to get a cure for your cancer and they would want to know if you had written your will, paid your debts, done any training and if your family were happy with what you intended to do.

My family think I'm nuts. That's all right then.

I'm also up to date with the will. Anyone want a Mallet?

I've got a clean bill of health, and I've paid the window cleaner.

I quite like the idea of getting permissions and encouragements, so after the bishop it also made sense to get a good luck message from my MP, who offered to come to my house and hear about my Camino. Theresa May is not the first female Prime Minister I've met. I once went to the House of Commons to play Mallett's Mallet with the children of MPs, and Margaret Thatcher turned up. She was not a tall person but had a handshake and a presence that made a mark. 'What's that?' she grinned, pointing at the Mallet. 'And what does it do?' I couldn't believe what I'd just been asked – the photo is in my hall. There's an official looking on slightly stunned as I demonstrate to a smiling Maggie what Mallett's Mallet does whenever there's a head within reach. Oh joy!

Prime Minister Theresa May and I have come into contact quite a few times over her 20 years as Maidenhead's MP. The first time was a month after her election, when Tony Blair's New Labour won their 1997 landslide. 'How do you think they're doing?' I asked her on air. 'Too many decisions are taken in number 10 Downing Street, not enough attention is paid to Parliament,' she replied. There's an observation that for some reason has become more prescient over the Brexit years. Then there was another time I was asked to be her stand-in at speech day: 'Well, you're both TM.'

As well as both of us having colourful shoes, Theresa and I had fathers in the church, and there's an unspoken understanding among clergy children as to how this may have an impact on your upbringing and your life. For a few years my parents lived in the Church of England retirement home next to the Prime Minister's country house, Chequers. President Yeltsin came to visit Prime Minister John Major, and needed a little drink before lunch. They walked across the fields to the pub, passing an elderly vicar along the way. 'Morning,' said the vicar to the President, Prime Minister and assorted bodyguards. Several hours later they managed to get Yeltsin out of the pub and headed back, unsteadily, for lunch at Chequers. They met the same vicar returning from a very long walk. 'Afternoon!' he called out conversationally. 'Nice day for it!'

The Prime Minister's armour-plated car pulls up in our drive and the rear door is opened by the bodyguard. Theresa steps out, beaming. 'Timmy!' she exclaims, with her arms out wide.

Oh. I'm not quite expecting such an exuberant embrace.

A split second later we have just one English-type kiss on the cheek, followed by a handshake (our British manners are safer to uphold). I make the introductions to the family and a couple of friends who are involved in my preparations, and we begin discussing my Camino, the reasons and terrain. I know the Mays are keen walkers and often spend their holidays hiking. 'Yes, Philip and I would like to walk this route one day – I'll be interested to know what it's like.' Immediately, I can't help wondering – with all the talk of how long she might last in her job and her own party scheming to get rid of her – whether this is going to be a whole lot sooner rather than later.

But as the year progressed and Brexit grew more and more extraordinary we began to say that less and less. Parliament has become the greatest theatre in the world. Across the globe more and more people watched with amazement the bobbing up and down of MPs, bowing respectfully to John Bercow, the speaker, and his glorious booming, 'Order! Orderrrr! The Ayes to the right, the Noes to the left.' It's an extraordinary example of the whole human condition. Strong, passionate, irrevocably held, ethical and honourable, contrasting opinions. I admire the tenacity of MPs to debate, occasionally listen, explore and consider something so bizarre as whether to be in or out of the club. I have friends with different opinions. They are still my friends. Democracy needs other opinions. The world would be a boring place if we all wanted exactly the same thing. I look at these politicians, some with high ideals, all with natural human failings, and wonder if this might be an advert to the next generation of students pondering what politics has to offer. Resilience. Brexit is surely a lot more interesting, though a lot harder to resolve, than discussing whether or not to fix the holes in the road.

Resilience.

Theresa and I discuss the route I'm planning to take and the training I am doing; then we inspect the bike – murmurs of approval – and talk about the paintings I am hoping to create – comments of admiration. Neither of us says so, but I am sure we are both wondering how Brexit might be received along the way through two mainland European countries. There is an understanding acknowledgement as I talk about brother Martin being my inspiration, the way he reaches his potential, even with language and learning difficulties.

'Yes, I know about your brother. And, like him, you just have to be the best that you can be.'

Theresa offers me a handwritten letter of encouragement to share with people along the way: 'Dear Timmy, travelling over 2,000 km across three countries like this is by no means an easy feat and will undoubtedly demonstrate your strength and resolve . . .' There's resilience right there in the letter she personally composed and penned.

'And Mrs Mallett, what will you be doing while Timmy is away for two months?'

'I'll be in Melbourne with my mum, Maisie, about to celebrate her one hundredth birthday . . . Would you like to send her a video birthday greeting?'

'I'd love to.' And straightaway the Prime Minister records a personal message of thanks to Maisie for her wartime contribution in the UK and her pioneering contribution in Australia. My mother-in-law is another one who reaches her potential every day.

'And what about you, Billy the Gardener?'

'It's my busy time in the garden. I've just come from work now to meet you. Here's my business card!' Now here's an opportunity for the Mays to have a knowledgeable plantsman maintain their garden.

Our MP wants to look at some of the photos in the hallway: Mrs Thatcher and Mallett's Mallet in the House of Commons, my grandfather's mention in the First World War dispatches signed by Winston Churchill . . .

'Forget about that,' says Billy. 'This is much more important. Here's me on the pitch celebrating when Maidenhead United won the league and were promoted!' And, of course, he is right. The here and now of living. Yesterday's history, tomorrow's a mystery, today's a present.

My painting, inspired by our meeting today, is of Theresa and Billy, a little head and shoulders portrait. Two generations, 35 years apart, held together by a common national thread. Both affected in some way by the other's action and opinions.

The Prime Minister takes her leave with a jar of my delicious homemade Mallett Marmalade and heads off for her next appointment, and another Brexit headache.

In the event, it's another 18 months before she will be cast aside by her allies and can consider her own potential Camino.

Sticking your head above the parapet and going into public life must be one of the hardest jobs ever. You are forever faced with people who want something. Some things you can achieve, but so much involves compromise and many things are impossible. All political lives end in failure, they say. All of life is negotiation – our work, the home – and you live with it until it's no longer what you want. You take the new job – the hours aren't great, the pay could be better and the commute is a bit long, but you can live with it, until the recruitment agent dangles something new and more enticing in front of you. My career has jumped about a bit and taken me in interesting new directions over the years. I've been a radio DJ, a TV presenter and producer, acted on stage, had a number one hit record, sell-out art exhibitions and now I'm about to cycle across half a continent on my own. I don't need to do this. I want to do this. Now, when the email lands with an offer of work, I am always grateful to be thought of. I ask myself, 'Does this offer challenge me? Will it help me reach my potential? Does it make me smile?'

Touchdown.

A new country.

Step off the transport and notice everything.

Tarmac is the same all over the world. Some countries collect more holes in it. The air is always different, the humidity varies, and there'll be a unique landscape beyond the airport perimeter. Head high, and there's snow on the mountains; head to the tropics, the palms are waving in the breeze. Land in the Scilly Isles and it used to be that the plane would touch down on the grass, while in Gibraltar the landing strip cuts across the road. Boat landings are different again. Dock in Hong Kong and everywhere you look there are skyscrapers; I've come ashore on sandy beaches and pulled up aside floating pontoons. Today we've arrived in gleaming St Malo, Brittany's most magnificent port. It's early morning with bright blue skies and a feeling of spring in the air. My spirits are high as we pedal over the cobbled stones to the old town for coffee, croissants and a pen and ink sketch of my first morning in France. I've made a decision to go slowly, paint and absorb the day. In fact, this is how I imagine many days will pan out: breakfast at a nice café, and plenty of stops for refreshment and reflection. (Weirdly that isn't going to happen very often. In fact, hardly ever. This is not a jolly, as it's going to take some time to realise. Most of my stops are to look at things, experience stuff; for some reason I don't have a very good nose for finding places to eat so I get into a habit of a piece of fruit at breakfast, and a sandwich during the day.)

Today I want to be a tourist.

'What are you going to paint, then?' Stevie asks, after I've sketched the old town square. The young woman in St Malo's flash new tourist information office is brilliant. I make it a habit to ask at every tourist office what the officer's own personal favourite view is and then go find it and try painting it. She offers us some St Malo stickers and little do I know that in three weeks' time the St Malo sticker on the front of my bike bag will get me a place to stay, in somewhere that's supposedly full.

I've practised painting in acrylics from the back of the bike all through the winter, so I'm confident this will work. I've been out in all conditions, experimenting with different paints, oils (too messy) and acrylics (just fine), and finding out what is the minimum I need to carry to capture this adventure. I set up on the wall above the beach, looking at the rows of oak tidal defences that resemble an ancient forest sticking out of the sand. The tide is low, the sea is blue-green and I have a happy hour in the sun getting to work on my first location Camino composition. I paint the drama of the sky, the light and shade of the walls and turrets, the ruggedness of the rocks. The rule is simple. Sharpen your eyes. See everything and assume you will never repeat this route again, ever. Remember every bend in the road, anything that makes you go 'Wow!' Stop and look, and if you can paint it, then do. If not, then a sketch, a photo, a lightning snapshot in the memory for later. That later may be in my accommodation, or back in my studio over the autumn and winter months to come. This journey on the bike is about here and now. And painting it is a way of fixing myself in the experience; interpreting the scene and how it affects me. This is something we often lose sight of in this high-tech age, where capturing a selfie can become more important than the experience itself.

My pal Gary always turns the radio on whenever he is abroad. 'I like to know I'm in a foreign country,' he says. When I was 23 and hitchhiking around Umbria with my paints, in the footsteps of Renaissance artists (yes, honestly, they were the inspiration to visit Spoleto and Orvieto), I kept hearing a funny little song called '*Mi scappa la pipì, Papà*', which translates as 'Oh Dad, I want a wee'! That quirky hit became the charity song of our record-breaking, non-stop, 66-hour radio show with Martin Stanford on Radio Oxford. Years later the kid's voice in the song inspired the weeing catchphrase of my Pinky Punky Mallet. 'Mr Mallett! Can I go to the toilet?!' So keep your ears open and your eyes peeled and see what inspiration unexpectedly comes your way.

Immediately it's apparent our antennae are in tune, because Stevie and I notice the trees being pollarded into weird and wonderful shapes. All along the French avenues those plane trees, which in a few weeks will be leafy green, are now knotted and gnarled, and we comment that they look like lollipop sticks with the lollipops bitten off. We shape our world and our environment in many different ways. The tourist office lady has given us a cycling circuit to explore and above the bay we stop to watch the weather rolling in. As we set out eastwards, the temperature drops with every minute. Watch out – the Beast from the East is coming back. It's been forecast. Enjoy the view of the sea, ma bubba – I put Martin's name tag behind the wire fence. Stevie makes an observation that resonates with me.

'Wherever you find a place to put a Martin name tag, do it. Share the photo on your blog and social media.'

'Are you sure? It's a bit personal, isn't it?'

'In years to come,' replies Stevie, 'long after Google has disappeared, when someone finds a Martin name tag, there will be a way to follow the story in whatever shape online takes.'

This is exactly what I will do.

We share a delicious seafood lunch with oysters in a popular family restaurant and step out into a biting gale. The wind whips the tears across my face and it's time to head back into St Malo to find somewhere to stay. The *Auberge de Jeunesse* has a nice room at a good price and then it's the moment for Stevie to head for his ferry back to England. From a spring-like morning it's now an arctic late afternoon and I really feel alone on this great adventure as I watch the impressive boat sail away.

In the old town I do what I always do: pop into the church and an ancient art gallery. Every town has something special and unique, and some sort of work of art, and I like going in search of it. Churches, often the largest public building in any town, are usually open. It feels right to call in for a moment of reflection. I like visiting galleries because there will always be a gem in them. The old gallery door creaks open and immediately I can see what the masters have painted along these coasts. Just looking at art fires me up.

Back at the *auberge* the bike is safely locked up, and I have a conversation with the woman in charge, who is interested in my adventure and not at all surprised by its scale. In my room I get out my paints to recreate that grey cold Brittany afternoon. The evening disappears late into the night, with paintings and some barmy texts about the football predictions. It's been a calmer day and given me a little courage for what is ahead.

I still ask myself, 'Is this what I really set out to do? How am I going to be on my own?'

4

Ancestral hero

Ever wondered what it would be like to step inside a real fairy story? It may not be quite as you imagine.

Reading Museum has a full-length copy of the Bayeux Tapestry, made by ladies of a Staffordshire sewing circle over tea and buns in the nineteenth century. Out of Victorian modesty some naked male figures have been given trousers – sweet! Early in the story there is a not very good likeness of World Heritage site Mont St Michel. Even 950 years ago the devout nuns of Canterbury, who made the original, had a fair idea of its impressive appearance. These days the distinctive shape of Mont St Michel is easily recognised. Perched on an island by the border of Brittany and Normandy it's one of the must-see sites in France – after Notre Dame, the Eiffel Tower and Disneyland.

The place pops up in the story of the Bayeux Tapestry because here in 1064 top Englishman 'Mr I'm in charge' Earl Harold Godwinson, a 'guest' of Duke William, rescued two drowning Norman soldiers from the quicksands of the river and the sweeping tidal bore across the bay of St Michael. It was an impressive and courageous act of bravery (or madness). In the embroidery, you see Harold the hero carrying the terrified warriors as the tide rushes in and everyone gets their feet wet. Duke William made a big fuss of him, and rightly so. Tidal bores are not to be messed with. When I was at boarding school on Morecambe Bay, we heard the signal for the bore every day, and every year someone would get stuck in the unforgiving quicksands.

A few years ago, for a summer thrill, we were led across the ten-mile stretch of the bay at low tide. It was deceptively, hauntingly beautiful and then we were brought up sharp, coming across the remains of the quad bike of the Chinese cockle pickers who were caught by the tide and drowned in 2004. 'Many water, many water,' they had pleaded on their phones. It was spooky and ominous. Those 200 square miles of sandy bay fill twice a day in a couple of hours. The way out to safety is never obvious and the tidal bore stops for no one.

These days the site of Earl Harold's heroics is easily viewed from the barrage on the River Couesnon; it's a great place to see Mont St Michel across the mudflats and salt marshes. It's also a fine place to paint one of the iconic views of my Camino as the wind carries the sound of the bells summoning the faithful to prayer.

Bells across the water . . . gulls calling. A New Year's Eve during panto season in the North East. The family are with me in a nice flat on the marina in Hartlepool. If I am doing a show near the sea, I want to be staying right by it. I love the sight and sound of the water and the smell of the air. I can see why Turner, Spencer and many other artists were inspired to paint the waves . . .

It's freezing cold, with thick snow on the ground and ice underneath. As we begin drifting off to sleep, Mrs Mallett nudges me.

'Is that someone crying for help, or a gull calling?'

From my position under the warm covers after midnight, it is clearly a gull.

Nudge, nudge. OK, I'll listen at the window – shuffle shuffle, draw back the curtain and hear through the icy night air a distant woman's voice: 'Help . . .'

I pull on trousers over PJs, a jumper and my coat. I struggle into socks and boots as Mrs Mallett says, 'Hurry up! I'll ring 999.'

Now I'm getting nervous as I go down two flights of cold empty stairs to the street. What am I going to find out there? Am I going to burst in on something I really don't want to see?

The street is completely empty. There's not a sound, apart from the wind rattling the masts of the boats in the marina, and I smell the crisp cold of the sea in the depths of a winter's night. I glance up at the open window.

'Have a look,' calls Mrs Mallett and I stand on the wall above the floating pontoon.

'Hello?' It seems foolish to call into the darkness. 'Anyone there?'

'Help me,' calls a thin frail voice.

'Where are you?'

'I'm in the water.'

The voice cuts through me. I look down at the icy floating pontoon ten feet below. I don't want to slip and break my leg or anything. I've got two shows on stage tomorrow and I'm top of the bill.

I jump.

There in the icy water of Hartlepool Marina is a head with two hands losing their grip on the rope on a boat's buoy. Instinctively I reach down and grab the person's shoulders and pull her out on to the pontoon. I'm wrapping my coat around her and hold her close as our teeth chatter in unison and the shock hits. 'What happened?' I ask.

'I fell in, after my handbag.'

'What's your name?'

'Geraldine.'

'OK, Geraldine, help is on its way.' I glance up and Mrs Mallett is on her mobile at the window, giving instructions as emergency services drive right past above our heads.

'You've gone too far. They're down below on the pontoon.'

There's a slope up from the pontoon to the gate. The gate is locked. We have a bizarre few minutes waiting for someone to get a key. 'Just break the lock,' I suggest.

'Can't do that; it's not our property.'

After far too long, Geraldine is wrapped in a thermal blanket and put into the back of the ambulance and driven away. 'Another five minutes in that water,' offered one of the rescue team, 'and she'd have been dead.' I'm left standing alone on the icy, snowy street when someone appears full of concern and asks, 'What happened there? I hope they didn't nick anything from the boat!'

Sometimes, being in the right place at the right time matters. If Mrs Mallett hadn't left the window ajar, if she hadn't heard the insistent cry, if, if, if. Befriending Geraldine afterwards was the easy, lovely, lasting legacy of that transient panto season. A six-week run of laughter and entertainment – that is here today and gone tomorrow. Did you deliver your lines to get the right reaction? Did you and Cinderella sing 'Oooh Baby' in the same key? Did you make friends with the cast and crew of the theatre? Did Tony Blair's family (whom I invited to the show) have a good time shouting 'Blaaah!' at each other? Did the meet and greets with the audience after every show make a difference? Did you enjoy getting to know the people of a new town, if only for a short while? All of these things matter in the Christmas and New Year of pantomime in a strange new town each festive season. But meeting Geraldine and enjoying a phone call, an annual birthday greeting and catching up on family news, has been one of the lasting blessings of decades of on-stage entertainment.

It's bitterly cold this Sunday morning. I'm wearing lots of layers and I take my time with St Malo. The hostel is busy and there are many different languages over breakfast; I pack my cycle panniers carefully, retrieve the bike from the locked shed and go into town to make sure I didn't miss anything yesterday. It's as if I don't want to leave yet. Maybe I'm daunted by the enormity of the journey. I know that every place I visit I may only see this once and I shouldn't be in too much of a hurry. I'm aware that finding places for lunch may not be as easy as in the UK, so I shop for snacks: baby cheeses, chocolate, a sandwich and a piece of fruit. I like the name of this area – the Emerald Coast – and that's good enough reason to take a longer route. Fields of green-grey cabbages, muted tones perfect for watercolours, glimpses of the sea . . . and I come to a tiny village called St Benoit des Ondes – my twin town is St Benoit near

Poitiers – so I share a photo of the spare St Benoit with my French friends in our twin St Benoit. 'See you in a week – hopefully!' I promise.

I'm cycling the verdant ways along deep and rugged sand dunes, crossed by treacherous quicksands and bordered with oyster and mussel beds and old windmills. There are long straight poplar-tree lanes brimming with mistletoe, and the air is cold and crisp. Then the World Heritage island of Mont St Michel comes into view and I halt on the new barrage to catch the colour of the afternoon. Painting this view makes me get off the bike, to look at, consider and become absorbed in the moment. Here's what I see.

Light and shade in the early spring sky. The meandering river below leads me to the mount with the tower and spire of the monastery, which appear like clasped hands making a plea. I'm going to telescope the view and make the mount larger in my painting. I want it to be monumental in the big sky. I can use the same colours to achieve different effects in the painting, and the purple underpainting will accentuate the drama.

I'm working with very few shades: Naples yellow, Wedgwood blue, burnt umber, tiny bit of azure blue and sap green, and then titanium white. By four o'clock the temperature is dropping, the bells are calling the faithful to prayer, the gulls are crying and I'm excited to cycle across the new causeway to my accommodation. This is the only place I've pre-booked anywhere along the route. No other day has this degree of planning. And the reason is simple. I want to stay on a World Heritage site and there's a timeless aspect to Mont St Michel. The pilgrim hostel has very few rooms; turns out I'm the only guest tonight.

The *maison du pèlerin* is at the top of the single impossibly narrow street, just beneath the monastery. What I didn't realise is that there are 40-something steps to struggle up with the heavily laden bike. I need a helping hand from a willing tourist. Andre the manager has assured me there's somewhere to lock the bike up and he leads me through the little gate in the wall by the monastery, down some more steps into the tiny cobbled courtyard beneath the town walls. There's just room for the bike in an alcove alongside the buckets of empty wine bottles waiting to be recycled.

Martin's name tag goes in between the mortar of the eleventh-century stones. I rename the place to myself: Mont St Martin. My little room is a tiny old monk's cell at the top of the stairs overlooking the courtyard and walls, with a little bed and bright pink blanket (a very Timmy colour). Across the corridor are the simple facilities.

It's a perfect afternoon and I'm instantly into something utterly unique. It's a joy to explore the island with my sketchbook. Climbing more steps, I discover an ancient statue of the Virgin Mary in the little chapel of St Pierre. There's a tiny gap beneath the statue and I slide Martin's name tag underneath her and say a little prayer. 'You me, ma bubba.' There's no way that statue will be moved in a hundred years and when it is, they'll wonder who Martin Mallett was. I smile as I recall what Stevie had said: 'This tribute will last for ever . . .'

I watch the tidal bore come rushing in as sunset approaches. In the Bayeux Tapestry, William the Conqueror wanted to show how Harold turned traitor just two years later, but I think his bravery shows his humanity. Some sort of memorial wouldn't go amiss. The events of the Norman Conquest are in my thoughts and I wonder if my Mallett ancestors ever stayed here at Mont St Michel. Our surname supposedly originated from around St Malo, and William Malet of Le Havre was the go-between for Duke William and King Harold in 1066. Related to both of them through marriage, he was given the task of burying Harold after the Battle of Hastings on Saturday 14 October 1066. William Malet wrapped the remains of the dead king in a purple robe and set the corpse above the cliffs at Hastings, beneath a stone cairn. 'He couldn't defend his country when alive,' said the duke. 'Let's see if he's any better at it in death!' Malet's reward was the honour of the small market town of Eye in Suffolk. I've often wondered whether it was Malet's idea to shoot the arrows over the shield wall. The arrow that supposedly pierced Harold in the eye and brought him down to be hacked to pieces by the Norman soldiers. The Battle of Hastings had been a touch-and-go affair and the decisive nature of that day is a reminder to me that every day counts; every day you can make a difference. For centuries now there's been a William in the Mallett family. My dad was Michael William, my older brother is Paul William and our son is Billy, which is, of course, short for William.

One of my favourite Mallett ancestors is the little noticed William Mallet on the Magna Carta. There were 25 barons who brought King John to account at Runnymede on the River Thames, and Baron Mallet of Somerset was one of them. It feels impressive to have one of my ancestors involved in something so important to universal justice. 'No free man shall be imprisoned except by the lawful judgement of his peers.' And there on the memorial is the Mallet/Mallett coat of arms: three scallop shells, the sign of a pilgrim. I've painted three scallop shells on my art bag. I'm cycling back through an ancestral landscape, wearing the scallop shells of a timeless pilgrim and the family coat of arms.

Talk about feeling the touch of history.

I'm intrigued as the island empties and the tourists head home. Just a few visitors like me remain and the town is shuttered up for the night. Footsteps echo on the stone steps.

Floodlights cast eerie shadows on the monastery facade and I sense a moody melancholy. That night I dream of medieval pilgrims, kings, warriors and adventurers.

'When I woke up I could not get up, but once I was up I was all right.' This is the opening line of my first diary, aged ten, from January 1966. I've always liked this line and it's surprising how often I hear myself say it.

Putting things off is delicious. It's that extra treat you give yourself, knowing you shouldn't, knowing you'll have to face stuff sooner or later, knowing that it's now or never, and it would be a lot better if it was never.

I'm back in the olden days, looking at the first little black and white two-inch photos from the Box Brownie . . . I can smell my clothes, feel the itchy wool, hear the splutter of breakfast frying. There's frost on the inside of our windows, behind the colourful steam-train patterned curtains. Jack Frost came last night and carved his wonderful intricate designs all over the glass. I peak out of the blankets and eiderdown and my nose is cold. There's a *hurr!* in the air. Dare to creep out of the blankets (careful not to let the warmth escape) and breathe on the window pane and scratch the patterns away. That screeching sound and the frost beneath my nails. It's a British thing, this frost. Our climate delivers beautiful frosts with all that moisture in the air. Take yourself off to America and they have much colder temperatures, but it's a dry cold. Ours is prettier. Jump back into bed and wait for the call up the stairs: 'Come on down, breakfast is ready!' Lie in bed and notice your own smells. From downstairs, I can hear big brother Paul singing, 'A fart is a breeze, that whistles round the knees, ruffles up the bedclothes and suffocates the fleas . . .'

It's time to get dressed – in bed. Everything is cold, so I hurry.

So many winter mornings, I've got up like this. The hot water bottle from last night is just bed temp, and the only warm place in the house is downstairs in the kitchen. Number 59 Station Road, Marple, had no central heating all the time we lived there. Just coal fires in the living room, dining room and the kitchen. A letter from my mum dated March 1969 says, 'Lots of snow last night. I lit a fire in the kitchen this morning to warm the house.' We had a cast iron coal-fired range which heated the water for washing and cooking and raised the temperature in parts of the house, or at least the kitchen. Uncle Wilfrid had talked about his new home in Skegness and how central heating was the thing that would transform our lives. 'Nobody will have coal fires in a few years,' he said. 'The change will be brilliant.' My mum liked the idea of a living fire with flames, and smoke that would billow into the room if the chimney was blocked or it didn't draw properly. Every morning in winter somebody had to rake out the old ash and try not to spill it on the carpet. The coal man would come around every six weeks with a black leather jerkin covering his head, back and shoulders. His face was always covered in coal dust. He would empty a ton bag of coal into the outhouse. 'This is the stuff, Mrs Mallett, smokeless coal. Costs a bit more and splutters a bit. Or you can have coke which is warmer but doesn't look as nice.' Our job was to shovel the black stuff into the coal bucket and struggle with it into the house. 'Keep the door shut, it's freezing out there!'

Clothes would be dried on the fire-guard and our pyjamas warmed at night when we didn't want to face the cold race upstairs. There was an iron poker in the living room which idle boys' hands might heat up to see it glow red hot. Wonder what would happen if we rested it against the mantelpiece? Oh look, there's a brown burn mark and smoke. Once I left it in too long and burned my hand. Didn't tell Mum about the blisters. But she spotted them, of course.

Weather plays a significant part in everyone's plans. It's a sorry soggy sight in the morning from the pilgrim hostel at the summit of Mont St Michel. The Beast from the East has returned with a vengeance. Howling winds rattle the windows; snow, rain and hail swirl about. The sound is terrifying. I'm staying in bed, cos when I woke up I could not get up . . .

But once I was up I was all right.

Better do something while I wait for the weather to clear, perhaps? I spend the morning in my makeshift art studio – the spartan, lonely kitchen/diner – painting watercolours and acrylics of the island, the bay and the view from the rattling windows in the squalls of winter.

I'm waiting hopefully for a break in the weather. Andre suggests I stay another night, but if I go today to please leave the key. He's already had a call from the St Malo Hostel asking for me to return the key to the bike shed I'd taken by mistake. Whoops! I post it back with a note of apology and a little drawing.

Should I brave the bad weather? The howling gusting winds and the lashing rain? I put it to social media, who vote 3:1 stay put and wait for better weather.

So I do

Until

Early afternoon.

The weather has barely eased but I head out anyway in case it's good enough to make some progress. I say to myself that if it isn't, I can always turn back and stay another night. I set off slowly, with the wind gusting fiercely across the causeway. The bike sways in the angry blasts. I'm constantly stopping and looking back through screwed-up eyelids, and tears from the wind and squalls of rain are streaming down my face. I know at some stage I'm going to paint this view of the wild Mont St Michel and capture this timeless island in today's moment. *Run that video camera in your head, Mallett. Look at the white caps on the water.* What a contrast to yesterday afternoon.

I know the next time I see the sea will be half a continent away on the Atlantic coast of Spain.

5

The Way of the Plantagenets

PONTORSON

MARTIN MALLETT

MARCH...

OBSTACLES

FOUGÈRES

VITRÉ

History is all around us, and occasionally it weaves its way into our lives. I love it when our story is wrapped up in something older than our own experience.

The little town of Pontorson is where William the Conqueror founded a church in grateful thanks for something – various military victories? For getting across the river without sinking into quicksand? For the fine weather? (For good Wifi and a phone signal?) It's an austere, bleak-looking church, but colour comes from a little pot of cyclamens and jonquils on the altar and a stained-glass window showing Earl Harold doing his bit to rescue the army. Let's give thanks and leave my brother's name tag. This time I hide it behind the stone chapel carving.

The staff in the tourist office on the main road are amazed to see anyone out in the wind and rain and snow flurries. I misquote a favourite saying to them: 'Wherever you may be, let your wind blow free!' They point me to the old railway line, 'Bonne chance . . .', and I'm on a green cycle way, the Way of the Plantagenets, or William the Conqueror's old railway line, as I like to call it. It's a stunning ride even on a wild March day. Winter is attacking hard. There has been a lot of rain and the fields are flooded, but the well-graded mostly tarmacked road is unaffected. I am alone all afternoon. In 60 kilometres there are perhaps three or four cars, a handful of pedestrians and one other fleeting cyclist. I try out my best French on a family walking their dog. 'Bonjour!' I smile and wave. Nothing. Not a word.

It's got to be my accent. Hey, I'll speak to anyone and I usually get some sort of response. Once I checked out of a Parisian hotel with Mrs Mallett. 'Bonjour Mademoiselle,' I said to the young woman on the desk. 'Merci beaucoup pour un nice stay. Aujourd'hui, nous partirons et . . . can I have the bill, please?'

'Certainly, Timmy,' said the English woman on reception, and Mrs Mallett beamed delightedly at my confusion.

I share this afternoon on my blog and make a few phone calls to my Camino encouragers. I need some company and we talk about the unusual emptiness of the miles without meeting anyone. It feels like an awful long lonely way. Maybe, just maybe, I've bitten off more than I can chew?

Someone suggests I break it down into little chunks. Get involved in the here and now – as far as the next cuppa, the next junction, to the next corner.

And that simple bit of advice is why I can recall every bend in the road, every village, every encounter, every view, every aroma, every flavour and every bit of weather on the entire journey. It's not the destination that matters; stay involved in the here and now of cycling, and that massive 3,500-kilometre, two-month, daily solitary adventure will be the biggest thing I've ever done. The richest most detailed journey of my life. Today I know it.

So, an empty old track for 60 kilometres, was it? Not really. There was the old station converted into a home, with chickens running around where the railway yard used to be. There were mistletoe clumps high up in the trees, exposed by the naked branches, and the fallen ivy-clad ancient tree blocking the path, which I had to scramble underneath and drag the bike with me. And then the everlasting cowslips in the cuttings. What are we used to seeing at this time of year? In Britain, daffodils along our verges, new shoots of green grass. Not in this place. Here is an everlasting, dead-leaf, dead-fern-covered grey emptiness, until I spot the primroses along the embankment. I cycle under old brick bridges between farm fields, through crossing barriers at every road junction, absorb the whirr of the wheels, make detours into villages, look in shop windows, step inside every church to see the image of St Jacques, listen to babbling streams, and even spot my first Chemin de Saint Jacques sign with scallop shell (EU route *Itinéraires Culturels Européens*) by a post office in a small town. Antrain is on the border between Normandy and Brittany, and the sign is shared with the Way of the Capitals and the Chemin de Mont St Michel. Clearly this is a crossroads for people heading everywhere.

I'm looking for somewhere to get a pilgrim passport stamp. The post office will do and it's in the queue that a delightful exchange occurs. Someone offers to lead me to the next part of the cycle track, as the old railway line is blocked off and there's a diversion to the green way. 'Follow me,' he says, so I pursue him on my bike as he drives a couple of kilometres and I can re-join the cycle track next to the house he is visiting. He's surprised I am keeping up with him in his car. But I'm on an E-bike and I make it my business to stay with him. We part with an enthusiastic handshake and his beaming smile at my adventure.

Just before closing time, I cycle into Fougères and it's time to find somewhere for the night. The young women in the tourist office call the Sanctuary of the Sisters of Rille, who can put me up. 'Is ten euros OK?'

'Really? That's cheap. Is there any actual bed? And do they actually have any sheets and blankets? Because I haven't got a sleeping bag.'

'Yes. Yes. And a towel.' They laugh.

The delightful retired nuns of the Sanctuary of Rille speak no English and the youngest would be about 900 years old. They are just up the road from the old castle and could be left over from the days of King Henry II. They lead me through a narrow gate in the wall into a tiny courtyard. There's a door and steep wooden stairs leading to some sort of garret. Inside a kitchen/living room with home comforts including tea and coffee, a stove, books, maps, a single bed, dozens of chairs (expecting some visitors, are we?) and another room with three more double beds and a bathroom. It's a suite of rooms for pilgrims on the Camino or for those heading the other way to Mont St Michel.

'Welcome to you who stay here for one night. Let it be restful and beneficial to lead you to new horizons . . .' Clearly in the main season this is always full. Tonight, I'm on my own in something magical. I fill up on delicious Breton *galette* pancakes at a small nearby café and think how lucky I am. These good nuns have been welcoming pilgrims since the Middle

Ages and I'm part of something that's neither new nor unusual, except that it is for me. All our lives are like this. We are each living a life that is unique to us; discovering its joys for ourselves. How we embrace what life has to offer will be the bit that is our own.

It's the spring equinox, with day and night the same length, and now the promise of warmer, longer days to come. The blue skies are stunning but it's bitterly cold and I'm wearing at least six layers again, so it's a promise that's unlikely to be kept anytime soon. On a bicycle you get to notice how brief the spring warmth is each day. On the Continent it's much colder in the winter and warmer in the summer. What about springtime? I'll reserve judgement for the moment.

I don't want to leave Fougères. It's got the best-preserved medieval castle in France and it was built by one of my favourites – Henry II. Is it a weird thing to have favourite rulers through history?

The Plantagenets were a rum lot. They ruled England and large parts of France for 330 years and they got their nickname from Henry's dad, who liked to wear a sprig of yellow broom flower in his hat. I like yellow. You'll find me, every day on this ride, with a sprig of something attached to the bags on my panniers. I think of Henry II as the lucky king who didn't realise how fortunate he was and so nearly managed to cock it all up because of his uncontrollable temper. Politics and anger – they aren't easy bedfellows (ask our politicians). He was the son of a pushy mum, the empress Matilda (the one who was given the Hand of St James as a wedding present), and great-grandson of the Conqueror. That's good warrior pedigree stock. Shrewd, pragmatic, decisive, Henry was fortunate enough to have masses of energy, good looks and the most fabulous wife in history: Eleanor of Aquitaine. But his volatile temperament led him to fall out with not just his best friend and archbishop, Thomas à Becket, but his whole family – his kids were known as the devil's brood. This is way better than any telly soap opera, or even Donald Trump or Brexit.

Among Henry's hobbies were swift successful military campaigns and building castles. There are some massive fortifications surviving that take your breath away. Fougères is one of them. Huge walls and towers with a sort of 'You won't capture me, so don't even try!' attitude. 'I'm the biggest and best medieval castle in the world. So there!'

Henry's Angevin empire stretched from Hadrian's Wall, on the border with Scotland, to the Mediterranean Sea, and through marriage and inheritance was the biggest and richest European empire of its time. I'm in the heart of that realm now and as I pedal, I'm musing on Henry and his family. In the midst of a periodic family uprising, his eldest son fell ill and died. King Henry was heartbroken and lamented, 'He caused me so much heartache; wish that he had lived and caused me so much more.' Then at the end of his reign, Henry heard that his favourite, youngest son, John, had joined a rebellion against him. 'He broke his father's heart . . .' were among his last words. Henry was only human. He may have suffered from those deadly human sins of pride and anger, but his remorse is the thing I notice. Like the tears he wept at the murder of his great friend Thomas à Becket, precipitated by his own rage and outburst at Christmas 1170. 'Who will rid me of this turbulent priest?' he is purported to have shouted. Don't believe a word of it. The language would have been a lot more vicious, colourful, violent and French! And so loud, Becket could have heard the yells across the Channel.

Henry was mortified to have prompted the shocking murder

and walked barefoot to Canterbury to be whipped by the monks. He even paid for anchoresses across the empire to pray for his soul and spare him purgatory and utter damnation. In our local church an anchoress nun was bricked into a cell with a single window on the altar, through which came her food and drink and out went the bucket. She lived like that for ten years. The smell would have been a little distinctive, and she would have known every bit of gossip in the village! The choir say that even now when practising on warm summer evenings a faint mysterious odour can sometimes be noticed . . . uncanny. Our anchoress is buried under an impressive stone slab outside the north wall of Holy Trinity Church.

I've always enjoyed history. It's about people and their foibles. Like, for instance, Cleopatra. That sultry, alluring, charming Queen of the Egyptians who seduced Mark Anthony of Rome and led the Mediterranean into a hopeless war. We recreated her story on *Wacaday* and called her Cleo-Wac-tra. I wore a gorgeous long black wig, dress and bright red lipstick, and danced as you'd expect to 'Wac like an Egyptian'. In our film she perished from a blow from Mallett's Mallet. That's a true story, Wideawakers – we made it up ourselves!

I stick a massive sprig of mistletoe on my pannier and share it on a little video with Mrs Mallett. I ponder a painting I'll work up when I stop later. The view is of a distant silhouette of a village on a hill, with sunlight glistening on the roofs. I prop the bike on the track, throwing its shadow towards me. In the middle distance are sheep in the field and I'm looking for an image to show me alone riding through sunshine and shadows. On the E-bike you never fear a hill, so I'm pleased to pedal up to an old village for the view and a Martin Mallett moment. There's a blue statue of the Virgin Mary in a craggy graveyard, so different from any churchyard back home. Speeding down into the valley in the sunshine the cargo net comes adrift, and paints and dry bag suddenly fly off and go crashing in a terrifying sound of ripped and smashed containers. Hmmm. That's not good. Can it be patched? Until a new one is found?

Going fast and having things break. They often go together. Like at the Silverstone Grand Prix in 1981, when Nelson Piquet's Formula One car crashed and pieces of the car flew into the crowd in front of me. I picked up bits of broken bodywork and gave them away on my Radio Oxford show next day. Sometime later, I did a kids' TV show on go-karts, at which I led the field until the nine-year-old future world champion Jensen Button sped past me. We met again in the pits at the Melbourne Grand Prix a couple of years ago, as he was about to race, and he asked me for a selfie. (Jensen likes to cycle, and takes his bike with him on the Formula One circuit, to ride the race tracks after the heats. He's still faster than I am!) It was the same race in which F1 driver Fernando Alonso had a horrifying crash, flying end over end; he told me afterwards that he'd only been scared for his family watching. Still, I don't imagine he slept easily after that.

It's a shame to break stuff. I know we're used to the throwaway society where we replace stuff regularly. The toy soldiers proudly given to us brothers one Christmas, bearing the label 'indestructible', didn't take me long to satisfyingly wreck. It hasn't always been like that. There's a set of wooden eggcups at home, crafted by my grandfather on a lathe a century ago. I'm pleased we still use them now.

Vitré has a stunning medieval quarter to rival anywhere. I pedal into the fine cobbled streets and expect to come across Blackadder, but there's no one. I've been mistaken in the past for Tony Robinson, who played Baldrick in the TV series. 'Lovely to see you again, Tony,' said the lady at the market stall.

'I remember when you worked in the newsagents. We love you in *Time Team*. Will you sign an autograph for my daughter?' I hadn't the heart to tell her she'd made a mistake . . . so I signed it from Tony/Timmy.

The castle reverberates to the sound of the church bells echoing off the witch's hat towers. It's strangely eerie when there isn't a soul to be seen. It's as if everyone has disappeared off on a Hundred Years' War. See you next century, or when the football season starts . . .

My ride is along another well-maintained, easy surface, an old railway, in the cold afternoon rain showers. I don't know it, but this day will prove to feature the longest distance I'll ride – and the most stressful. The desire to paint everything is being overtaken by the need to find somewhere to stay. I've ridden at least 80 kilometres and the options on my accommodation list don't answer when I ring. I got the list from the Confraternity of St James, who help pilgrims plan their trips. They have partner organisations across the world, and they put me in touch with Graham and Carol, who had tandem ridden this route in the middle of summer. They both had good advice and were encouraging about what I might expect to encounter. Tonight, though, I find that the two hotels in town are strangely full. It's a Tuesday night, almost a fortnight before Easter. What's going on? I'm a bit stuck and wonder if I should be worried. Patrons in the bar make helpful suggestions. 'There's a hotel forty kilometres away.' Er, I'm on a bike . . .

I'm not worried about cycling at night. I do it every year. It's usually around midsummer – the overnight bike ride. 'Who's in?' I ask, and I usually have around a dozen takers. We start out by taking the train to somewhere and finding a pub. I've done a recce and prepped the route and made sure there's entertainment for the evening. I find a cheerful pub with some live music. We want a sing-song. Let's rip into our version of 'Sweet Home here in Berkshire!' or 'You're Just Too Good to be True!', and give us the Monkees; we want the Shrek song: 'And Then I Saw Her Face'! Remember when the German band came to visit and played in the English pub and sang 'She Loves You Ja, Ja, Ja!'? Whatever it is, make it loud and we will sing along with it. Sometime after midnight we leave the pub and head off slowly on our bikes along empty country lanes and tracks. Our bike lights pick out the occasional wild animal – a badger, deer or prowling fox. Our senses are upside down and everyone is laughing, cos we have to go slowly, especially through the woods. At the top of Coombe Hill the security cameras around the Prime Minister's country house, Chequers, pick out a bunch of cyclists who have stopped for a sandwich and a drink. A patrol car comes out to investigate. 'Got any ID?'

'Of course we haven't; we're on our bikes! Timmy Mallett's in charge.'

'Are you all a bunch of comedians?!' And they send us on our way.

Down to West Wycombe's Hellfire Caves, where I've arranged for Jack the manager to scare the living daylights out of us. He's there in costume, with hair-raising tales as we are taken down into the depths of the chalky Chilterns. Then we catch sight of the first light in the eastern sky and by half past three the dawn chorus has begun. Daylight swiftly follows and before we realise it, we've gone from late night to early morning in less than a dozen miles. We end up with the early mist rising on the river, and a breakfast feast by the outdoor fire pit, courtesy of Mrs Mallett and friends. We slope off to bed by half seven and some embellish the tales of what we saw when we meet up. It's a fabulous tradition and I love it. But those rides are planned. They are looked forward to. This ride is very different.

Celine, the bar manager, takes pity on me, makes a few calls and then hands me the phone. An English voice, Roger, says, 'Yes, we have a room in our gite. It's nearly thirty kilometres away in the middle of nowhere; you'd never find it without GPS.' It's my only option; somehow I'm going to have to make it work. My phone says it's an hour and a half away. I always said I wouldn't rush anywhere. I'd take my time and absorb it all. Not tonight. Tonight, I'm stuck. I need to get there. I'm hurrying off the main road as the sun goes down and the sheep bleat for home. The little lanes have no signposts and I'm getting cold even with all these layers on, and I'm anxious. Over a highway, come to a crossroads – there's no signpost. As it goes dark – or, as Mrs Mallett might say, 'black as a bat's bum' – I'm aware my phone battery is on 5 per cent, there hasn't been a dwelling for 20 minutes and my E-bike battery shows just three kilometres left. I'm exhausted, can only see the pool of illumination in front of my wheels and need to rethink things.

Is that a light across the fields? I ride gingerly along a track. Thank the Lord, it's the gite. Roger comes out to greet me. An English voice. Relief. I'm safe. But phew, I don't ever want to have to do that again, unless it's a planned overnight ride with friends in midsummer!

Roger and Sue have set up a boutique, upmarket B&B in southern Brittany. It's my unexpected bit of luxury on this trip and quite a contrast to the retired nuns the night before. In the morning I discover I'm not the only guest. About midnight last night a weird Frenchman arrived by taxi. He sits all morning at the breakfast table, saying nothing. We try to coax him into telling us who he is and what he's planning to do. There's a strange story about a sister perhaps coming to collect him and take him to where he lives alone a hundred miles away. Sue asks the mayor what to do with the strange guest – and the

Frenchman! I spend the morning painting from my sketches and photos from the day before. Mental health needs our attention. It's World Down Syndrome Day. I think of brother Martin, born with Down's, and how much we enjoyed cycling together. As long as we were doing things together he was content: 'You me', 'I'm happy'.

I overdid the cycling yesterday. Massively. Today I'll paint first, pedal later and I'll go much slower and stop sooner; remember what my friend Judy said: 'These are the Golden Years. Be kind to yourself.' It's a nice instruction and a good excuse to pause. Take stock. Be in the moment.

6
Noire Loire

Acts of random kindness are always more noticeable when we are alone and vulnerable. I am delighted when my Camino brings me nuggets of generosity at unexpected moments.

I once had a black Renault 5 with a glorious piece of artwork sprayed on the side. It was French (obviously) and my name for it rhymed. I called it 'Noir Loire', but I spelt it wrong! I missed the 'e' off Noire. 'We were going to tell you,' said my friends, 'but we wanted to see if you'd notice!' When I pranged the car, and the panel needed replacing, I nailed the beautifully painted name bit to the wall of my garage, as a souvenir of my love of imaginative language.

The soft and gentle Way of the Plantagenets that I have chosen to follow southwards weaves into Anjou and I'm greeted by the formidable castle of Pouancé, built to protect against intruders from Brittany. It would have been one of the places those pesky Plantagenets stayed on their journeys across the empire. There's even a turreted medieval gatehouse for sale. 'What would I do with a medieval turret house?' I'd collect bits of medieval stuff to put in it!

It's threatening to be a spring morning with a bite. It starts cold and overcast, and clears and warms to a balmy 10 or 11 degrees as the route drops down into the valley of the Loire, which isn't *noire* at all. It's warm rich farmland with sprigs of white. The first bits of hawthorn blossom make me think spring may be on its way. Sadly, there's no apple blossom, just a chap cutting down several acres of apple orchard, not far short of 200 trees.

'Why are you doing that?'

'*Pommes. C'est mort.*'

'Are you going to replant the trees?'

'*Non. Agriculture.*'

It doesn't feel right.

This afternoon I want to be better prepared and I ask at the tourist office for help for this evening. No problem. A few miles on, in the next town, Lion d'Angers, there's the perfect place. A special pilgrim hostel with free rooms for pilgrims. The phone rings and rings . . . 'Oh, hang on; it's closed on Wednesdays.' Everything is closed on Wednesdays, except a delightful *chambre d'hôte* (B&B) by the river. This little town surprises me. First with Eric the organ grinder and his little dog, Jumper. They look like something out of another era, another century. Jumper the dog has clearly never jumped for anything in his life. Eric slowly turns the organ handle and I'm their sole audience in an otherwise deserted street. The music is quaint and it's all so perfectly here and now. My friend Michael, Canon at York Minster, makes it a rule never to walk past a street entertainer. If someone is prepared to do something to entertain you, then stop, look, listen and enjoy. It's a good lesson on a day like today, with nobody about because everything is shut. But I am here, so Eric and Jumper play for me, and I applaud.

Tonight, I eat alone in the only place open – Lion Pizza. A tiny immigrant-run café where, by chance, a profound and thoughtful conversation follows that includes brother Martin, Down's syndrome and being made welcome in a strange land. I am the Turkish man's only customer that night, and for both of us it is a brilliant evening.

I'm a week into my journey and today the air traffic controllers are on strike. No flights, trains full, busy roads, but I'm on my bike. Why should this affect me on quiet lanes? Mrs Mallett will not be able to fly out and join me this weekend. We had planned to be together in our twin town, but that's all off now. Shame, I was looking forward to some much-needed gentle encouragement from home. It means I haven't got to be any-where today. In that case, I'll just be here instead. Cutting out the importance of being somewhere else is liberating. My day is not defined by where I need to get to but by what I'm seeing and experiencing here and now.

Laura, my hostess, encourages me to paint her view of the River Mayenne from her garden.

This is a very good suggestion. The air is soft and I can smell the celandines and the river. There's the hint of the aroma of spring; the flat light is smooth, the reflections are perfect, and the dark ivy on the black tree trunks gives a moody look. I reflect upon my family, and on the tree where I sit with the watercolours, I plant a Martin Mallett name tag. At home, when Martin and I walked down to the River Thames we would feed the ducks and skim stones. When he was little, I told young son Billy that the *Titanic* sank near the bridge. Martin perked up; he liked the film and readily agreed. Billy still points out the place.

The Loire Valley is chateau country. Around each bend, it seems, another impressive castle comes into view. This is where anyone who won the lottery, all those centuries ago, built a chateau.

And today I learn a lesson about why it's good to be on a bike. Because it's easier to stop. If I'd come across this in a car I'd have had to find somewhere to park and that's too much of an effort. If I'd been walking, I'd be going out of my way. On a bicycle, and especially an E-bike, it's easy to stop, because getting momentum again afterwards will be straightforward.

I've stopped because of something I've seen in a field. Something that takes me back to before those chateaux were even thought of. George and Damian are cutting up and splitting the most enormous fallen oak tree. It's well over 600 years old and would have been a sapling before our Henry VIII was on the throne, a mature tree when Louis XIV was prancing around as the Sun King, and an ancient thoroughbred when Napoleon was rampaging across Europe. Now the tree is riddled with Capricorn beetles – enormous big bugs with massive antennae – that chew their way through anything wooden. The oak has fallen over in the middle of the field and these two men are chopping and splitting it into firewood. There's another lesson here. Don't get too confident – all things must pass, and it doesn't always end with the tree as a fine piece of furniture, or timber for a building. These two men have several weeks of constant chopping and splitting before them and they offer me the axe. It's immensely satisfying to smash the logs into pieces. But then I'm used to hitting things with Mallett's Mallet. In my painting of this scene there's a neighbouring tree overhanging the workmen. Don't get too confident, the painting says. Those beetles must find somewhere to go . . . This tree will end its days as a refuge for bugs and creatures before finally keeping people warm in winter when it's consumed on the fire.

I am rummaging for something in my cycle bag and come across the St Christopher medallion that has made its way with me, courtesy of my thoughtful friend Irene. A little prayer card: 'It is not the distance travelled but the quality of the journey. Leave behind a trail of hope, love and peace.' I like that – makes me feel good about the trail of mud I seem to be picking up and dropping.

Last time I was in Angers was over a decade ago with the Wanderers five-a-siders, when we all pretended to be 'dead flies' lying on our backs on the football pitch. Today, in front of Angers Castle, I surprise the tourists by lying on my back, waving arms and legs in the air, to celebrate this acrobat having cycled here all the way from home. These little moments of achievement feel wonderful and I leave a Martin name tag in the candy coloured stripes of the castle walls. 'I'm happy!'

I can almost hear the whistle.

Whoever had the whistle could blow it at any time and set a task for someone else in the group. Someone had to run around the football pitch backwards, then in the city centre Scotsman Colin had to wear an English wig and sing 'En-ger-land'.

It's a fun game, and we had played it all weekend in Angers. Originally it was my best man Andy's idea. On my stag week-end I'd come off-air on *Wacaday* at half past nine on the Friday morning and we'd hurried across London. A dozen of us took the boat train from Victoria station to Dover and across to

Ostend for the usual beer and fun-games weekend. The whistle was blown and Solly had to carry everyone's bag from train to ferry (wheeled cases hadn't been invented). In Ostend, he blew the whistle and Peter had to crawl on his hands and knees across the beach to the sea and back. The tide was out; he was gone for 45 minutes. The whistle was blown. Glover had to stand under the icy outdoor shower getting brain freeze, then the whistle screamed and someone else was instructed to swim to England, or that buoy over there, whichever was nearer. Another one had to feign death on the pavement. It was an imaginative weekend, though by the end Solly had consumed a little too much and was feeling sick as three of us squeezed into the back of the taxi, with him in the middle. Suddenly he needed to be sick. '*Arrête!* Stop the car!' I jumped out quickly to let him out, but he didn't follow. Instead, the door slammed and the car sped away with my 'friends' waving and cackling. It was only a couple of miles or so to the port and I hurried along, smiling. Good gag!

I arrived, presented my passport and told them I was part of the party of 12 on the 4:30 p.m. ferry. 'That's it there, on the horizon,' I was told. It had gone at 3:30 p.m. 'You'll have to buy another ticket for the next ferry at six p.m.' And so it was a very late and lonely trip home, without my friends to share the gag. I missed the captain's tannoy announcement on the earlier ferry as it made its way across the Channel – the chart news and congratulations that my hit 'Itsy Bitsy' was number one. My friends all felt a little sheepish but were still invited to the wedding the following week. The moral is: never get into a vehicle with someone who feels sick – or keep hold of the whistle.

There's a swimming gala in town and every hotel room is taken. I can't believe there's nowhere to stay in a big city like Angers, but Cecile is my angel today in the tourist office when she mentions somewhere called the diocesan house on an island in the Loire. 'There's room there,' she says, and – pause – 'the path should be OK . . .'

I cycle along the embankment of the River Maine as it heads towards its junction with the mighty Loire. Sure enough, the pathway completely disappears under flood water. The recent heavy rains mean no alternative but a substantial detour carrying the bike up and over the footbridge. How's this for serendipity? A young jogger named Max stops to help me. The brief conversation reveals he's from Poitiers and knows my friend Dom the mayor. We wouldn't have spoken if the track hadn't been flooded. It's an encouraging signal.

Late in the day I reach the island of Béhuard, 25 kilometres from Angers. The island is famous for the rock of St Peter Church that has survived countless floods. It's built into the only high point on the island – the rock – and nearby there's an impressive three-storey Catholic diocesan mansion, raised up in case of flooding and with accommodation for more people than I've met in a week. Stephanie and Claudette look at me quizzically. 'We didn't know you were coming . . . Yes, there is room. You are the only one here.' I rattle around in an empty building with space for several hundred. Smiling Claudette, in her late 60s, has encouraging comments on this adventure. She walked from Mont St Michel to Santiago on her own in 73 days. Gentle Stephanie finds me something to eat – wine, bread, eggs and cheese. She has adopted an autistic daughter, Maria. 'That was brave to take on someone with such challenges,' I offer.

'Not really,' she replies. 'We all have to do what is best . . .'

Our dear brother Martin – ma bubba – was born with Down's syndrome in Marple, Cheshire, in August 1953. He was the second son of Michael and Nan. It had been a troubling pregnancy and in her own way Mum knew there was something different about this child. She was a tearful, fearful new mother who confided in her doctor, 'What's wrong with us?'

The doctor paused – 'He'll bring his own welcome.'

And what a welcome. Martin was an inquisitive little boy who grew up exploring, digging, finding, losing, trying, always with a smile.

When the third boy – me – came along two years later (that was brave of my parents, wasn't it?) we were a little band of brothers ready for anything. We formed a pop group together and called ourselves the Kettle Holders. Martin was the drummer. The drums were saucepans, and the cymbals were their lids. Paul played the toy Chad Valley three-string guitar and I bashed the tambourine.

Paul couldn't remember the words.

Martin couldn't say the words.

And I just made them up.

We had one song, which went like this . . .

Comer comer, I got some love so true.
Comer comer, I got some love so true.

Not quite 'Itsy Bitsy', but Martin lived that song. He had love in abundance, and an extra chromosome. We sometimes wondered if that extra chromosome, which defines Down's syndrome, is an extra chromosome of love. You can't have too much love in the world, can you?

But it wasn't just Down's syndrome for Martin. He also had language difficulties. These weren't helped by having a tongue a little too large for his mouth. There was the dreadful day he fell off his bike and bit his tongue so badly he needed stitches.

Today a young Martin would have had all sorts of educational support. It was our mother who patiently taught him basic reading and writing. He learned simple Makaton sign language. It might not sound much but there is great dignity in being able to sign your own name, 'Martin x', except that the kiss was always done like this: '+'.

Brothers are not always as kind as they are told to be. It took an uncomfortable episode to learn our teasing could be cruel . . .

Martin was a lot stronger than either Paul or me and we liked to goad him into picking on the other one. We'd push him to see how far we could go. Then he'd explode and chase us up the stairs and we screamed. There was a glass window in the door and Martin put his fist through it. He lived with those awful scars on his arm and if anyone ever asked how they came about, he pointed directly at Paul and me to remind us. We never stopped apologising – or blaming the other one.

It was useful having an older brother who would play my games. Aged ten and eight, Martin and I went to cubs together; the other scouts protected Martin and he belonged to the pack. 'Dib Dib Dib, we'll Dob Dob Dob.' One night on our way to the cub meeting some big kids picked on us in the street. 'He goes to our school,' said one of them, pointing at me. 'Get the other one . . .'

'Leave him alone,' I pleaded as Martin was targeted. We were in tears and the big cubs came running out to chase the kids away.

The best cub week was bob-a-job, and Martin somehow raised the most. He liked earning his badges. He was a lot better than the rest of us at cleaning and tidying, and he liked to wash and brush diligently and thoroughly. Being neat and tidy was something he did himself – everything else was a shared pleasure – 'washing up, you me'. We three boys would wash, dry and put away. Probably not best to get Martin to put away. Things could end up anywhere.

Look in Martin's room. Everything is always neatly folded and put in its place. Often in some other place that made sense to Martin at the time but which nobody else could fathom.

To Martin there was dignity and delight in doing chores. Especially shared chores. How often we heard him say, 'Me work hard!'

Being tidy and neat meant that things were often lost.

Not least himself. Our parents tried locks on the gate, wire netting in the hedge, but still Martin got out and went exploring. He had, though, a very good sense of direction and would amazingly find his way home for tea. As he got older, our parents were happy to let him go to the shops with a list, to get bread and eggs. In his teens, he learned to take a bus and on one occasion, when the bus was a long time coming, got in a taxi and gave the driver directions to his home. Left and right. Was this a more trusting age? Or a more empowering time?

Our parents certainly worried. Dad often found himself searching down by the canal for little lost Martin. 'Every time I came to a canal lock I hardly dared look over the edge.' There was the time Martin had gone out and was away too long. Suddenly there were dozens of police around the place, far too many, and there was a very anxious atmosphere in our home. I was sent to bed early. 'It's not fair,' I pleaded. 'I'm not the one in trouble.'

It was the time of the Moors murders. Brady and Hindley had not been caught, and Mum and Dad's fears grew as the host of uniformed officers asked questions and looked at pictures of the missing lad. Martin had gone past the canal down to the station, got on a train, headed into Manchester and hours later was picked up by a concerned stranger, a very Good Samaritan. Why did our brother Martin do that? It's a big world out there and he was keen to explore.

It's a cold, grey, damp day. A day to wear lots of layers and expect to get wet, with not a chance of painting or sketching. But I still decide to zig-zag, to go back on myself and explore . . . That's another way of saying I am happy to get lost, trying to find my way back on to the signed Camino Way of the Plantagenets. I'm doing a Martin thing here, without realising. Let yourself get lost and see what happens. As long as you are vaguely going in the right direction, the route may become apparent again.

And there's scope for serendipity . . .

Downton Abbey has apparently gone on holiday to France. The enormous stately home at Brissac has graceful cedar trees spreading their shade over the parkland. Someone lets me through the gate into the private grounds and I wait on the bench for Carson or the Dowager Countess to confront me. Carson, that is Jim Carter, did arrive. Only not in Brissac. I met him at Windsor Castle cricket pitch, when I played in a charity match with Jimmy Anderson, Graeme Swann and Andrew Strauss, stalwarts of the England cricket team and their pals. Carter was the umpire. I bowled out Peter Reid, the footballer, and took Swanny's wicket in dramatic circumstances. He smashed my bowling high in the air and the ball was caught by a youngster six feet beyond the boundary. The highlight of my cricketing career. Up went Carson's finger. 'You're out, m'lord!'

Drizzly weather means I have to concentrate. The slippery road can be treacherous. But I'm distracted on the ride across to Doué-la-Fontaine by a landscape of Hobbit holes, or troglodytes as they are known. Homes, farms, wine cellars all underground. The Camino route through here meanders and I like that. Meanderings reveal things . . . as I get wetter. A soggy donkey comes up to me to have his nose rubbed. We like the way animals give us love and attention without prompting. This moment in the drizzle reminds me we are both out in all weathers and sodden wet.

This is not a jolly jaunt. It's strange how vulnerable you feel away from familiar surroundings. When at home it's easy. Hungry? Open the fridge. Tired? Go to your bed. Every day on this adventure I wake up not knowing who I'm going to meet, what I'm going to eat, where I'm going to stay or even which detour I'm going to take. They say that being a pilgrim is to make yourself vulnerable. To be prepared for the unexpected. Indeed to welcome the unexpected. Is it naivety? I wouldn't do this if I were travelling with someone else. An extra person would mean I'd have to take account of someone else's energies and wants. To travel alone in this way is both liberating and a little scary.

I'm in vineyard country. It seems right to find a spot for brother Martin, and I choose one of the gnarled trunks and attach his name tag, entwined in the ancient vines. Let me tell you, this year's wine will be a fine vintage.

It's the end of my seventh day in France. Late afternoon I reach Doué, the 'Rose capital of France', and my usual charming way with the tourist office produces nothing. I am an unwelcome hindrance and sent off to a local hotel. There's nobody to check me in. Told to wait an hour till the manager returns, I remember the accommodation list from the Confraternity of St James and find the number of an English couple who aren't doing overnight stays any more but invite me for a coffee.

The cuppa and a chat turns into delicious homemade soup followed by beans on toast flavoured with blue cheese and balsamic vinegar. 'Please stay,' say Katie and Malcolm. 'I used to work for George Harrison,' offers Katie, 'and you're welcome. But we'll have to fix the shower first!'

Such simple kindness is a massive boost to a travelling pilgrim. Generous expats with hearts of gold. Smiling company offering hearty food, a warm bed and a shower. What more can you wish for?

I'm blessed on this journey.

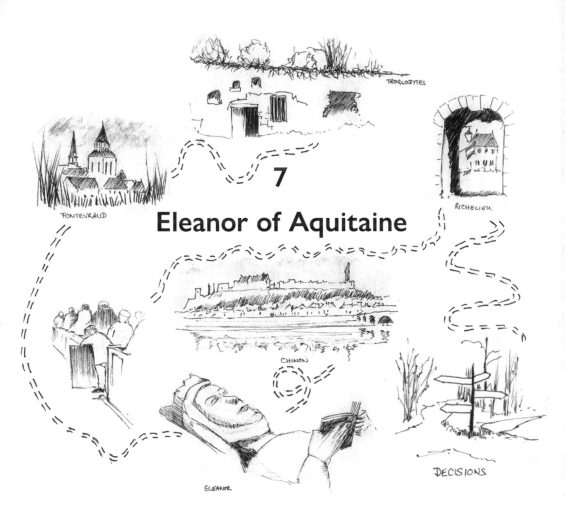

7

Eleanor of Aquitaine

How does someone who lived more than 800 years ago have an impact on a bike ride in the twenty-first century? We all have heroes. I happen to look up to a woman from the Middle Ages who reached her potential and then some.

It was all over the news. Guest celebrities commented on the scandal. The Queen of France got an annulment – the gossips say because King Louis was more interested in going to church than going to bed. She left him with a daughter and took her lands and money. Gave him a goodbye peck on the cheek on the way out. No hard feelings, dear.

Two months later she stunned everyone by marrying an

eligible catch 12 years her junior with the finest pair of legs, a wicked laugh and no qualms about making the goose feathers fly. What a woman! Eleanor of Aquitaine knew what she wanted and she knew how to get it. She had the best pre-nup ever and got to keep the province of Aquitaine when she left the King of France. A few months later it got better still. Her new husband inherited the crown of England, and now Henry and Eleanor were the richest, smartest, sexiest couple on the planet. Eleanor began delivering children, lots of them, and two of their sons would become kings in her lifetime.

I would love to read the gossip columns, the social media, of the twelfth century. They would be absolutely alive with this extraordinary woman. Forget Madonna and Lady Gaga; Eleanor was the greatest woman of her age since . . . well, I'm hard pressed to find someone to shine as bright. Cleopatra? Hardly. Boudicea? Not really. Elizabeth I is getting better. Marilyn Monroe? Lovely but not a chance.

Eleanor's story is amazing in any age, but for the twelfth century it's extraordinary. As a child she inherited her father's hugely wealthy duchy of Aquitaine after he died on the Santiago de Compostela pilgrimage in April 1137. (Hey, the Camino has been working its magic on people for centuries.) All the lands between the Atlantic Ocean and the Mediterranean Sea became hers. She learned immediately that a teenage woman with money is an attractive catch. Young King Louis of France came courting and the couple were married within a few weeks in Bordeaux Cathedral. There's still a carving of Eleanor's face above the main door, where she keeps an eye on every visitor. The honeymoon was cool – Eleanor and Louis went on crusade. Hmmm, that sounds appealing. It wasn't a great success. Eleanor had more fun with (let's call him Uncle) Raymond (which made very juicy gossip for the tabloids). However, her ability to travel in tough conditions and put up with disappointment showed she was robust and determined. Remember that, Mallett: be robust and determined.

The next wedding, to her toy boy Henry, in Poitiers Cathedral, was a massive affair. Poitiers was the capital of her province of Aquitaine and Eleanor liked music, poetry and entertainment. Hers was a colourful court; indeed Eleanor was the catalyst for the twelfth-century Renaissance. Behind the flourishing of arts, the growth of chivalry and the building of grand cathedrals lies her wealthy and glamorous patronage. It's still on show all along the Camino.

And then came chaos. Henry had a roving eye and was more interested in the young Rosamund Clifford than his wife, while his sons began a series of rebellions for more expenses and power. Eleanor, feeling slighted, encouraged the rebels and even joined in. There's a delicious story that she was captured fleeing dressed as a man. What followed was that the Queen of England was locked up by her husband, the king, for 16 years. Now that's a scandal. But don't write her off yet. In 1189 her favourite son, Richard the Lionheart, inherited the crown, and his first act was to let his mum out of prison and make her regent over England while he went off on crusade. Richard loved fighting, and to go on crusade and win battles made him very happy. However, it wasn't a great return trip for Richard and by bad luck he was captured and held to ransom in Germany. The price of his freedom was six times the Gross Domestic Product of England. Ouch!

Amazingly, England raised the money in 18 months. So the price was upped to include the Hand of St James (the same hand that is in St Peter's Church, Marlow). It was Eleanor's idea to instead offer something that wouldn't cost much but would be expensive to receive – a decorated, fancy, travelling gazebo.

It was a massive affair, covered in gold embroidery, designed to wow visitors. Of course, there were no spare parts, and like all gazebos it only lasted a couple of seasons. But it got Richard home again and kept the Hand of St James in the Thames Valley. Meanwhile all that English silver flooding Europe led to rampant inflation and stimulated the English economy. Go Eleanor! Yah boo to continental rivals.

The Camino connection continues . . .

When Richard was killed, it broke Eleanor's heart (we are never meant to outlive our children) and she retired to live out her years in a convent not far from where I'm cycling today. At the grand age of 80, her youngest son, King John, had one last job for her. To cross the Pyrenees and select a princess for a diplomatic marriage. That should be inspiration for me in a couple of weeks when I'm attempting to cycle over that massive mountain range.

Eleanor lies now, in dignified effigy, alongside tempestuous husband Henry and beloved son Richard the Lionheart, in Fontevraud Abbey. It's worth cycling a 50-kilometre detour to see this great figure of world history and one of my all-time heroines, who stands head and shoulders above all the men of her age.

Dream big and your life can be big. Dream small and your life will be small. Eleanor dreamed exceptionally big.

I like the idea of dreaming big dreams. Do we dream that big these days? I would say the nature of being human makes us dream the big dreams. But getting them to come true is the trick. For dreams to come true, you need to work at them. Hard work is usually associated with success, and that means tackling the things you might not want to face.

I've got a big dream to cycle on my own across Europe on the Camino de Santiago.

To make your dreams a reality you have to have a plan and follow it through. And that means doing your prep. Prep's important.

I learned this lesson well at the school debate: this house believes we should do away with school uniforms. 'OK, Mallett, you're opening in favour of the motion.' This is easy. School uniforms are pointless, we don't like wearing them and they cost money. 'You'll be great at this, Timmy,' say my friends. 'Can't wait for your speech; you'll win easily.' I walk around confident it will all come good on the night; then the day arrives and I start to feel a little uneasy. But I know it will be fine. I'll think of loads of things to say.

I'm opening the debate, the hall is packed, and everyone is waiting eagerly. I look at my associate speaker – he's got notes, and so have the opposition. Er . . . should I perhaps have thought about this?

We are introduced on to the stage and the English teacher, Mr Sharpe, smiles and sets the debate in motion. I'm first up to the podium. Round of applause. 'This house believes that school uniforms are a waste of time, because we don't like wearing them, I hate doing up my tie and tucking my shirt in and', my voice starts to waver a bit, 'they cost money . . . er and another thing . . . they don't look good . . .' And I sit down, embarrassed. I had nothing to say, no argument and I was utterly rubbish. The other three speakers have jokes and lots of good points. The teacher wraps it up. He mentions the others; then turns to me with a gentle, disappointed smile and the smallest but most damning of rebukes: 'A little lacking in preparation there . . .' We lost the debate and the embarrassment still hurts.

Next chance I get, I work at it. 'This house believes there are fairies at the bottom of the garden . . .' I'm opposing. After tea, my dad kindly offers me a closing statement and I write out my arguments and work on my delivery. Punchlines need to be practised. Most successful punchlines don't come out of thin air. I've written a two-page speech. I learn it, rehearse it and walk around the house delivering it. I need to have a memorable punchline that will sum up my argument and be remembered by all. Come the day I am a transformation from the uniform debacle. 'There is washing on the line in my garden and a smelly compost heap at the far end of that thing called the lawn. There are weeds and an old bike and there may even be a rabbit in a hutch, but fairies at the bottom of the garden?' I boom in triumph, 'Fairies, my arse!' Nailed it.

Prepping things is worth it. At Radio Luxembourg, on a two-month, stand-in gig, I was interested to see Rob Jones writing in his big blue book. 'What's that?' I asked.

'I'm doing my prep for the afternoon show on the community station.'

'But that's just a couple of hours of meaningless filler, on the tiny little local service,' I remarked.

'I know,' said Rob, 'but I like to get my one-liners rehearsed for the evening show, because my audience is Europe wide. Few DJs can think of a punchline on the spot. You have to write them down and practise them.' It was the clue my dad had revealed and I seized on it. Without realising, I'd actually been prepping gags and ideas since my very first radio show ever on University Radio Warwick. I had walked past the open door of the radio hut the day I arrived and heard a voice say, 'Would the next DJ turn up soon, please? I want to go for my breakfast.' Because I showed an interest, I was given an hour's slot the following week. That first ever broadcast would set me on the way to my career.

In my first show, I talked about the student accommodation I was living in. My student house had one of those hotel toasters, where you put your bread on the tray and wait a minute for it to drop off the end all brown and toasty. I worked out that at full speed it would deliver a slice of toast every 15 seconds, which meant that it took only 8.75 minutes to feed all the residents in the hall, and 12 and a half hours to feed the entire student population. Utterly useless and quirky.

Skip forward a few years and there I was on my first show on Radio Luxembourg. I was Timmy on the Tranny firing in the jingles, talking fast and playing smash hits like 'Town Called Malice' by the Jam. I introduced it 'Clown Called Mallett'!

I found the show on an old reel-to-reel in the loft and heard my voice from December 1981 booming out again: 'I'm a great tea drinker . . . I bought some liquorice tea bags today. There's research out this week that says in the last eighteen months we've drunk twenty per cent more tea, so by my reckoning in thirty-six years' time (2017) we'll all be drinking a cup of tea every two and a half minutes.'

I noticed that all the presenters I admired did their prep. Something mildly amusing happened to you today? Write it down, think of a punchline and deliver it. There's also a feeling that putting out lots of gags means something is more likely to hit. They don't all have to be belly laughs. We prepped gags on *Wacaday*, looked for funny word plays and used them over and over again so that the audience – Wideawakers – would feel they shared a private language. 'Kenya believe it? Course you can!' 'There's Norway you can do that!' 'What are we? We're wide awake!' 'GoBots Go Botty!' 'Blaahlin – capital of Blaaahmany!' As Mrs Mallett's father used to say, 'You don't have to be funny. Just be quick!'

If ever I was stuck for something to say, I'd have a look through the preppy book for a line from a year or so ago and re-use it differently. That preppy book was the best thing going.

My young Timmy helper, Chris Evans, and I discussed the never-ending list of ideas our preppy books offered many times as he went on to do new shows at new stations.

I like prepping. It's about putting your mind to things. Things may still go wrong but at least you are prepared.

I plan my Camino, and the lovely Eleanor of Aquitaine appears all over today's ride. In one church there's a relic from the Holy Land brought by her grandfather. I love the idea of a bit of holiday/pilgrimage souvenir being kept in the church. In Montreuil-Bellay there's a castle rich in her chivalrous architecture and I'm inspired to set up my watercolours on the bridge to capture it on a grey, damp, freezing day.

To detour or not detour? You betcha! If it's to see an all-time historical hero!

There are works going on around the regal effigies in Fontevraud, and it feels like the perfect time and place for a Martin Mallett moment. I like my big brother being among kings and queens, high achievers and those who strove to reach their potential. A Martin name tag goes into the joints where they are relaying marble flagstones next to Eleanor. They'll keep each other company. 'Soft lady,' Martin will say. 'My friend. You me.' And if I were to meet Eleanor of Aquitaine today, guess what I would ask her?

'Can I paint your portrait? And do you fancy coming on a bike ride?' Bet she'd say 'yes' to both.

It's so worthwhile doing the diversion that I go on a further 30 kilometres to their massive royal castle. Under purple clouds, Chinon stands above the river, dominating the town and putting all the other castles, towers and fortifications that I've seen into perspective. Nothing comes close to the real deal. Out comes the sketch pad and I'm in the moment. It's a great image with that craggy silhouette. Storm clouds gather. The river is still, pensive and reflective. It feels like a metaphor for the tumultuous Angevin empire, or maybe it's Brexit looming. Live big, dream big. This should have been a lesson.

Because then I do something I regret. I'll only do it the one time, and it will sound foolish and maybe you'll go 'So what?' This is the moment I cycle past a photo/painting opportunity.

Whenever I'm on the bike I'm looking for things that excite my eye, maybe a painting, a photo, a moment to absorb, a moment of magic. Not everyone does this and there's a very good reason. Momentum. You come around the corner, you see something, you think about taking a picture or having a look, but there's a hill ahead or you're going a decent speed and it'd be an effort to get going again. Not on my Timmeee E-bike. Stopping and restarting again – no problem. The bike is the means to an end, not the end itself.

My last hour's ride today is along the brand new cycle path on a converted railway line to Richelieu. It's so new, there isn't a leaf on the trail and no tyre tracks in the gravel. It will be officially opened in a few weeks and I'm possibly the first cyclist to ride it. This tells me France loves its cyclists, and as I'm riding, the sun comes out from behind the clouds to bathe the whole landscape in a glorious golden evening sunlight. The colours are sensational, and turning the corner I get a vision of heaven through the trees in that low winter sun, backlit and majestic. I can already picture the painting. 'Stop,' I tell myself, 'and set up the image.' It'll only take a few seconds, but I hear my own voice say, 'I'm tired. I'll do it tomorrow. There'll be another opportunity.' But there never will be a sunset like this again on the whole journey. Maybe it's because tonight the clocks will change and the seasons and the sunlight will move on. Today I learned my lesson. Seize every moment. Never miss an opportunity, because life only comes around once. This is it. It's not a dress rehearsal. This is the real thing.

I needed a job. I had a dream. I wanted to be on air and make a name for myself. I was finishing university (History with History of Art) and I fancied doing more with that radio bug. I'd written to every radio station in the country and had a string of rejections. Except for one letter. Keith Salmon at BBC Radio Oxford wrote: 'Sorry, nothing right now, but if you are ever in the area . . .' I didn't read the rest. Just fired back a reply saying I would be in the area on Friday. I put on a suit and hitch-hiked to Oxford and talked about my ambitions and willingness to do anything. He gave me a week's work. It became two weeks, a month, and I did whatever I was asked. When Elvis Presley died, I was allowed on air to play the hits of the King of Rock 'n' Roll. I had a go at the request show. Someone asked for a song by Nancy Sinatra, which we didn't have so instead I played her biggest hit, 'These Boots Are Made for Walking', with lots of love from the listener to her dad. She rang me up in tears.

'Why did you play that song? Anything but that song.'

'What's the matter? It's a massive hit.'

'It's my dad – he's got no legs!'

The role that worked best was being a kids'-show host every afternoon, after school. 'Will I be typecast?' I asked.

'You'll always be in work,' was the reply, 'because there will always be kids.'

That's when I became Timmy on the Tranny and each day the airwaves were alive with pop, jokes and excited young-sters. In the adventures of Prince Timmy and the Quest for the Golden Tranny there were hilarious nutty battles against borons and baddies. Directed by the Great Trannyoid in the sky, Prince Timmy and his pet Octocat (a grown-up octopus) always needed the help of the heroine Susan Zinc (she's always on her metal!), who was charismatically portrayed by seven-year-old Emma Boughton – better known these days as the wonderful DJ Emma B.

And while I was having a great time making a name for myself, I was practising my art and enjoying the interesting people I came across through my love of history. People have different ways of leaving a legacy. It's unusual to come across a politician whose legacy is a town named after him. I change my Camino route today to take in that town.

Cardinal Richelieu is a cartoon character in *The Three Musketeers*, the delicious, evil, scarlet villain in the stories, though in real life he was so much more than that. The cardinal was a Charlie I lookalike reformer and the money man for the ambitious plans of King Louis XIII. One of his schemes was a model town, built on the grid system that the Americans so admired and copied. Richelieu designed it, made a model, got the nobles very excited and they all wanted to be in it, as near to the heart of the action as possible. The catch was, they had to pay for the construction, which they did! Bingo!

Today, 350 years later, Richelieu is still an impressive place and the crowds have come to promenade around the town and to pack the church for Palm Sunday. There isn't a spare seat in the building. I'm standing at the back, smelling the incense, looking at the expectant assembly listening to the priest chanting. A young boy swings on the door of his pew. Why? Because he can – because he can cling to the top of the door and drag his feet across the bit between floor and door. An adult may tell him to stop in due course. But everyone secretly wants to do the same thing. Break the rules, why don't you?!

One of the sights people notice today is a cycling artist

dressed in scarlet – I imagine I'm one of the three Malletteers: Timmyos, Mallettos, Wackyos – sketching at the main gate!

The clocks have changed and the light is different. Spring is in the air and under a cool blue sky I ride down long and winding roads that lead straight across the big landscape of southern Loire into the prairies of the Charente. People are playing petanque, flowering yellow forsythia is attached to my bike. On a large memorial waymarker with a crucifix I place a Martin name tag. Martin had a strong faith and it seems right to put a tag looking out on the big sky and everlasting landscape. This is a crossroads in the middle of the country and the stone sign-post dwarfs my bike, reminding me as I paint the junction that every day is full of big decisions. Which way will I go? What will happen next? Who will I meet?

8

Twin town

What's the point of getting blessings and encouragement? Is it any different from collecting stamps or autographs? Possibly not – except sometimes the people we meet give us more than just words.

My first experience of France was the school trip to Paris in 1970. InterCity from Manchester, boat train from London Victoria, ferry from Dover Marine, odours of Gauloise cigarettes on the SNCF train from Calais to Gare du Nord, school kids running up and down the corridors being told to behave. We stayed at the modestly named Hotel Perfect near Anvers (it's still there) and were quick to discover the Moulin Rouge and Pigalle were nearby. There was a girls' school trip staying at Hotel Bristol. We stood outside and shouted. Someone came on to the balcony and we ran away. Culturally, there was the Louvre and the metro, but they just aren't as memorable, are they?

Town twinning was something dreamed up after the Second World War to see if Europe could find a way of getting on with its neighbours. Continental Europe took to it with enthusiasm. It wasn't until the 1970s that the UK started to consider the idea. Cheap flights and overseas holidays made it appealing; as did joining the European Economic Community – the EEC.

Hyde, in Tameside, where the Malletts lived, was twinned with Colmar, in Alsace, and in 1974 we teenagers went along and met Germans, Italians and French. We learned important things like Italian drinking songs, and a very useful German phrase, *Ich liebe dich leidenschaftlich* (I love you passionately). It was the sort of thing to shout out at the top of your voice, to see what happened. However, it wasn't for shouting that I got arrested, but for banging on the nice round metal street tables to make a lovely din after 10 p.m. Volume has always been a Mallett thing. Next moment I was in handcuffs, being escorted to a local *gendarmerie* lock-up.

Twenty minutes later, after some diplomatic intervention from our twinning hosts and a sheepish apology from me, I was released, lesson learned. Apart from noisy tables, Colmar has one of the masterpieces of the Renaissance – the Isenheim Altarpiece and its utterly brutal crucifixion. It's appalling to see the cross bending under the weight of the dying figure and the agony in his outstretched hands. There would have been a lot more noise and shouting at that event.

My current twin town, near Poitiers, wisely puts the metal

tables away each evening. We've been staying there with the mayor of St Benoit and family since the noughties. Mayor Dom and Sophie Clement have an ancient family holiday home in the woods, an hour south of St Benoit, near the intriguingly named town of Champagne Mouton (translation: 'Sheep Champagne'). There are photos of his father there in the wartime resistance. At the back of the woods is a sunken lane going over a ford past a small quarry. 'Before my father and his friends used it to escape from the Gestapo, this was an old Chemin de St Jacques route,' explained Dom. The Chemin de St Jacques is the French name for the Camino de Santiago, and visions of young vigilantes and ancient pilgrims stirred my interest. At the back of the quarry there is a small tunnel to hide in or where a hermit might live. I imagine ancient pilgrims stopping and chatting on their way across Europe. On the Clements' wall there is an old map from the Middle Ages of various Europe-wide routes to Santiago. So many different routes. I'm intrigued. Which should I choose and why?

It's an interesting thought that the original concept of Europe comes from the inquisitive citizens of the Continent. Not the spiritual and political leaders, even though they might take credit for it. Long before the first tentative steps in the 1950s that led to the treaty of Rome, the European Economic Community and eventually the European Union, ordinary people were exploring the idea of Europe. Curious people, travellers, traders and pilgrims from all across the Continent took it upon themselves to go in search of something special, and perhaps even something different to eat! All those strangers wandering around encouraged a growing economy, and the different cultures that have flourished across the Continent were the effect. I like discovering these new experiences (even though I occasionally find myself wanting something to eat that I understand). Even today there are so many different nationalities among the ever-growing number of travellers. It seems natural curiosity is inherent in all of us. Perhaps that's something to remember in the midst of Brexit?

In the past I've travelled by plane or train to Poitiers in hours. This time I arrive in ten days, cycling from home. I'm feeling very proud, with a huge sense of achievement, and Mayor Dom has arranged for a great big banner across the street: 'Go Go Timmy Go!' Everyone is asking what it means – is that encouragement or an instruction?! They even lay on a civic welcome in the town hall and it's really touching to have my adventure recognised in this way.

Dom has also shared my story with his friend, former French Prime Minister Jean-Pierre Raffarin. Jean-Pierre was Prime Minister to Jacques Chirac and he's sent me a wonderful email of encouragement in English: the second Prime Minister to support this adventure . . .

Dear Timmy
Dominique told me your beautiful trip. He said you are a good guy! I always believe him.
I walked to St Jacques for several years. I loved it.
Only one advice: drink the wine of Dom it's the best on the way.
Bon Chemin.
Jean-Pierre Raffarin

Thank you, Jean-Pierre. *Magnifique!*

There's an interview with a regional journalist. At midday, Daniel arrives with macaroons and when asked what he'd like to drink replies, 'Pernod please!' The aperitif helps the interview go swimmingly; I fall asleep immediately afterwards.

Interesting how I have to correct Daniel on the word 'handi-capped' when describing my brother. The condition is Down's syndrome; it has a name. 'Handicapped' is a comparison, and not appropriate any more. My mum used to give talks to different groups, entitled 'Being the parent of a mentally handicapped child'. It sounds so odd these days, as does the description that Martin was born a 'Mongol'. I'd like to think we are more thoughtful and hopefully a little less patronising now. The story obviously means something to him, as Daniel asks for a name tag, and of course I give him one.

History plays an important part in the way I see this Camino because the human aspect of the stories it encompasses res-onates with me through the years. They pop up unexpectedly, as now.

Near St Benoit is the site of the Battle of Poitiers, a great English victory over the French, when the Black Prince captured the French king in 1356. There's also the other great historical site – Châlus-Chabrol – where in the early evening of Thursday 25 March 1199 Richard the Lionheart met his match in the Man with the Pan. This is a *Wacaday*-type story, so Dom, Sophie and I have a brilliant afternoon re-enacting it with props.

King Richard was a man who had cheated death so many times. This particular early evening, he had just finished his meal, and went to inspect the tiny fortress to see about finish-ing off the simple siege. The castle had some impressive towers and a handful of defenders. Among them a legendary young-ster who had been seen on the parapet batting away arrows with a frying pan. Pierre Bassin was the name of the Man with the Pan (I love the fact that over eight centuries later we still know the name of King Richard's assailant) and right on cue there he was – pan man! To applause, Pierre batted away an arrow from the king's party. 'Show us what you can do then!' cried the king, and Pierre fired his crossbow from 150 metres. It hit Richard smack in the shoulder – great shot! (or just a lucky hit?) – and he wasn't wearing armour. The surgeon made a terrible hash of getting the arrow out and the shaft snapped off. The king could smell the onset of gangrene and called for young Pierre to come and see him under truce.

'Why did you shoot me?'

'You killed my father and brothers. It's revenge.'

'I forgive you. Here's a hundred schillings and you'll be spared.' Hmmm. It didn't last long . . . King Richard the Lionheart, warrior king of England, ruler of most of France, the legend of Europe, died 12 days later, in the arms of his mother. Poignantly, Eleanor of Aquitaine had dashed 120 miles in three days to be by his side.

In the room where he passed away, we imagine the scene: Richard, with his last breath, announcing his successor and agreeing a will with his wife and mother. Pierre is dispatched, of course (who can trust these promises?), and we recreate the whole thing in a *Wacaday* way with a bow and arrow and a frying pan. We should have used Mallett's Mallet in the story, but I forgot.

And after a two-day rest with my friends, it is time to move on.

It is raining . . . Proper all-day-long, never-going-to-stop rain. Woo, that's weather. Before leaving, though, there is an important thing to do . . .

Across France today there is a minute's silence for a gendarme with a young family, killed in a terrorist attack. He said to the terrorists, 'You can die in your struggle against France. Well, I can die for my country,' and he offered to change places with the hostage. The terrorists accepted and shot him. Such courage resonates across the world. It's right to stand still in the everlasting rain and honour a hero of our time. I imagine Richard the Lionheart would have saluted him.

Next is a blessing from the Archbishop of Poitier's vicar general, Jean-Paul. Vicar general sounds like a military figure, but in fact he's the archbishop's fixer. We meet in the impressive room where Joan of Arc pleaded her case to her judicial investigators. The poor young woman never stood a chance, though her dignity and faith shine through the centuries. There is a lot of history and world events surrounding me today. I had the support of President Macron at the start of my journey, and now the encouragement of a former Prime Minister and a French archbishop's vicar general. That should do me well across this country. Let's see, shall we?

I say farewell to my twin town, St Benoit – 16 of my paintings are to be shipped home – and I cycle south-west on the route known as the Chemin de Tours. There has been a discussion with Dom about heading south via Périgueux to Bergerac, but I decide instead to go further west through Saintes and Bordeaux along a more recognised Chemin de St Jacques route. Either way will be wet and windy. I recall Dom's comment last year when I said I would be starting in March. 'March? There may be a little wind . . .'

I thought that springtime would be fresh and different; that the colours would be emerging and the newness of the year would be an inspiration. 'Why don't you go in September when the weather is always good?' asked Mrs Mallett. But my heart was set on springtime and for the last five or six years March and April had been the sunniest and driest spring months. 'But how are you going to do it?' I didn't know. I needed help, advice and practice. All through the preparation months I discussed my thoughts and plans with the family; although it was some time before I had an answer to 'How will you lug all those paints and boards?'

I've always carried a set of watercolours. On *Wacaday* filming trips, whenever we were short of a story the director would say, 'Paint a picture, Timmy, and tell us what you are doing.' Those film stories were, without exception, challenging to do and gripping to watch. The crew loved them because it meant they wouldn't have to haul their gear very far and for some reason it's always interesting to see a picture emerge from a blank piece of paper. Except for my mother-in-law, Maisie. She would sit there and say, 'Hmmm. It's just like watching paint dry!'

I knew the watercolours would be relatively straightforward. A small set of a dozen colour pans, three or four tubes of vibrant, everyday colours and at least three watercolour pads. I wanted to take oil paints but they take too long to dry and are notoriously messy. I decided, instead, to take water-based acrylics, which are easy to use and quick-drying – a small bag of less than a dozen colours. For the painted surface I wanted to go A3 size (30 x 42 cm) and tried light and easy foam boards covered in acrylic paper, as well as slightly heavier art boards in a pack. I could carry over 30 surfaces, which I felt would serve me well. They sat in an A3 plastic box which also acted as the easel. The art kit was kept in a dry bag held on to the bike rack by the bungee cargo net. All I needed now was some drier weather to set up the easel and start painting.

This is springtime.

The wind is in my face, the rain coming sideways from a filthy sky, and ooh this is a tough day. It's unrelenting. I hope for a hedge or two to take the edge off the rain lashing sideways. No such luck. The French don't do nice protective English hedges. They like their open, exposed prairies. There must be somewhere to shelter. I struggle into a village, Saint-Sauvant, where someone disappears inside the converted stately home. It looks like one of those scary *Hammer House of Horror* locations or the *Psycho* house! Now it's the village library, only open a few hours each week, and this afternoon I'm in luck. I follow inside, if only to drip on to the nice floors. There are frescoes on the ceiling, ancient furniture throughout and the sound of children's voices laughing. It's a treat to find the library with kids and seniors all playing games and reading books together. I take off the poncho and gently steam and drip wet puddles across the floor.

I love libraries. They are places to explore and discover. I always gravitate to the maps section in my local library, which has the facility to loan out Ordnance Survey maps of the British Isles, useful for planning cycle trips. Last year I borrowed a big guidebook of Umbria and Tuscany to rediscover an old painting and pilgrimage trip around St Francis of Assisi. I lost it in an Italian castle and sheepishly owned up when I got home. 'Ah yes,' said the librarian. 'It's been found and returned by a woman to her library in Kent, and we've got it back!' Amazing! What a lovely, generous thing to do. Wish I had her name – I'd sign her a copy of this book.

My favourite library is in North Wales – Gladstone's (residential) Library in Hawarden – a gothic masterpiece with 150,000 books at one end of the building and 26 bedrooms at the other. It's the only prime ministerial library in Britain and it was here that the old boy, William Gladstone PM, transported his personal collection – many with his own scrawled notes in the margins – in a wheelbarrow from his castle a mile away!

After a career as a graphic artist with a Manchester textile company, my dad studied here for two years in the 1960s, to become a clergyman. From his letters, which read like a personal diary, I know more about these couple of years of our family life than almost any other period. Dad wrote home to Mum every couple of days with engaging anecdotes and tales of student hijinks, what he and his fellow students were learning, what the visitors were like, the entertainment, and expressing his hopes and fears about what becoming a parish priest might entail. The college had a blind warden who led motor trips into the surrounding countryside. How did he manage that, when he was blind? 'Around this bend you should see a farm on the left – very good cheese from there – and on the right coming up, a stile with a path that leads to . . .' He remembered every bend in the road. (Weirdly, I'm also able to recall every bend of this Camino!)

Dad would spend his mornings studying, learning how to concentrate on the relevant chapters of a reading list before writing an essay. All this for a man who left school without those all-important qualifications we need these days. Dad's afternoons were spent exploring the North Wales landscape. He'd describe his walks in the letters to Mum and she had a map on the wall at home to follow his routes. The letters are full of little family jokes and hopes and railway timetables (we lived the other side of Cheshire, at least two trains and a bus ride away).

One noticeable thing is there was never a bad word written about anyone. People that Dad found difficult or challenging were just that. (It's a good example to remember when I'm feeling crabby about someone.) At weekends, there would be practice church services to take and sermons to preach. 'Better go and check if I can be seen over the pulpit,' said little Michael. Then the students had jobs to do, fixing bits of the library that needed repair, keeping the gardens tidy, booking films to watch together, which came on reels needing a projector and sound system. No DVDs or streaming in the 1960s. There was a choice of village pubs to relax in (try them; they are still very welcoming) while coping with the inevitable ups and downs of everyday living. When not reading religious tracts Dad had other books to enjoy. D. H. Lawrence's *Lady Chatterley's Lover* was publicly and controversially decriminalised in 1968, so he and my mum discussed it by letter. It's a fascinating insight into how people thought in the late 1960s. My dad thought the sex, though graphic, was appropriate, because sex is an important part of human love. My mum said it was rude!

I'm pleased to be a patron of Gladstone's Library, and I love the variety of people I meet there. It's no longer a theological college, although it encourages the study of faith. We used it as a film set for young Billy and his pal Alex to make home family thriller movies with titles such as 'The Blue Pencil' and 'Knights of Chester'. Fun family creations that usually ended in a boys' bundle in the nearby graveyard!

Over Christmas we were caretakers at Gladstone's. It was a little like staying at Hogwarts (without Voldemort); and Martin joined the family fun. On Christmas Eve, Father Christmas came to visit, and Martin was concerned that one of our party – Santa himself – had missed meeting Mr Ho Ho Ho. Our Christmas Day service put Martin at the front, leading the procession around the library building wearing a cassock and carrying his homemade crucifix. We loved how his faith played so strongly in his life.

An hour later, the rain hasn't stopped. Nor the wind. It's a wild wet day with scudding wet clouds blowing through me. I have to get to the accommodation that's expecting me – I think. The bike battery is flashing 3 per cent after 65 kilometres into this headwind.

The blessing comes at the end.

I meet my first pilgrim.

Gretel from Ghent. She is a godsend. Gretel is staying at my first private *albergue*, in Melle, a peculiar tatty place with an unusual chap who offers to cook something simple for us. Gretel and I spend the evening in conversation while I paint scenes from my wet travels today, including a self-portrait in the rain. I include the water dripping off my glasses and face, the grim look of determination under ominous wet clouds. The opposite of the universal happy selfie. Gretel had left from her home in Ghent a week before me, on foot. It's her sixth or seventh Camino and she will take the route to the coast and along the Camino del Norte. It's a very reassuring conversation when I'm wondering if all pilgrim hostels will be this odd. 'No, don't worry. It'll be fine,' Gretel says and, many weeks later, on my way back, we will meet again, and discuss if it was.

WIND!

CLING FILM TIME

ST. JEAN D'ANGELY

FENIOUX

SANTES

9

When an Australian asks for your address

Some people you meet you will never see again. Others, whom you may think you are bumping into ever so briefly, turn out to become lifelong friends. It's strange how we have no way of knowing which.

Friends are our lifelines and come into their own when we are miles away from home.

In spring sunshine the town of Melle looks a lot nicer than it appeared in the winter rains of yesterday. The graceful church across the valley is one of my favourites and it boasts the pilgrim shell and statues of St James. Richard the Lionheart and

Eleanor of Aquitaine visited here 800 years ago on one of their many excursions to protect twelfth-century pilgrims from the thugs and bandits who preyed on them. Some of those ancient landowners were an unpleasant lot and thought nothing of robbing travellers as they passed through. Incidentally, today's the anniversary of Richard meeting the Man with the Pan in 1199.

On that cheery note, I stop to sketch the church, leave a Martin name tag there, and then head along lanes wandering between my pre-planned route and the way markers for the Chemin de St Jacques. This is usually a walking route, so it follows footpaths, tracks and ancient bridleways, which can be very muddy and tricky for a heavily laden cyclist. I tend to alternate a lot between the track and the tarmac road. They both head in the same direction; one is just a different, often winding, way of getting there.

During this fine spring morning I record a little video message for friends Joan and John's wedding. My Mrs Mallett and Joan were at high school together in Melbourne. They've been best friends from the age of 11 and now live only ten miles apart in the UK. As I'm missing Joan and John's big day it's good to let them know I'm thinking of them in this place. I begin painting the scene, sketching in the bare trees and thrilling to the light and shade filtering through the branches. It's progressing well, then the rain starts and the painting is soaked.

Musing on that wedding back in England, where I know friends will be gathering from around the globe, I'm transported back over the years . . .

He's standing at the rail of the ferry to Mykonos wearing a striped T-shirt and black beret. The hair is green and purple, the glasses are bright red. 'Take a look at that weirdo,' say the two Aussie blokes backpacking around Europe. It's April 1980

and the one in the T-shirt and beret with a backpack, paints and easel is *Timmy on the Tranny* from BBC Radio Oxford, the aspiring DJ on a painting exploration of Greece.

I've been travelling around the world with my paints for as long as I can remember.

On the island we bumped into each other again, in a bar, and Aussie Steve and his pal were delighted to find their room cost a couple of drachmas less than mine. Booming out from every bar was the soundtrack of the trip: Pink Floyd's 'Another Brick in the Wall'. I'd stashed my easel and paints under a bush so we could have a merry evening, unencumbered, and next day we were to go our separate ways. The parting shot was, 'Give us your address and we'll come and see you in England.' All Australians want your address. They are all looking for somewhere free to stay. And be warned: they always turn up.

Always.

Months later I got a call. 'Remember us? We're just down the road from you on Regent Street.'

'You're in London. You're thinking of Oxford Circus. I'm in Oxford the city, a couple of hours away.' Crikey, what have I done?

They offered to go to the supermarket and bought bread, eggs and milk; and they had stories. Good tales of places they'd been, people they'd met. They were funny. Australians have a way with words and these two were easy going and entertaining. They showed the right degree of interest in my job at Radio Oxford and I put them on air once on an outside broadcast. Only once. I very quickly took them off again when Steve's idea of a typical Aussie greeting turned out to be 'G'day mate. It's a bloody ripper!'

'Bloody is not an adjective, Steve; it's a swear word and not acceptable on the radio.'

'Bloody sorry, mate!'

Over the summer they dropped in several times as they

criss-crossed the country. Then Steve's dad died, he headed home to Oz and that was the last I heard of him for a year or two. But this was a friendship that just wouldn't fizzle out. Steve went travelling with the American girl, Jan, he met the week after me in Greece. They got married and their first stop was . . . with me. By then I was in Manchester at Piccadilly Radio. While I was pursuing my radio career, Steve had taken to seeing the world. He and Jan did 18 countries in six months and every time they came back to England I was louder, faster and brighter, and my shows were growing bigger. I put American Jan on air as Nancy Reagan. 'In tonight's top song Ronnie and I would like to vote for "Ronnie (or should that be Frankie?) Goes to Hollywood"!' We loved the funny way Steve and Jan spoke, in particular his Aussie rhyming lines:

Linga longa in Yarrawonga,
there ain't no work in Burke;
things are crook in Tallarook
and water ain't flowing in Batley's brook.

My shows have always experimented with language. On the radio, *Timmy on the Tranny* developed its own code phrases: Borons, Trannyoids and Zapheads, and borrowed Frank Zappa's nonsensical phrases – 'Barf me out', 'Gag me with a spoon', 'Grody!' On TV we inventively put WAC (as in the Wideawake Club) in front of everything. Wactors and Wactresses; Wac Snax; Wacamakes; Wacamoats (seaside sandcastles) and Wacawaves (hands as a 'W' to greet fellow viewers). It was a fabulous time to try out an idea and develop it.

When I went to Steve and Jan's place in Denver I met the top DJ in the city, who was doing stunts to get noticed on TV and in the local press. It was easy to try something similar back in Manchester where it made a big impact. I broke the ice to plunge into a frozen lake on the coldest day of the year; I did a radio show in a bath of custard (to get the lumps out, of course) and then the big one – Seat Aid (more on this later). It was our contribution to the Live Aid appeal. I was offered a backstage pass for Live Aid and turned it down. *It'll just be another rock 'n' roll gig*, I thought. Instead, we watched it on telly. Status Quo kicked off, Rocking All Over the World, and I knew I'd made a mistake then. Bother! Why had I not paid more attention? Queen had the crowd going nuts with 'Radio Gaga' and Bob Geldof held everyone spellbound, for what seemed like a lifetime, as he held his hand aloft –

'And the lesson today is how to die!'

Phil Collins attempted to do a live interview on Concorde over the Atlantic, David Bowie said it was so good we should do it every year, and Paul McCartney's mic didn't work on 'Let It Be'. What a glorious lesson in worldwide live entertainment. Pop came of age on that glorious July Saturday in 1985 at Wembley, when the power of popular music and culture was extraordinary. Who would have thought then that it had reached its pinnacle?

On Boxing Day 1987, heading to California to spend New Year with Steve and Jan in their new home, I called into the TV-am studios on my way to the airport. There I greeted the cheerful producer Peter Van Gelder, a great friend whom I'd first met on a BBC training course a decade earlier. Peter laughs at my jokes, and on his piano he has one of the best *Wacaday* props ever made. 'We need a wacky pirate ship with a flag with crossed mallets, and a wacky pirate to walk the wacky plank,' he said to the props department. We were expecting a toy. Instead a work of art was carefully crafted with masts, rigging, pink sails, cannons, poop decks and every other wacky detail you could think of. It cost over £800. Peter gulped and kept it to remind himself to always be careful in the brief and now he's very much better at sticking to budgets!

The first thing that happened when I arrived in the USA was the phone rang and it was Peter. 'Ten minutes after you left I was sent to LA too. Are you ready for some fun doing some pop video links around LA and San Francisco?'

It was the time of an infamous strike at TV-am. Bruce Gyngell, our boss, and his managers were manning the cameras and tape machines. The presenters had to bend down to get into shot. We were showing endless episodes of *Batman* and cartoons such as *Galaxy High School* and *Pacman*. Mrs Pacman had an affectionate American nickname for Mr Pacman – 'Paccy'.

Language issue!

Someone had to frantically look through the episodes and cut out that bit before it went to air and was misinterpreted. Because of the cartoons and the chaos, the ratings soared. Bruce decided to send the presenters abroad to film some fun bits. I was already in California on holiday, so Peter was sent to produce a pop programme or three with me. The freedom was blissful. We chose our favourite songs – 'California Girls' by David Lee Roth of Van Halen, 'Heaven Is a Place on Earth' by Belinda Carlisle and U2's 'Where the Streets Have No Name' among them – and off we went on a travelogue of the famous sights. We found a crazy California dude cameraman, Neil Antin (with an actor brother in the movie industry), who knew all the places for us to film the links. That's how we got the best shot of the Hollywood sign from a private garden. Then we went to Grauman's Chinese theatre where the Oscars happen and stuck a cardboard *Wacaday* star on the walk of fame – I wonder if it is still there.

Next we flew up to San Francisco and in one day filmed all the sights. Wac-Catraz the infamous prison island; the Golden

Gate Bridge, Fisherman's Wharf and the famous zig-zag street, from the back of a trolley car and in a pink Cadillac. I put on a cheap wig and beads, and went around the hippy district – Haight-Ashbury – going 'Hey man!' It all seemed to work so well. Dream up a gag, do it. It was the catalyst for an extraordinary period of *Wacaday* film stories from around the world.

Inserting the videos into the programme was a little bit more complicated, and this is where another bit of serendipitous magic happened. My first Piccadilly Radio helper, Andy Bird, had followed me to London to work at a new music channel. He fancied seeing Los Angeles, so we went together to stay with our friends. For the videos, Andy was the man. Everything needed to be transferred from the US to UK formats, and somehow Andy managed to get the videos set up correctly and sent across the world. 'I like it here,' he said. 'One day I'm going to work in LA.' It was a great declaration of intent. Within 15 years Andy was the head of Disney worldwide. It nearly didn't happen. On our first drive down Highway 405 the car skidded in the rain and did a full 360 degrees at 50 mph. We hit nothing and resumed our journey, relieved and incredulous. Mickey Mouse was keeping an eye out that day for his future boss.

My overseas adventure continued. 'Don't come straight home, Timmy. Go on to Australia for the bicentenary,' said Bruce, 'and have a little stopover in Hawaii on the way.' Here I cycled 10,000 feet down from the summit of the volcano Mount Haleakala, on the island of Maui, after painting a watercolour of the sunrise. My favourite things again, cycling and painting. Actually, it was more like freewheeling – 26 miles from a moon-like landscape, through a rocky descent, a eucalyptus forest and finally to the ocean breakers on the Pacific.

Unforgettable.

'When you're in Australia,' said Jan, 'wouldn't it be great if you and Steve's sister got together?' And they set up a blind date. It was 26 January 1988, the bicentenary of the first fleet landing at Botany Bay. TV-am broadcast live overlooking Sydney Harbour. Captain Phillip of the first fleet had described the harbour as one of the finest in the world, with enough deep water for a thousand ships to shelter. There were over 10,000 ships in the harbour that day and several million people lined the foreshore to watch the re-enactment. The tall ships led the way, with the flagship proudly bearing a top sail with an awkward 'Drink Coke' sponsorship (talk about incongruous!). TV-am had a glorious set-up in the zoo, and my date and I enjoyed the thrill of being in the right place at the right time with all the world looking at the view and wishing they were there. That evening we watched the Harbour Bridge explode into a firework display that even now makes my heart skip when I recall it. Beside me was a funny woman with a quick line, a great smile, ready to embrace the world and enjoy what's on offer. She joined us on Bondi Beach, where I filmed *Wacaday* stories as a lifeguard and tried surfing on the hotel ironing board. 'Better take the ironing off it first, Timmy!'

'If you're not doing anything this summer,' I said to her at the end of the filming trip, 'you might like to come over to England for a visit.'

The Future Mrs Mallett (TFMM) arrived in April with more suitcases than I'd ever seen. 'How long are you planning to stay?'

'Don't know. I suppose I'll see how it goes . . .' Now this was interesting. We had to learn to get to know each other and I was surprised to find she was unaware of quite a few obvious things. There's a shared culture from being brought up in the same country and although TFMM had seen plenty of English TV and we, in Britain, had just been introduced to *Neighbours*, Kylie and Jason, lots of things were alien to us. TFMM didn't know who national legend Terry Wogan was and I didn't know his Aussie equivalent, Bert Newton. She started talking about 'Manchester' as in cotton goods or something to put on the table, like table linen, and a 'doona' for a duvet. There were other intriguing phrases too: 'Off like a bride's nightie', 'Dry as a dead dingo's donger', 'Cold as a witch's tit', 'Bangs like a dunny door in the wind'. So many things to be learned by both of us and that's where you need patience and time.

Except those were in short supply. My career had jumped into top gear, and I was travelling the country every weekend for shows, personal appearances and filming fun. 'We're up and down like a whore's drawers!' remarked TFMM trying to learn the geography, the language and the culture of the UK, to say nothing about trying to get to grips with Mallett's Mallet, WacaWaves, constant autographs and photos. 'Hang on, I've got to wind the film on. Just a minute, take your finger out of your nose. Not you, Timmy; I mean Nathan.'

This was a hard, challenging world to fall into when we were still trying to learn about each other. It's amazing that TFMM stuck to it. That took a degree of determination, patience and perseverance to cope with it all. In addition, my little house in north London was in the throes of being renovated and we lived on a building site for almost a year. My friends said, 'She's got you, Mallett,' and I still thought it was a long summer visit.

For my parents' fortieth wedding anniversary her mum flew over from Australia. Nothing happened. Then there was Thanksgiving in America, where eyes turned towards us questioningly. Was I missing something here? Could the future Mrs Mallett cope with the chaos of fame? Being in the public eye?

There still needed to be time and room for two people to get to learn about each other and like what they saw away from the glare; and the looks from family and friends.

Then.

I bought an engagement ring in a hurry while she was choosing a sandwich. And that's how we came to be a couple, though right now we are on opposite sides of the world. Straight after her best friend's wedding, Mrs Mallett is flying off to see her mum for her hundredth birthday and I'm on a European bike ride in the rain.

The afternoon is dominated by the wind. My agent of 35 years, John Miles, rings me and can't believe the roaring sound down the phone. He's trying to tell me something but I can't hear him over the furious howling and his voice blows away in the gale. Maybe John just wants to cheer me up with the great story of how he booked the Beatles for £25 in a hall near Bristol in 1962. He gave them a pile of 50 photos to autograph and John Lennon whined, 'How many of these do we have to sign?'

'Oh, all of them,' said agent John.

Over a 60-year career, John Miles has managed over 300 rock and pop bands, had hundreds of chart hits and at least two different number one acts, including me.

John has always been supportive. He came to one of my shows at a holiday park, in his Rolls-Royce. 'You sure you've got the right place?' asked the man on the gate. He was given directions to the stage door and managed to crunch the Rolls on a bollard. Ouch. That was an expensive night and even my brilliant show probably didn't make him laugh much. We never signed a contract with each other, 'because a handshake,' said John, 'is the strongest contract you'll ever need'. He was right.

Having people who understand what you are wanting to achieve, and are patient and persistent in working with you to bring it about, is worth its weight in gold. His attention to detail has been good for me, Noel Edmonds, Carol Vorderman, Martin Bashir, Keith Floyd, comedian Jethro, Tommy Cooper and Des O'Connor, among dozens of others he's represented over six decades.

'Take a punt,' he'll say; 'it may just lead somewhere.' He works in his office, sometimes in his greenhouse, and makes fair deals, creates a buzz and lives by his motto, 'Yesterday's history, tomorrow's a mystery and today's a bonus!'

I'd like to find somewhere to stay tonight. The tourist office and pilgrim help centres in the next two towns are shut and I'm feeling frustrated. St-Jean-d'Angély is a pretty tourist place with lots of accommodation, but nowhere seems to have a vacancy. Even the hotel in the square that shows availability online is full, says the manager. Eventually, I find a room in a motel on the edge of town. The bike takes up all of the space at the end of the bed.

Dinner is a take-away pizza, with three young kids silently waiting while their father, a shouty, stressed Frenchman, gets upset on the phone. In the morning, when he yells at his silent, well-behaved kids again, I ask him not to. He kicks off at me then, in broken English. 'You're just painting nice pictures, while my family and me are homeless and I have no job, and you should pay attention to other people first.' Hmmm, is that a wise intervention from me?

It's a 'cling film on my shoes' day. I wrap myself in a poncho and then the E-bike starts having issues. All the rain of the last few days is affecting the switching between power assist modes, and the on/off button works only intermittently. I have to reboot regularly throughout the day, and I feel the weight of the E-bike when it can't give me that essential extra assistance up the hills.

I'm so relieved to receive some friendly reassurance. Big Dave rings me from home. He's known as 'Big Dave' because he's nearly twice my height, has a heart of gold and always makes me smile. It is a very welcome, cheery call. 'How's it going?'

'Wet.'

'Just thinking of you and keep going, you are doing fine.' So reassuring, and I like the fact that in the comfort of his own home, he took the time to sympathise with someone struggling to pedal alone in the rain in a foreign country. Immediately afterwards there's a call from another friend, Paddy, saying my pals want to give me a bench in memory of Martin. 'You don't need to do that,' I say, 'but that's very kind and thoughtful of you.' And I start to choke up. Now there's moisture on the inside of my specs as well.

It's Good Friday and my friends are caring about me. I feel empowered as the sun comes out for a minute. My mum always used to say that Good Friday and Easter Day never have the same weather. It's funny how your mum's sayings stick in your mind: 'Visitors and fish go off after three days'; 'Little boys, please do not shout, and never throw the earth about'; 'Ignore Timmy; he'll be all right when he's 18'.

Here's what I notice now . . . The first substantial Camino pillars with stones on top next to a terrifying scarecrow dressed in curtains. That'll make a painting, with storm clouds building and blowing overhead – typical April-showers sort of clouds.

There's a Martin Mallett moment in a little village with a couple of houses and an ancient church. Bizarrely, the church at Fenioux has an ornately carved doorway a metre and a half above the ground, with no steps to it. How bonkers is that?

There's also a strange matching lantern tower in the field nearby. It's the lantern of the dead. Ooh er, this is eerie.

My dad had a good friend who was a funeral director – 'Peter the Undertaker'. Peter used to book my dad when he needed a priest for funerals, and they would drive to and from the service listening to favourite organ recitals. Peter had a bunch of sayings that we've adopted: 'Ordinary folk, such as yourselves'; 'We'll eat at the Golden Trough, I've had a policy mature!'; 'If you can't be the boss, get a job near the till'; 'Just like mother's milk – could eat it with your granny's teeth in'.

My dad liked to be prepared and before he died sent a list of things to do, including who to call first and their telephone numbers. He suggested hymns for the funeral, location for the wake, notices in certain newspapers – even where to return the library books! It was an amazing list. But still Mrs Mallett rang him when we got it: 'Michael, you've missed something...'

'Ooh, I thought I'd done it all. What have I missed?' said Dad, very concerned.

'You haven't put a date!'

10

Be kind to yourself

Surprises can light up our lives. Sometimes, it's an unexpected visitor . . . like the time I'd just taken an international call from my friend Andy in the States, when seconds later there was a knock at the door and there he was, phone in hand – surprise!

Some surprises are planned; others are . . . a surprise. Paul McCartney was both of those.

My big brother Paul came rushing home in 1965 with the book of the film *Help!*, which even had pictures in it. This was the second movie by the Beatles and it was in colour. We loved the Beatles in our house. We also loved the Rolling Stones, though it was supposed to be one or the other. Growing up we had radio but no TV and our favourite show was broadcast every Sunday afternoon: *Pick of the Pops* with DJ Alan Freeman. When I was away at boarding school, big brother Paul would post me the pop charts every week, along with a second version of what he thought they should be. Climbing eight places, Engelbert Hunk of snot – 'There goes my last clean hanky', and top of the lot, Long John Baldlegs – 'Let the fart aches begin'. Chart positions, climbers and fallers, mattered to us, and I looked forward to laughing at Paul's pop letters: the Rolling Twits – 'Get off my cow'; the Beatles – 'Mummy won't buy me gloves'.

June 1987 was the twentieth anniversary celebration of *Sgt Pepper's Lonely Hearts Club Band* album at Abbey Road studios and I went along in my scarlet braid jacket and musical-shaped specs looking the part. Paul and Linda McCartney came into the big studio where all the press were waiting. 'Hello there! You all right? Nice to see you, Timmy – love what you are wearing. Can I have your autograph?' They climbed part way up the stairs to the control room, turned and said, 'Come on up, Timmy. I want that signature.' Everyone looked on in amazement as Paul ushered me to follow him up the stairs.

I know my big brother will want every detail.

In the master control room, drinks are offered. I pull out Timmy pics from my jacket pocket. 'Er, who would you like me to sign this to?'

'One for me, one for me nephew . . .' It's a moment of magic, and unthinkable as it will sound, nobody thought to take a photo. Just take my word for it – or ask Sir Paul.

We had a camera, and a film crew, when Beatles producer George Martin had me singing 'The Laughing Policeman' for a charity album organised by Anneka Rice's TV show, *Challenge Anneka*. 'Bit more hopeless, helpless laughter, please, Timmy.'

We did no more than three takes, each with increasingly helpless uncontrolled laughing at his insistence. What a gentleman, George Martin. Generosity. It's wonderful to witness and when you are on the receiving end it's the most magical thing in the world.

I cycle into the Roman city of Saintes in Good Friday sunshine. It's a stunning city and I'm delighted to see the cherry blossom is out by the cathedral. I always double-check cherry blossom. Never rush past it, because five minutes after perfection, the wind will blow all the blossom into scattered heaps all over the ground.

I'm sitting outside a café when I hear a voice: 'Hello, got room for any more?' It's Stevie and Lorraine Kelly, driving to Spain, stopping off just to see me. It's the most welcome brilliant thing, and we eat and drink and talk and look at each other, chuckling in amazement. I'm halfway through France on my bike and my friends have taken a detour on their journey to Spain and are here to see me, cheer me up and bring me some things I may need. Mrs Mallett has sent them with a new dry bag to replace the one patched with tape, some more paint colours and the small round palette (the cardboard one has fallen to pieces). I need a spare adaptor for the plug. I've got two but one has bust. Spare sunglasses, a tripod mount, and some heat pads for my gloves. There's also some new clothes and masses of toiletries. Woo, hold on here.

Do I need the short-sleeved Lycra shirt? Not sure, but it's arrived anyway.

There's even an Easter egg and a loving card from home.

I'm really encouraged by Stevie and Lorraine's appearance, but all too soon they need to get on their way. In the car park we do a transfer of goodies. But it's too much for me to think about and I get into a fix. I mislay the camera tripod that the mount was for. I've now got too many paints and stuff; then when they drive off I feel desperately alone and over-packed. I need to leave things behind, but our friends are the one thing that we can't ever do without. They make the world a better place.

I'm staying with Philippe and Anne, French friends of Mayor Dom. I need a bath and a really good rest. But the worry starts to get the better of me and I'm sending WhatsApp messages like this . . .

'I've got a huge pit in my stomach. Feeling dreadfully anxious and terrified of going anywhere with the bike so heavily loaded; the switch is not working as it should and I'm not finding any time or energy to paint. This is nuts. I want to ditch stuff, stay in bed and hide.'

Back comes the message of helpful common sense: 'Have a proper sort out and ditch some stuff. You only need to do a painting every three days; leave any excess with your friends and I'll pick it up on the way back . . .'

I've become dehydrated today and can't think straight. My pals Robin and Judy make an unexpected call and their words resonate across the miles: 'Be kind to yourself . . . Less is more. Pause and rest. Know your limits. . .'

Philippe and Anne have left a lovely message on the door: 'We're out at work; let yourself in, have a shower, explore.' Later they feed me, make sure I drink enough water, and show me their gorgeous city of Saintes. I'm glad I decided on this route southwards. The Romans liked this part of France and built the usual: an Arc de Triomphe, amphitheatre and temple or two. Later the locals used the stone for their churches and castles. It's such a fabulous city on the Camino de Santiago, I'm staying an extra day.

Philippe has a look at the bike issues. There's a Giant shop in Bordeaux, which should be open after Easter, about Tuesday. On Saturday night I paint a little watercolour for him and Anne, of the full moon reflected in the ancient street. Full moon. That's it. I'm often edgy, anxious and short-tempered around the bright full moon. So it's really no surprise at how I'm feeling and the day's rest is good for me. The next day is the first of April – April Fool's Day.

Last summer I was sorting out the loft and found more than 200 old reel-to-reel quarter-inch tapes. Full of odd snippets and shows I'd kept over the years. They are in the process of being digitised by radio presenter Stephanie Hirst and are revealing all sorts of little memories. It seems to me now that when I started out I was searching for my voice. What sort of broadcaster/presenter was I going to be? Would I be a news journalist? A pop DJ? A story teller? It wasn't obvious at all. I was experimenting and I'm glad I kept our April Fool's gag from Saturday 1978 when BBC Radio Oxford went independent for the morning and starting playing home-made adverts. 'Fly Griffin Air direct from Oxford, England, to over thirty American destinations. Book today. Our number's in the book!' As the show resounded around our house I heard this young enthusiastic voice saying, 'You're listening to Independent Radio Oxford,' and then Mrs Mallett walked in. 'Is that you? I didn't know BBC local radio had adverts.'

'Mrs Mallett, it's the first of April . . .'

'Yes, but there's no such airline as Griffin Air. Oxford Airport doesn't do any flights to the USA! I'm looking on the internet now!' How delicious. The gag still worked, decades later. We must have been better than I thought.

On 1 April 1985 I did a fun little piece on TV-am about needing a licence for a push bike. 'Make sure you have a licence for your bike. They don't cost anything, and you get them at your local police station . . .' The head of the Metropolitan Police went bonkers; he didn't see the funny side at all. He demanded retractions and on-air apologies. So in the afternoon my colleague, Arabella, went on TV's *Splash* to explain that it was all a joke. Trouble is, that just compounded the whole thing. Somehow, repeating the story got more kids than ever dashing to the police stations of Britain! Over 20 years later, I was stopped by someone reminding me of how he'd been taken in and is still worried when he's on his bike and a police car goes past with its siren going. Long live April Fool's Day!

Easter Day I check the bike. I don't need a licence or the tyres to be pumped up. Philippe and I cycle around the city to see the sights he wants to share with me – such as the blue door of Anne's family home where they courted (we all have our personal landmarks that make our home town special), and the church where they were married 40 years ago. We notice how flooded the river is and Philippe comes with me for a few miles to make sure I leave town with a smile and a dry bike.

Friends – they really are a lifeline.

Martin has a name tag safely in the crypt of the ancient pilgrim basilica in Saintes. It's Easter all over the world. People are with their families, and it's a happy new beginning for people with faith. Have faith, have a bike, have a smile and a 'wide-eyed wonderment at the world', as my TV-am boss Bruce Gyngell used to say, and all will come right . . . Just remember to be kind to yourself and laugh at April Fool's gags. Gyngell was one of the best bosses I ever worked with. Like all real Aussies, Bruce would go walkabout every morning to greet his staff. He knew everyone's name and always met you at the door of his office, knowing that seeing him behind his desk could be intimidating. Though for some reason he had a trampoline in the office. Maybe he got his ideas from bouncing a bit? Bruce loved the colour pink, which may be why Mallett's Mallet always got his approval. 'Be bright, be colourful, and have a big smile,' he would say. 'You can't go wrong, fella.'

The day warms up and the sky is blue with some lovely early-April sunshine. I mark the moment by changing into shorts for the first time on this trip (in the village bus shelter). My pink knees can finally enjoy the surprise of fresh air and I'm instantly happier. How can a change of clothes make such a difference?

Today I pay attention to friend Terry's good advice. Drink every 20 minutes whether you need to or not. If I am splashing and dashing lots, then I'm drinking enough!

The Chemin de St Jacques is well marked and at St Léger, where I'm expecting to find horse racing, instead I'm surprised to come across a stunning pilgrim shelter. The little town has spent 25,000 euros turning a run-down barn into a great pilgrim facility, with shelter, tables, benches and space to relax. It really is a highlight. How hospitable to build something like this for people who are just passing through. It shows a real generosity of spirit. That gets me thinking . . . Cast your mind back . . . A lot further than that . . .

Think back to the golden age of Aquitaine – and my heroes, Eleanor and Richard the Lionheart. The latter years of the twelfth century were a golden age for pilgrims on the way of St James. People yearned to travel, prompted by a spiritual longing, the inquisitiveness that is integral to us as humans and a passion for art, music, poetry and adventure. The Camino de Santiago was growing in popularity and 800 years ago a quarter of a million people walked there and back across Europe every year. That would be a big boost to any economy and the Middle Ages thrived on pilgrimage.

Centuries later that would seem to explain why a regional government would invest so much money in something for temporary and transient visitors. They probably believe it will benefit the area economically and encourage more people to visit it for walking and exploring. It's an example of planning for the long term and investing in infrastructure. Naturally I find a home here for a Martin Mallett name tag and a little moment of reflection.

The enormous ancient castle at Pons attracts my attention. As does a group of life-size pilgrim statues in the middle of a roundabout on the outskirts of town, where I see my first signpost to Santiago. Only 1,200 kilometres to go! I'm not even half way yet. I've reached somewhere that attaches great importance to the Camino. I ride through the ancient cobbled arches of a medieval pilgrim hospital, and a grim thought comes to mind. How many people have come to the end of their journey here? On the way to or from Santiago? Better keep going. There may be a surprise coming up, and sure enough . . .

Ahead of me are two people walking with rucksacks along the muddy track. As I get closer, I spot their pilgrim scallop shells. '*Buen Camino!*' I call out and they turn around, startled. This is a first time for us both, to meet other pilgrim travellers on the road in this way. I've been going for several weeks, and Pascal and Françoise have been walking from Brittany for two months, and suddenly here we are together. We take a photo to share the moment. We know that such meetings will be commonplace within days. But right now it feels very special. Let's mark the spot in Saint-Genis. They and I have met on a rugged farm track with newly planted crops either side. Little to distinguish this from anywhere else. 'I've walked all this way and then someone passes me on a bike!' says Pascal. There are big smiles. Where are you staying tonight? How far have you come today? How's it going? When do you expect to be in Santiago? How will you get home?

This last question produced an amazing answer from the pair of pilgrims:

Santiago to Santander
Ferry from Santander to Cork in Ireland
Then another ferry to Roscoff in Brittany
Roscoff to Home.

Wow, that's a roundabout route – that's dedication.

At the end of the day, everyone in the village, the bar, the shop, on the street, finds it difficult to direct me to the ad-dress where I'm hoping to stay tonight. 'It's down the *rue* of three windmills . . .' I'm lost and forlorn when I come across Fabianne, who has walked out to find me and smilingly lead me over a kilometre to her and Bernard's home; and a lovely, welcome, chatty 'Franglais' meal. Phew, what a relief.

Good food makes all the difference. Mrs Mallett was in charge of feeding everyone through the rehearsals and shooting on *Timmy Towers*. This was the panto-style children's TV show where we had to battle the Abominable No Man (Mark Speight), who loved capturing kids in the audience – 'Pick me!' – and flushing them down the giant toilet to a fate worse than death – The Room with No TV! I love the pantomime gags where you know what's going to happen – and then it does! Through my own Brilliant TV production company I made various series of *Timmy Towers* with my co-stars Miss Thing – gorgeous Alex Lovell – and Aunty Knobbly Boney Knees, who liked to knit her way out of trouble (and the plot). It seemed that TV should be creative, co-operative and funny. Even a neighbour's son was roped in for the theme tune. It was a pleasure to give a platform to talent such as the young Stephen Mulhearn and legends like Rod Hull and Emu. The young work-experience lad, Jamie Wilson, became my webmaster and is now producing top CBBC shows like *Crackerjack* (back from the 1970s) and the live *Saturday Mash Up* (he asked about *Wacaday* ideas and we discussed reinventing them). Every single person on the show was very well fed; in the next-door studios the *Art Attack* and *Thomas the Tank Engine* teams looked on enviously.

I cycle into another town with a historical connection to my adventure. Blaye used to be famous for its ancient abbey, where bits of Roland, one of Charlemagne's heroes, are buried. More than a thousand years ago, Roland was a tragic general who was ambushed and slaughtered by the Basques when he took his army over the Pyrenees to invade Spain. Tragic figures are always fascinating to us. 'If only?' and 'What if?' are among the great questions we ponder. It's always easier to see what should be done if we aren't having to make the decision ourselves. Roland, whose gruesome end at the hand of pesky guerrilla fighters became a symbol of Charlemagne's greatness, was brought down by baddies not fighting by the rules. There was a famous eleventh-century hit called the 'Song of Roland'. It's not quite 'Itsy Bitsy', of course, but pilgrims used to stop at Blaye Abbey to see the bits of Roland that were on show and sing to him. The abbey is a grass-covered ruin now. Back in the seventeenth century Louis XIV got rid of it to build a vast fortress. One of squillions of impressive fortifications that the Sun King put up along his frontiers to defend his kingdom. Fort or abbey? Nothing lasts for ever, of course, but it seemed like a good spot to remember the 'Song of Roland' and then to sing one of the big hits of the twentieth century:

She was afraid to come out of the locker,
She was as nervous as she could be . . .
Two, three, four tell the people what she wore . . . !

For the video of 'Itsy Bitsy Teeny Weeny Yellow Polka Dot Bikini' we had an artificial beach set made in a north London warehouse. 'How many pairs of glasses can you bring, Timmy?' I carted along several dozen and had some palm tree ones made especially for the occasion. The video was huge fun and I've since found myself unexpectedly recognised all over the world. Zulus in South Africa, Saamis in Scandinavia, surfers in Australia, guards at the Kremlin have all stopped me to ask, 'Are you the "Itsy Bitsy" man?' Today I'm the 'Itsy Bitsy' man performing on a grassy mound by a castle!

I still get regular royalties from the hit every year. Thank you.
It's enough to buy a new bike . . .
bell.

I'm ringing it as I ride through the wine region of France. Years ago the Romans loved this region's wines and then for over 300 years, during the Middle Ages, this part of France was English owned. Even today the major foreign owners are the English, with second homes all along the Dordogne. And the reason? Sunshine and fine wines. Fine wines and sunshine. And fine wines.

Along the way I stop at a car boot sale, because you never know when one of these will throw up a little gem. I remember I once found a First World War French helmet for a tenner. It wasn't quite a bike helmet, but it looked the part when we cycled the Western Front in honour of our family warriors during the Great War. (My grandfather Mallett served in the signals and rode a bike carrying important messages during the conflict.) At this car boot sale, one of the stall holders greets me like a long lost friend. Apparently, we saw each other yesterday at another sale more than a hundred kilometres away and although I didn't recognise him, he certainly knew who I was. I suppose a cyclist stands out when he's wearing a tie covered in badges.

This is bridge country. There are at least four crossings in less than a mile and they are all spectacular, and I enjoy painting them positioned by the water's edge in a park. Think of your favourite bridge – there's the Forth Railway in Scotland, the Severn River Crossing, London's Tower Bridge, Sydney Harbour, San Francisco's Golden Gate, Ribblehead in the Pennines, Bristol's Clifton Suspension, Pontcysyllte Canal Aqueduct in Wales, the Gateshead Millennium Bridge, the Ponte Vecchio and Bridge of Sighs in Italy and, on the Camino, the Hospital de Órbigo. Start adding your own and in ten minutes you'll have at least 20 bridges you love. But how many have you cycled over? And will any of them be like Skyreburn Bridge?

There's a painting by my dad that the family has always admired of a bridge over a dark cascading stream, and it set me on another pilgrimage to find the 'where and why'. In his diaries there was a clue. Inspired by the Dorothy L. Sayers murder mystery *Five Red Herrings*, which is set in Galloway, Michael and Nancy had gone to south-west Scotland on holiday. In his 1966 diary Dad has written: 'Took a taxi to Skyreburn to look for painting motif. Find a lovely cool woodland stream and paint 'til 4:30 p.m. Then walk home over the moors. Lovely day.' So I took the train to Dumfries and cycled 40 miles across to Gatehouse of Fleet (what a great name for a town) and searched for the woodland stream and bridge. With some difficulty, but aided by curator Rachel at the nearby Kirkcudbright Museum, I found it, and scrambling down to the water managed to locate the exact moss-covered stone Dad had stood his easel on. Nancy would have made the fish paste sandwiches, and while Michael painted she would have got water from the clear mountain stream, boiled a kettle on a campfire for tea and then knitted. As he continued painting, Mum may have dozed in the afternoon sunshine. It was fabulous to search and find my dad's inspiration over 50 years later and I then recreated his painting in the same, secret spot. Now our two paintings of the bridge and stream are side by side in one of Scotland's finest national galleries in Kirkcudbright. It was a pilgrimage of inspiration I'm very proud to share.

Bridges bring us together.

After the crossings, I follow the tramlines through the Richelieu-inspired, old Bordeaux gateway into the pilgrim hostel. It's in an old wine cellar next to the Frog and Rosbif pub, which is handy! Happy days.

The cellar isn't big, with just a dozen or so pods to sleep in, but it has the original stone arched roof, and I fall asleep dreaming of rolling wine barrels and counting imaginary bottles. Next morning, half a dozen pilgrims are up and out of the hostel at four in the morning for the early train to St-Jean-Pied-de-Port and their walking Camino. I'll overtake them in a week or so. Today I want to get the bike checked out and be a tourist in this classy city. Giant has a big bike store here and I'm confident any problems will be simple to fix.

But I shouldn't be surprised to find that in France things work differently. There are public service strikes all over the country. The bike store won't open until midday, and then closes again for a two-hour lunch. I know the controller for the E-bike is the issue and my contact at Giant UK confirms there have been a number of incidents of heavy rain affecting the switches. 'It won't be a problem; they have your bike's serial number and they know it's in warranty, so just ask them to speak to Jean Marc the national service manager.' Jean Marc is in Paris – at lunch. 'Come back at half past two or three.'

My lunch is fast food followed by watching and slowly sketching the old boys playing boules.

Finally, the controller is switched over in less than ten minutes. The chain is replaced – I've done 1,500 kilometres, and it's lasted well since that first day's drama. They check the tyres, brakes, gears and I'm good to go. Four hours in total, most of which was at lunch. Patience, Mallett. Everywhere works in its own way.

In Bordeaux's pilgrim church of Saint Sauvin there's a Martin Mallett moment by the statue of St James. I'm counting my blessings and the bike is one of them. It's important to remind myself that there are only two things I can rely on. Myself and my bike. Everything else is chance. It may be a blessing; it may not. Then I receive an email from Mat, the chaplain to the Bishop of Winchester. He's worked his magic and got me contacts for the Archbishop of Santiago's vice chancellor and the archivist and dean of the cathedral. It's up to me to get in touch when I'm nearer . . . now that's encouraging.

I paint today and absorb the Eleanor of Aquitaine links in the cathedral. I'm soaking up the history, admiring the city, sharing a glass with Michel, the hostel host, as my paintbrushes dance across my boards, depicting the vineyards I've been cycling through. 'Dream big and your life can be big. Dream small and your life will be small.' It may be the wine talking, but it's a phrase that is sticking with me . . .

Time to be on my way, but 'never have regrets'. I never want to say, 'I wish I'd seen that . . .' So I have an artistic morning in the city art gallery and go for some performing artistry at the outstanding piece of public art: the giant water mirror by the river. A huge lake of water no more than a centimetre deep, which reflects the city. Standing on it I appear to be walking on water. Even cooler to cycle over it. Cycling on water? Now that's something special!

I've got a big grin on my face, and as I turn to leave Bordeaux I catch sight of my first cycle sign for Spain. It's still many days away.

11

Life is what happens while you are busy making plans

It's never the destination, always the journey.

The difference between a pilgrimage from the Middle Ages and one today is expectation. Nowadays we all expect to reach our destination and to come home again. How you come home depends on you, of course. Will you be changed somehow? Enriched spiritually, physically, culturally? I'm asking a lot of this journey and I've set myself specific targets. To reach my potential by cycling alone across Europe with my paints, without prebooking accommodation, and painting whatever I encounter.

I've cleared the diary for a couple of months, and it's only as

126

I carry on with the training and preparation that Mrs Mallett says, 'It would have been nice if you'd asked us first . . .' Oh crikey. I've been selfish here. That makes me realise that this journey involves attendant fears for my nearest and dearest. Someone mentions the inclement, unpredictable weather in the Pyrenees (they miss out the rest of France and England, though). Better get prepared with those good luck blessings, like this one from the Archbishop of York, John Sentamu: 'In your television career you have had a wonderful way of connecting with people to bring life and laughter. On your journey I pray that you will know much joy and laughter on the way.'

I'm carrying photos of brother Martin, including a favourite one of him on his bike. Ever since we could walk, we've ridden bicycles. Martin is concentrating hard on the business of pedalling. Holding on to the handlebars, keeping the bike steady, pushing on the pedals, moving the bike forwards and balancing. He's absolutely engrossed in the moment. Not thinking about where he's heading to or where he's been. This moment, the here and now of living. We don't do this very often. Usually we're absorbed in what we've done and the hoping for what's about to happen. But the moment is everything.

The priory at Gradignan has an enormous statue of a seated barefoot pilgrim (I'm glad I'm carrying spare shoes). He dwarfs me as I stand beside him, and I feel smaller than usual in the vastness and timelessness of this journey. This is south-west France, Les Landes, and now the Chemin de St Jacques is bigger and more important in the landscape. Just how far I am from Spain becomes very clear as I ride into the forest against a huge headwind.

The Way of St James never lets you get lost. The signs are

everywhere: large, EU-funded *routes culturelles*, smaller scallop-shell stickers stuck on road signs, wooden regional 'Chemin de St Jacques' signs, and occasional yellow arrows. Just keep your eyes peeled through the never-ending trees. I go past a grove of mimosa, and I put a large sprig of it on my bike, to remind me of Mrs Mallett, whose Australian national flower is the beautiful fragrant wattle.

The wind is solid, immense and deafening, and adds to the enormity of what I am undertaking. I'm inspired to follow the tough and rough pilgrim route rather than take the tarmac road, and wonder if I'll come across any pilgrims.

Not a soul.

Nobody.

It's as if this is a path to eternity and I'm the only one on it.

It's while I'm thinking of nothing in particular that I come around a corner of the track and fall off the bike. Ouch. It lands heavily on my knee. I don't know if I've hit a rock or a muddy pothole, or perhaps I just slipped, but the fact is that I wasn't concentrating. I wasn't paying attention. I was looking around, thinking of something else other than this moment in time. I was on autopilot when the track just deteriorated. Now I feel foolish. I've got a graze, some blood and a bruise, but I'm not hurt badly. I know this, because I take a photo and resolve to paint this spot.

After checking the bike and wiping the blood off my knee, I have a few words with myself, because I know that there's nobody else looking out for me on this ride. I have to take responsibility for each turn of the pedals. Who can I rely on? It's just me and the bike.

But here's the thing . . . Around the next corner is a village, and in the village is a pharmacy . . . and amazingly it's open and has some arnica cream for the bruising. Then I have a little rest, a snack and a drink, and resolve not to tell anyone at home in case they worry. So if you see any of my family or friends, don't tell them about this, please. They don't need to know.

Just up the road is a little rural pilgrim shelter, but it's not for me; I haven't got a sleeping bag and I want some comfort after that little shake-up. I ride on to a lovely Logis hotel, which is the perfect place to stop tonight. Joy and Isabelle welcome me and lock up the bike in the conference/function room. They even do my laundry. I need these home comforts just now.

Be kind to yourself.

As usual I spend part of the morning painting. This time I'm painting the crash spot. Isabelle is a sweetie and makes me a packed lunch. I don't want to leave.

But I'm feeling better after Joy and Isabelle's thoughtfulness and it's a warm and sunny morning in south-eastern France. My first stop is a disused football stadium, though 'stadium' is a bit of a generous description. It's named the Stade Louis Pasteur and was at one time the home of FC Poulet. It's weed-filled, over-grown and derelict. What a shame. Public sports grounds are to be used and celebrated. Son Billy and I love football. So did Martin. At Oxford United we met the manager, Chris Wilder, who went on to guide Sheffield United to the Premier League and when Martin announced to him, 'Me play!' Chris replied with a smile, 'That's the best motivational team talk ever!'

My experience with Premier League football managers has been mixed. When I met Eddie Howe of Bournemouth I didn't recognise him and asked him what he did at the club – he graciously explained he was the manager, to chuckles from those around me. At Turf Moor, Sean Dyche, the gaffer at Burnley FC, interrupted his post-match press conference to ask me for a selfie. It made us smile that no one there in the press room was quick enough to take a photo of the moment.

On our cycling adventures my friends and I have taken to visiting football grounds from various leagues. Someone suggested the joys of Scotland's Highland League and I'm so glad he did. We cycled to see the 'Mighty Can Cans' – Forres Mechanics – where Tommy the groundsman recommended macaroni pie for lunch. Delicious! At Buckie Thistle – the 'Mighty Jags' – we were proudly shown the modest dressing rooms; at Turriff United the kit carer, Pearl, showed us the ladies loo with flowers in a vase. In North Wales we took penalties on the pitch at the 'Lilywhites' Rhyl FC and again at the 'Wingmakers', Airbus UK. In Northern Ireland we cycled to see the 'Candy Stripes' – Derry's football club, who play in Eire. It's on my list to one day visit Fort William, who finished the season on a record minus 245 goal difference, no wins and minus seven points.

At this weed-covered stadium in France I remember my favourite football Lord's Prayer:

Thy moment's come,
This match be won
Give us this day our three-nil win
And forgive us our sliding tackles.
Lead us not into penalty shootouts . . .
For thine is the victory,
The final and glory
For ever and ever
Our men!
#Itscominghome

This pitch is in the small but important village of Moustey. It boasts twin medieval churches side by side (is one of them the substitute?) and the black wooden pilgrim statue next to the all-important sign showing 1,000 kilometres to Santiago. I'm over half way from home. Say it quickly and it doesn't seem too bad. I've met three pilgrims along the road so far. I know I'm going to meet a whole lot more soon . . .

But I can't leave. I'm here for ages. Drawing, having my lunch and putting ma bubba's name tag into the crack of the wooden statue. 'You me, Martin.' We've come all this way; and now there are a thousand kilometres to Santiago somewhere over the Pyrenees. It's an odd sensation. Am I meant to feel joyous that I'm so far on when in fact I feel strangely empty thinking that it's all going too quickly?

There are Dutch St Jacob cycling stickers marking the way now. This is encouraging as I ride along straight flat roads through everlasting pine forests. Row upon row of pine trees with black trunks and grey-green branches, which go on for ever. Planted in uniform rows across south-western France, the 10,000 square kilometres of pines make up one of the biggest forests in Europe. The occasional tiny village tips its hat to the wood-lands by pollarding its trees in the squares . . .

I'm reminded of the tale of the two blokes picnicking by the lake in the forest a long way from the nearest town. They've run out of vodka. It calls for desperate measures. They find the can of paraffin with a label 'Do not drink – you'll go blind'. They look at each other and one says, 'We've seen enough trees . . .'

This evening I'm lucky to discover the village *albergue*. I knock on the door. Nothing. Then the window shutters open and 79-year-old pilgrim Hans from Switzerland pops his head out. 'Hello, come in please.'

Hans has been walking since February from Mont St Michel and he's carrying a massive 15-kilo backpack. I'm the first pilgrim he's seen. There is something really comforting this evening about sharing a meal of fried eggs, fish fingers, cheese and tomatoes, and a bottle of rosé, from the little grocery store around the corner. Hans has the Camino bug. He's walked to Santiago six times already, and says each spring he gets itchy feet and needs to set off again on a different route to the city. He will be away for at least three months. I tell him to watch out for Gretel from Ghent, as they're walking the same Camino. In a week's time, he'll hear a voice cry out, 'Hans!' and he and Gretel will meet in a village and exchange stories about the strange cycling artist they've both met.

Tonight, we are staying in a delightful renovated half-timbered house in the middle of the village of Lesperon. Kitchen, bathroom, dorm with five beds, sheets, pillows and blankets. Martin's name tag is pushed into the low bedroom beams on which I banged my head. In the morning I pop into the town hall to pay them for my lodging. 'Thanks for a lovely stay in your *albergue*,' I say.

'You're very welcome. We like to look after our visitors . . .'

Hans and I meet again unexpectedly for coffee later after I've helped push start a stranded motorist – get a bike; it's easier – in a village with the brilliant name of Taller. There's a great photo opportunity by the town sign. When I grow up, I want to be Taller (except when it comes to low ceilings).

I cycle into the Roman city of Dax, famous for its thermal baths. The mineral water comes out at over 60 degrees Celsius and would have been a place for pilgrims to have a wash and tidy up. I like Roman towns and Roman roads; they take me back to *Wacaday* adventures when I met my cousin 'Spaghetti Malletti' at the leaning Tower of Pizza. Climbing the tower is really weird. The higher we climbed the more the walkway went strangely up and down as it went around and around. I tried to straighten the tower with a little bash from Mallett's Mallet and with some simple fun camera trickery the tower appeared to collapse into a pile of rubble – or was it a pile of pizza?

In Rome, we re-enacted a gladiatorial fight with Mallett's Mallet in the Colosseum. Thumbs up, thumbs down; Mallett's Mallet always came out on top.

Our stories usually began with a joke. Think of a gag, or even a simple wordplay joke, and see if it would develop into something visual and funny. In the Bond film *View to a Kill*, Grace Jones sky-dives off the top of the Eiffel Tower – 'That tower's an eyeful!' We thought we'd try something similar, but on a smaller budget. Tim, the cameraman, was an ex-Rhodesian army bloke who always wore fatigues. He had every conceivable attachment he could get on this camera – night-sights, cross-wires in the viewfinder, camouflage film canister. I carried it for two steps and dropped it. Whoops.

Two hours later we'd climbed to the top of the tower. It took two hours, because we had to go up and down shooting it all from a million different angles . . . Pretending to paint the metal struts, and counting all the rivets: 'One, two, missed a few – 99 – a squillion'. Then the last shot at the top. I jumped off the Eiffel Tower.

And this is how I did it without a parachute, permission or insurance.

I stood on a box, leapt up and dropped six inches out of the shot. The crowd lunged forward, staring down and gasped!

Then in a wide shot we drew in a little stick Timmy doing a loop de loop before I landed perfectly from a jump approximately 18 inches high!

It looked very silly and very homemade and we were all delighted – so was the audience. Everyone except the person ringing to complain that I was encouraging kids to jump off very tall buildings. Hmmm.

Wacaday and Mallett's Mallet grew organically from the Saturday morning show the *Wide Awake Club*. In the creative chaos of TV-am, the breakfast channel at Camden Lock, WAC, had started in autumn 1984. My good friend Arabella Warner from Radio Oxford days had introduced me to the children's department and together with James Baker we three did the Saturday morning kids' show, based on the idea of being wide awake and in a club. The very experienced presenter Tommy Boyd joined us and, soon after, one of the girls from our dance troupe, Wacky Feet, became an instant hit on screen – Michaela Strachan. Michaela is a dream to work with, and I'm delighted our friendship has grown over the years. The team of presenters all looked out for one another. At New Year they played Silly Senses with me blindfolded and I can still taste the clove of garlic they gave me to chew! We had lots of TV games, including Bonk 'n' Boob, the spelling game; Singing in the Shower – essentially this was karaoke before karaoke was invented. If you won a prize it was likely to be a WAC PAC lunchbox or a WAC SAC backpack with T-shirt, records and autographs of the team. Comedian Keith Lemon, host of *Through the Keyhole* and *Celebrity Juice*, proudly told me how he'd won two competitions when he was a young Wideawaker – to design a dinosaur (complete with a fish's head from *Star Wars*) and a pair of Bermuda shorts each for Michaela and me. 'You're a legend, Timmy. I've still got the VHS from when my name was read out,' he exclaimed. 'Best moment of my life!'

The show attracted another pair of aspiring comedians to perform an occasional skit they called the Sound Asleep Club. This was Mike Myers and Neil Mullarkey's first adventure in TV and there are elements of the hit film *Wayne's World* in some of Mike's characters. We all start somewhere and Mike began on the *Wide Awake Club*. We met again at the premiere of *Shrek* and he told me, 'People always ask me here about those days on the *Wide Awake Club*, and you . . . Thank you.'

Pop music was always important, and among the record pluggers who came to visit us was someone who wanted us to feature the singer Sinitta, and his new band – Bros. They both made regular appearances on WAC and in our annuals. The plugger was a very persuasive visitor. I never heard a critical word from Simon Cowell.

Simon never got to play Mallett's Mallet. But Jason Donovan and Kylie Minogue both did, on separate occasions. I presented her with her proud loser's prize – an enormous Wacky plaster on her knee – with the line, 'I should be so wacky!'

When the song-writing, record-producing trio Stock, Aitken and Waterman were at their peak in 1990, Pete Waterman came to talk about presenting the *Hitman and Her* dance music show with Michaela. Someone made a comment that he might want to produce a Timmy hit. 'That'll never work,' Pete said. 'I'll pass on that, thanks.' A few months afterwards Andrew Lloyd Webber had the same idea. When Pete saw me later at *Top of the Pops*, he came straight up and said, 'Fair play, Timmy. I missed an opportunity there! Good luck!'

Mallett's Mallet was never meant to last more than a couple of weeks. In one of the early school holidays around 1986 we needed a game of some sort. Producer Nick Wilson and I were in the office bashing ideas around (bashing – get it?!). 'Let's try a word association game,' said Nick.

'What do you mean?'

'You know – apple . . . banana . . . orange . . . er . . .'

'Or school . . . homework . . . teacher . . . the whack . . . WAC . . . Wide Awake Club?!'

'That's it and when the kid gets the answer wrong you can bash them over the head with something . . . a mallet . . . we can call it Mallett's Mallet.'

Great idea. And Billy Pond, the props man, and his team went away to make a large yellow and pink foam mallet. The first couple of prototypes were far too heavy, but by the time we went on air, it looked massive and weighed next to nothing.

At the end of the meeting Nick asked me, 'Are you all right with this being called Mallett's Mallet, Timmy?'

'Of course. It's a fun idea and we'll do it for a couple of weeks and then try something else.'

'It's just, you'll probably have it for ever, and I mean for ever.'

And lo and behold, he was right. For the record, my name came first, before the Mallet. And as props go, it's very simple. It's foam, not inflatable, with a cover that can be washed; it travels in a black bag labelled 'Top secret'. And it resonates with people of a certain age who swear that it means their childhood to them. Mallett's Mallet has hit the heads of Prime Ministers, politicians, pop stars, celebrities, kids, parents, teachers, dignitaries, actors, sportsmen, professors, bishops, royalty and a few million others along the way. It was the oddest thing to see kids tearfully plead with their parents, 'Not yet; I don't want to go. Mr Mallett hasn't hit me yet!'

You always have to go through the rules of any game before you play (in case someone is new to it and needs it spelling out) and I looked for a way to hurry through them as fast as possible. Mallett's-Mallet-is-a-word-association-game-where-you-musn't-pause-or-hesitate-or-repeat-a-word-or-say-a-word-I-don't-like-otherwise-you-get-a-bash-on-the-head-like-this-or-like-this-and-the-one-with-the-most-bruises-loses. Look-at-each-other-and-go-Blaah!

'Blaah' came out of nothing at all. It's a funny, useful,

expressive, thinking word. Something to say while I'm searching for something better than 'look at each other and say hello', or 'good luck' . . . or 'my name is . . .' The other saying that became a catch phrase and the title of this book was 'Utterly Brilliant'. Two fine, over-the-top, expressive words – an adverb and adjective. When I'm thinking of what's coming next, and I'm not sure what it is, I'll say, 'It'll be Utterly Utterly Utterly Utterly' (for as long as I like until the director has shouted in my ear the next thing that we are doing . . .) 'Brilliant!'

Word association is a simple game to play for all ages and abilities, and over the next few years I began to wonder if there was a way to bring Mallett's Mallet to life. Someone suggested a puppet, but I wanted a soft toy Mallet that would have a character of its own. I met a helpful Welshman, Robert Lewy, at the toy fair at Olympia, and he made a couple of prototypes with a face and fluffy hair on top. We set an on-air competition to name the little Mallet and the winning suggestion was 'Pinky Punky' – cos he was mainly pink and he was definitely punky. The props man wiggled him up and down in front of the camera and suddenly little Pinky Punky was a member of the audience, hopping up and down in excitement. I recorded a set of Pinky Punky sayings and never knew which they were going to play out.

'Mr Mallett, I'm so excited I want to go to the toilet!' How many little kids have wet themselves with excitement?

'Mr Mallett, I know the address . . . it's *Wacaday* TV-am Blah Blah Blah, NW1 9TQ!'

'Mr Mallett, what's on next?'

'Mr Mallett, can I be on the telly now? Me Me Me please!'

'Mr Mallett, you've got knobbly knees!'

'Mr Mallett, my favourite bit is . . . all of it!'

These phrases were fun to do, and the sound department

would speed up the pitch and 'Mr Mallett! Mr Mallett!' became a popular, soft and funny, cuddly Mallet; the biggest selling soft toy for years. I'm delighted to say he still sells to this day. The face and stem are now beautifully embroidered, and even kids who have never seen *Wacaday* on TV still pick up a Pinky Punky Mallet and know what to do with it. It's hard to identify why it's lasted these decades, but there was a little clue from my old broadcasting pal, Peter Powell, who commented at the height of 'Itsy Bitsy' fame: 'You have a unique name; make sure you look after it. There's the warm and friendly Timmy coupled with the hard and determined Mallett. The two parts are what will always be memorable and make you stand out just by your name.'

The key elements of *Wacaday* that stand out for me are storytelling, fun and a wide-eyed wonder at the world. Let's get back on the bike and see where wide-eyed wonder takes me next . . .

My ride has brought me the first glimpses of the Pyrenees – their snow-capped peaks only 80 kilometres away. I find myself gawping and feel a lump in my throat. The Pyrenees are not just a mountain range. They're the great border between France and Spain, one of the great dividing ranges of language and culture, and somehow I've got to get over them. Everyone warns me the weather can be changeable. But if Eleanor of Aquitaine managed to cross at the age of 80, on horseback, hopefully I'll succeed on my Timmeee E-bike.

I take another call from my friend Big Dave. 'When will you be in Burgos, Timmy?' I laugh. I have no idea where I'll be tonight let alone somewhere in another country. 'How about I come out to Burgos in a week and ride with you for three days to León?' Dave's been working out my daily mileage and suggests this stretch would be doable together. It would involve him flying to Bilbao on Spain's north coast, renting a car and driving to Burgos (200 km), then renting a bike, dropping it three days later in León (220 km), renting another car and driving to Oviedo (200 km) for a late flight back to the UK. It's an extraordinary gesture and I'm really touched.

But I don't want to be tied to anything; I want to have the option to stop and paint, or spend another day somewhere. This is my journey, and I want to be able to stop as often as possible, see everything, experience everything and be engrossed in the way. I'm not lonely. I'm comfortable by myself and it's easier on my own, with no timetable, no one asking, 'How about we stop here? Shall we go and look at this?' Sorry, Big Dave. This is not that sort of shared trip . . .

As it transpires, Big Dave isn't far off in his calculations. But that doesn't leave any time for the unexpected, like yesterday, or indeed the next ten minutes . . . Next time, Dave . . . and thank you for the lovely generous offer.

Along the undulating way, with its new green verges and blossom in the hedgerows, I stop briefly to photograph some-one's house. It won't take a moment. It's a ten-second photo opportunity – inspired by the cobalt blue gate, the shutters and the flowering wisteria all around the windows. Here at last is a garden. The sort of garden we recognise, ablaze with the colours of sunny France. There are camelias, azaleas, rhododendrons, all in a fierce show of colourful glory. Cherry and apple blossom, bluebells and a pond. I've just been focusing on the big picture – the mighty mountain range I've got to cross; but before I do, it's important not to miss the details, the little here and now that makes up the rich tapestry of every day.

As I take the photo there's a *'Monsieur . . .'* I turn around and two women – mother, and grown-up daughter in an Oxford sweatshirt – are looking quizzically. 'I love your garden,' I offer. 'I hope you don't mind . . .'

They speak perfect English. 'Come and see . . .'

It leads to something very special: first a cuppa, then a guided tour.

'Would you mind if I paint your garden and would you care to be in the painting?' Marie Lise and Monelle look at each other and rather like the idea. Monelle sits by the blooms, and I suggest she read a book while I paint.

'What shall I read?'

'How about *Cyrano de Bergerac*?' And that's what I get – in French. I don't understand a word but it sounds great. As the afternoon progresses and the delicious smells of the spring garden mix with the smell of the paints, Monelle reads aloud the great tale of comedic romantic love from the big nose Cyrano (played by Gerard Depardieu in the original film and by Steve Martin in the Hollywood version *Roxanne*).

It is an easy painting to create. Dark mysterious windows, purple wisteria, blue shutters and a cascade of colourful plants. As Cyrano himself says: 'sometimes I wait, in the blue evening; I enter a few gardens where the hour is perfumed with my poor big devil's nose . . .'

The day is full of little treats. Marie Lise's husband, Gerard, has a collection of hundreds of model Dinky cars, Monelle adores cats (she has seven of them in her apartment), and after living for a time in Oxford the Rigaber family have fallen in love with gardening, the English way – Marie Lise has the most beautiful garden in France.

Then it's six o'clock and time to pack up and head on. Mother pops her head out of the window: 'You must stay for dinner, and there's a room for the night . . .'

This act of random kindness will stay with me for ever. The

painting is my mobile phone screensaver, to remind me I'm on a pilgrimage of encounters. Go slowly, and notice everything, because it's never the destination . . . always the journey, and a ten-second photo opportunity can lead to . . .

Kind words . . .

A painting . . .

And fortuitous meetings.

Tomorrow, in the rain, I hope to make St Jean at the foot of the mighty Pyrenees.

FRANCK'S FLAG

SUMMIT!

ST JEAN PIED DE PORT

GERRY

PAMPLONA

12

Reach your potential!

Games are a favourite Mallett thing. Especially when winning them.

We were brought up on hectic patience – the card game patience, with multiple participants all playing on to any pile. It's hectic. And when we wanted a calm game it was Martin's favourite – dominoes. He could recognise the pattern of the numbers and enjoyed the satisfaction of a long trail of tiles across the table.

This clearly helped me win Cluedo Detective of the Year 1977, in the Midlands. (It was a bonus that my opponents were no more than ten years old.) I left the competition loaded with all sorts of board and dice games, and our flat at university became adept at playing these instead of revising. Later, I collected dozens of Monopoly sets from around the world, along with homemade *Timmy on the Tranny* board games and the Utterly Brilliant Magic Spell game brought out during *Wacaday* (you'll probably find it on vintage collectors' sites). Hey, the thing I'm most associated with is Mallett's Mallet and that's a game. I wonder if this Camino will involve any games?

In the early morning I leave a Martin Mallett name tag in the home of the Rigaber family, who had made me so very welcome. (I can hear Martin saying, 'Nice house. You me.') I head to the nearby village of Cagnotte, with its ancient twelfth-century church and pilgrim hostel, paid for by Richard the Lionheart. He had come visiting, with an army, to knock some sense into the thieving barons who were making life hard for the visiting pilgrims. I liked this interest in humble travellers from the medieval statesmen back in the day. My own visit has been touched by so much honest kindness and generosity.

I ride past ancient abbeys, a Saturday market, cherry blossom just asking to be painted and multilingual road signs in French and Basque, then wind my way through valleys, and up and up the steaming hills. It's lush and fertile in the foothills of the Pyrenees. Everything grows. Because of course it rains . . . Not all the time – it stops for ten minutes every now and then – but when it does rain, I know it.

Mountains in the rain are always steaming and breathing. I can see the earth and landscape exhaling great puffs of cloud. It's a lovely thought and matches my panting as I pedal onwards and upwards . . .

My thoughts meander today, just like the road. I'm cycling a medieval route, wondering how much ancient travellers would have worried about who they might meet. I try shopping for yummy local foods in the Saturday market. Stock up on local delicacies while I can, as tomorrow's menu may not be as tasty. As you'd expect, I detour to admire the ancient abbey nearby surrounded by cherry blossom. How to describe these scenes without trying to paint a picture? They're difficult to capture in watercolours; I try crimson mixed with violet for the cherry shadows, and drops of pure white for the highlights in the sunshine between the raindrops. Through the trees I can see the Naples yellow, raw umber stone of the abbey and behind that the rainclouds in a wash of Prussian blue and burnt umber.

I come to the waymarker for the meeting of three Camino routes from across France that begin in Paris, Vézelay and Le Puy. It's a modest lump of stone at an easily missed place called Gibraltar Point. The rain closes in and the wind rises, and any view is swallowed up by rainclouds, the mountain ranges swathed in mist. This is not a jolly. This is tough. Cars throw up spray, and I glimpse bent figures trudging up the pathway ahead, draped in massive ponchos to protect them and their backpacks from the elements. Walking pilgrims are beginning to appear more frequently, with plentiful and more noticeable Camino route signage.

The last 40 kilometres of the ride today is a long slog on busy roads, filthy, wet and treacherous. I make the effort and do a detour to a lonely chapel. Am I trying to make sure I see everything in the guidebooks? I'm already wet. What will another half-hour of downpour do? I can feel the rain on my glasses – I'm peering through raindrops. They drip off the helmet; my balaclava and neck buff are sodden. The winter cycling gloves are drenched, and I rely on the hand-warming gel packets to keep the moisture warm. I've got my rain jacket on under the poncho. My shoes are wet, and everything is soaked. Every car going past throws more spray over me. I feel like Dory in *Finding Nemo* – just keep swimming, just keep swimming.

As I reach the top of a long hill there's a wayside stone crucifix and I stop under a tree. Looking down the wet valley towards a little town, it feels like a good place to give thanks for my ride through France. In a few miles I'll be into St Jean Pied de Port, the pilgrim capital of the country, and everything will change.

I want to have a little Martin Mallett moment and I plump for the top of the stone cross under a stone. Pilgrims are always leaving stones on wayside markers and memorials. The more stones I see piled up, the more I want to add to them. It's a way to mark my journey and add to the never-ending number of travellers. I have to stretch up to reach the cross and make sure the name tag is secure. Then I turn around satisfied and see a monster tractor and trailer come within a whisker of my laden bike. That feels ominous. Don't get complacent! Even resting on its stand my bike needs to be watched.

The bustling tiny medieval town of St Jean Pied de Port, at the foot of the pass over the Pyrenees, thrives on the Camino. St Jean is a steep cobbled street or two between three ancient stone gateways. I feel as if I've come into some forgotten time zone, because I've ridden up and over the hill from the next village, past the ruined citadel fortress and instantly I'm transported back to the early Middle Ages as I come under the archway. Narrow street, bumpy cobbles, Camino marker in the road, a gateway wide enough for two people . . . just. Today it's full of damp and soggy pilgrims searching for shelter. The pilgrim HQ is right at the top of the steeply curving hill, with adverts for *albergues*, refuges and pilgrim gear. The pilgrims I see milling around are about to start their big adventure. I've been on the go for weeks . . .

We are all wet and dripping and queueing to ask questions.

What's the path like over the pass? What's the weather forecast? Can you stamp my passport? Where will I stay tonight? Everyone has a different budget. The two women from Germany want to pay five euros each, Jenny from Melbourne is happy with a dorm, and a man from Wales wants some comfort tonight in a hotel.

Maddi from Holland is one of those answering the questions and giving helpful smiling encouragement. She is doing this as a volunteer job for a week. Everyone in the pilgrim office is a volunteer. Most have experienced the Camino themselves and want to give something back. All cheerfully answering the same old questions over and over again.

Maddi and I shake hands – mine are sopping – and she scans her list of accommodation and starts ringing for me.

'Thirty years ago,' she says, 'we hardly saw any pilgrims. Now there are thousands every year.' Possibly 100,000 starting here in St Jean.

Everyone wants their pilgrim passport stamped. I'm on to passport number three, and Maddi offers maps for the trail, apps and tips and a list of accommodations all along the Camino Francés. There are places to stay every few kilometres of the 800 kilometres from here to Santiago. It's become an amazing organisation as the numbers are growing each year. The thing is, even with all these people, it doesn't feel as though you are part of a crowd. As in real life, I suppose. Generally, we only really notice the people around us: our family, friends and associates. We don't consciously think of all the people busy around us every day. It's the same on the Camino. You travel in a bubble of the people you are with or you meet each day; and that's fine. Every nationality under the sun seems to be heading here, including squillions of South Koreans, who have all been inspired by a local TV presenter's pilgrimage.

Timmy (7) and Martin (9),
Cubs in the garden

Mallett brothers, Paul,
Martin and Timmy, 1980

Mallett formal family portrait (slightly awkward!), September 1969

Funday Sunday Piccadilly Radio at Heaton Norris Park, 1983.
Nobby No Level (Chris Evans), Curt Smith (Tears for Fears)
and Andy Bird (later my Best Man and Head of Disney)

Warwick Uni student
Timmy, 1975

If you can't see the colour,
turn up the volume! 1980

Beating off a scary attack by Dervishes with
Mallett's Mallet! *Wacaday*, Morocco, 1989

Prime Minister Margaret Thatcher meets Mallett's Mallet!
House of Commons, Christmas 1988

Together with Michaela on
the *Wacaday* set, 1987

Kylie Minogue played Mallett's
Mallet on *Wacaday*, 1989

Itsy Bitsy Timmy in tune with Andrew Lloyd Webber! Christmas 1990

Lorraine Kelly on the telly in *Timmy Towers*, 2000

An Itsy Bitsy wedding
day, 8 September 1990

'One day, young Billy, this
Mallet will be yours'

You Me! Ma Bubba!

Piccadilly pals – Nobby,
Timmy, Prof. Brian Cox

When Prime Minister Theresa May
came to our house to admire my E Bike!

Painting from the back of
the bike on the Camino

Top:
Windswept – this will
be a huge journey

Above:
Mont St Michel – echoes of history

Left:
In the moment – everywhere
has something special

Wood cutters – in the Loire Valley, capricorn
beetles and axes vs ancient tree

Camino crossroads. Where will
my journey take me today . . .?

Martin's Vineyard – his
name tag among the vines
makes this vintage special

Above:
Blue shutters – a ten-second
photo that leads to paintings and
an act of random kindness

Above:
In the village albergue,
Hans and I celebrate our
meeting with *The Toast*

Left:
St-Jean-Pied-de-Port –
traditional start point for many
pilgrims. I've already cycled
twice as far as they will walk

Forbidding Pyrenees – 'Don't take these mountains for granted' for good reason

The Hill of Forgiveness – a significant Camino spot in all weathers

The plains in Spain – the moody Meseta is wild and windy

Above: *Salome the Donkey* – every creature is on a journey . . .

Left: *Ruined monastery* – how small we are in the scheme of things

Bottom left: *Long and winding road* – to snow-capped mountains of León

Below: *Listening and observing* – is always revealing . . .

Top: *Sheep in the road* – a natural Camino traffic jam

Above left: *Heading home with the herd* – my home feels a long way

Above right: *Iron cross* – everyone leaves a stone from home

Left: *Card players* – everyone needs friends

Hórreos in Galicia – the weird storage barns on stilts

Hard at work – there is dignity in a job well done

Today's task – he sharpens his scythe in his slippers!

On the road to Santiago – crowds of eager hurrying pilgrims

Storm approaching – the promised land

Santiago skyline – the gleaming destination

The Botafumeiro – to fumigate smelly pilgrims!

Final waymarker – Finisterre

End of the world – Muxia and the never-ending sound of the sea

Puncture point – on the Camino Primitivo as the weather closes in

Camino morning – the analogy of my adventure

Built on faith – the Camino Chapel is always there – just in case!

For most people this is their start for the Camino de Santiago. People fly into France and take the train to St Jean. Others walk from Le Puy or Paris; some even start from home on their bicycle. I made my first decision at the end of my driveway. Left or right? Now here I am nearly 1,450 kilometres into my journey. Not far off double the length of the Camino Francés. There's a little bit of me that looks at these beginners as green-neck rookies. I tell myself to keep quiet, listen and not be smug. Because this isn't my first ride along the Camino de Santiago. It's my third . . .

It was my friend Gary's idea. We've known each other since university days. We are of the generation that were given a grant and had our tuition fees paid. Yep, we were paid to go to university, to learn how to learn. I did History with History of Art; he did law. Gary became an expert in equal opportunities and wrote for a magazine that had no pictures; so I never read it. I became an entertainer with a love of quirky stories through history, and if there weren't any pictures, I'd paint them. We are still quite different when it comes to cycling. A few years ago, we did a week's trip from León to Santiago – 800 years to the month since St Francis of Assisi walked barefoot from home. Not that Gary cared about that.

Accommodation and bike hire were arranged by a tour company and every morning they collected our bags and transported them to our next hotel. We told them the mileage we'd like to attempt and everything else was do-it-yourself. Inspired by the Martin Sheen film *The Way*, we got the bug. We didn't expect other things – a broken chain, multiple punctures, torrential biblical floods, fascinating fellow travellers and a sense of achievement like no other.

Six months later we were back to cycle the Via de la Plata from

Seville to Caceres in April. It was Holy Week and the trip was an unholy disaster. We barely rode together at all. You know that phrase 'The rain in Spain stays mainly on the plain'? We must have been on the plain . . . because the rain was wetter, the Camino was emptier and the journey was flatter in all sorts of ways. We probably met fewer than ten fellow travellers all week. We came home barely speaking to each other, feeling a sense of disappointment. Gary said it was because we hadn't reached Santiago, and I'd done a daft detour through the floods. I think we went with the wrong kind of expectations.

The thing that did stand out on that adventure was Holy Week. It's a big thing in Spain; parades happen every night of the week in every town and village. There are bands, statues, noise and excitement. It's the most watched show on local TV – the Semana Santa festival broadcast every evening from a different town. The whole village comes out to watch the parade of relics and statues from the church. There will be up to several hundred people involved in carrying the enormous statues of the Virgin Mary, Christ and the local saints. Costumes are ornate; in Seville they have a multitude of colours in the strange pointy hats that the Ku Klux Klan stole and made their own. It's a shame, because it changes the way we regard them. The parade is usually quite late – 10 p.m. would be an early start – and goes on past midnight, with huge crowds. It's an amazing spectacle of culture and religion right at the heart of civic life. It really made the week's highlight, and despite everything else that happened we were not put off the Camino.

In fact, the one thing we agreed was that we'd do it again, properly. By that, Gary meant to cycle all along the Camino Francés. I meant I wanted to cycle from home, without the back-up of pre-planning my stops. Plus, I wanted to paint it. On our first two trips, I'd stopped along the way and taken photos and later made paintings in my studio. I found lots to inspire my art. I could have gone slower and been more involved. But our sense of achievement in cycling is measured differently. I judge a day on what we see or who we meet; Gary judges it on the distance travelled and effort expended. We both judge the evening on who wins at dominoes. Doesn't everyone carry a box of dominoes?

Over the next few years, it was always there at the back of my mind. Gary had challenged me to ride the Camino again with him in my sixtieth year. It was one of those dreams that was too big to speak of out loud (unlike me, I know) until I was ready to undertake such an adventure. Once out in the open and declared, then I would have to complete it.

The Camino gets into you. I don't know how or why; it just does. It's like a metaphor for your life. Everything is super-heightened. There are the four aspects that everyone talks about: the physical, cultural, historical and spiritual. Physically, you are making your way over hundreds (or in my case thousands) of miles of rugged high mountains, vast plains and everlasting vistas. Culturally, you are experiencing people, food, manners and attitudes. Historically, it's quite something to be travelling in the thousand-year-old footsteps of our ancestors, and stepping into the buildings they erected and the monuments to their dreams or achievements. And then spiritually. The questions it asks of you about how you relate to family, friends and work, and that wonderful mysterious concept – the meaning of life. Which is obvious, of course: welcome refreshment, a glimpse of the infinite, a comfy bed, a sense of achievement, playing games and something to laugh at, please . . .

When I announced my plan last summer, I got plenty of comments and good advice. Who are you going with? No one. What are you raising money for? I'm not. It's for charity, right?

No, it's to raise awareness of reaching your potential. Just like my Down's syndrome brother Martin does each and every day.

I told Gary about my plans. 'Bugger, now I'll have to do it . . .' he said. It's not as easy for him. For some reason you can't rent a bike in France and drop it in Spain. Can't see why, when they're both in the EU. Today he's on a flight to Barcelona, then the train to Pamplona, where he picks up a rental bike and sets off on his pre-planned ride to Santiago. 'I hoped I'd be behind you, chasing you, Mallett,' he said, 'but it seems I'm ahead . . . Have you got the dominoes?'

I stay with Franck (from St Malo, who finds me a bed when he spots the St Malo sticker on the bike) and Patrizia (from Italy), the happy couple who met two years ago walking the Camino. Now they run this pilgrim refuge with smiling faces and big encouragement. There's room for the bike, good showers, a washer dryer and a good home-cooked meal. There's entertaining, cross-cultural company, with eight of us in total, including two Americans, an Australian, a Frenchman and a silent Italian. We play a game of 'Where are you from and why are you doing the Camino?' Then there's a conversation with Gary on the mobile. A sense of expectation – the journey is about to begin . . . again. 'Don't suppose I'll see you in Pamplona then?' I doubt it . . .

Our chat is just what I need to encourage me to set off over the Pyrenees.

Thanks, St Jean.

My next stop is the forbidding mountain range and the forecast is . . . utterly wet and miserable, solid constant total rain all day and all night, and on again some more for the next week.

The dormitory has five bunk beds in it. It's not my first Camino experience of multiple sharing, but in the old wine cellar in Bordeaux I felt as if I had my own space. At La Vita è Bella I am sharing with the Australian bloke, the Italian couple and the American woman. The rain and the sense of anticipation make it a restless night all round. I watch them pack up and head off first thing Sunday morning to walk up the pass over the Pyrenees to Roncesvalles. Not me. I'm going to wait, and hope the rain may ease, even though the forecast says it won't.

I set up my paints in the dining room while the hosts and their guests, the newly published travel writer and his wife, sit and chat over coffee. I work on the watercolour painting of the Pyrenean foothills steaming in the clouds. I wet the paper, drip the greys into it, do a wash of Prussian blue and burnt umber.

Along the way I'd been struck by the fields of oilseed rape blooming in the rain. The electric Van Gogh yellow is accentuated by the dark grey-blue clouds. I've always loved these yellow fields. They arrived on our shores back in the early 1970s when we joined the EEC. I remember being struck by the sight of them early one summer term at Warwick University when we had what turned out to be the first European referendum and I was out exploring on my bike. 'Van Gogh would have loved these,' I said and, ever since, I've enjoyed the way this colour marks the explosion of spring. I wonder if we will still have these fields after Brexit? Could this exuberance of colour disappear as one of the casualties of that process? I'm reminded to enjoy the sight now and paint the landscape. It may be time limited.

I found some of those 1975 referendum pamphlets in a box in my attic. The reasons to vote Yes and No were roughly similar 40 years ago, except for one. Vote No to keep food prices down. What? That was all about butter mountains and wine lakes. Whatever happened to them? Things we worry about today may seem laughable in years to come . . .

🚲

Around midday, I've run out of reasons to stay. Time to make my move. Wrapped in my poncho and my feet in cling film against the rain I get the bike ready to go. Franck comes out with his St Malo flag to see me off. The fact that I've cycled from his hometown on the English Channel to his *albergue* at the other end of the country impresses him. It is an encouraging send-off. By the gateway under the tower is a chapel full of pilgrims attending Sunday mass. It's a good time to remember my family and ask for a blessing for the next stage of the journey to help me through the gate and up the mountains.

Slippery cobbled stones, laden bike, rain and wind. Hmmm. *Buen Camino!*

Kings and princes and simple pilgrims have passed this way for centuries, and today it's my damp turn. I choose to keep to the tarmac and avoid the Napolean Pass, much of which is closed because of snow and rain and I know it's not worth running any risk. I cycle past trudging pilgrims, including a man in medieval trench coat with ten-gallon hat and gardening gloves, who's carrying an eight-foot-tall staff, backpack and sleeping mat. 'I want to make a statement,' he offers . . . as his coat gets heavier in the downpour. On the outskirts of St Jean, I pass recent landslips, with trees and bushes hanging precariously above the newly exposed rock. Gushing streams and rivers cascade down the mountains, and a car is stranded in the bank after being washed away. Look where you are going, Mallett.

The border is a few kilometres from St Jean. It is time to say *au revoir* to France and *hola* to Spain. I am reminded that everywhere and everything has a beginning and an end. In these conditions both the end and the beginning are dramatic and distinctive.

I stop for a sandwich and become aware of the difference between these two countries. It's extraordinary. Just a few kilometres apart and yet the two towns are utterly contrasting. The language, the culture and the food. What I'm eating is not a sandwich; it's a slice of cheese between two pieces of dry bread. If this is Spanish food, I'm in for a tough time.

The climb is relentless. I'm glad I have the E-bike; it just gives more power to the pedal. There are taxis shooting past around each hairpin bend, some carrying dispirited pilgrims who can't manage the walk with their big heavy backpacks and others just ferrying backpacks to the next stop. Everywhere all along the road there are pilgrims wrapped in ponchos, some carrying umbrellas. I pass three exhausted cyclists pushing their laden bikes. 'E-bike, E-bike,' I call out encouragingly . . . as I go past with my 25 kilos attached. Hairpin bend after hairpin bend. Oh yes, this bike is a joy and I'm trying not to be smug. No, I'm not at all. I'm happily, smugly pedalling past them.

There are countless rushing streams and then patches of snowdrifts. I can't see much across the valley, as its obscured by low cloud. But I hear my breath, I feel the pressure as I drop down the gears and pedal. I still have to pedal; this is not a motorbike. The three power settings of Eco, Normal and Sport give a little extra boost to my own hard work and are just a guide as to how steep the road is as it twists and turns ever upwards. Yet at the top, fifteen hundred metres up, I still have 50 per cent of my power left. I haven't gone above Normal mode. I never need the extra kick of Sport mode. Through the snow and drizzle and mist, my patient pedalling gets me where I'm headed – eventually the roof and crucifix of the chapel at the top of the pass come into view. It's the most amazing feeling to cycle up one of the world's great mountain ranges. Talk about reaching your potential. This is a day that will live with me for ever! I stop to take in the hugeness of the achievement.

I'm higher than the highest peak in Britain and the sense

of satisfaction is profound. I've pedalled up 28 kilometres on my fully laden E-bike. I need to celebrate, or at least mark the moment. The chapel is sadly closed but there's a gap between the wall and the roof just wide enough for a brother Martin name tag.

Ma bubba.

Reach your potential, Mallett! Yes!

It's now a short ride down to the ancient monastery at Roncesvalles, where all those hardy ones from St Jean will stay tonight. I call in, of course, for my stamp in the pilgrim passport. The place is packed. It's three o'clock in the afternoon and I look in the chapel to see the famous statue of St James, but something is ringing . . . it's my mobile. Up here on top of the world I've got a signal and my pal Gary is ringing me. He's just arrived from Barcelona into Pamplona and the sun is shining there. Pamplona is a massive 50 kilometres away. I wonder . . . Should I?

And while I'm considering I look across from the monastery to the road and see 'Santiago de Compostela 790'. It's the famous signpost, the first in Spain, that's in all the photos of the Camino. I set up the camera and consider my options. Stay here tonight in the crowded monastery? Go on to a suitable town or village and stop and paint? Or ride for Pamplona and my pal? The one with whom I first discovered this adventure. There's no contest. I need to see Gary. I need to reach the next part of my potential. I'm off again for another 50 kilometres to the capital of Navarre.

As I descend the mountains the sun comes out! It's a sign. I start singing loudly at the top of my voice. Then I'm howling with joy; whooping and laughing as I freewheel down the looping bends on the western slopes of the mountains.

Along wonderful fast empty roads with glorious views and

154

warm sunshine, I'm in the happy zone. This is a tree-lined valley ride. 'Come and meet me, Gary,' I say.

'But I'm in Hemingway's bar . . .'

'Come on, it's a beautiful day; you need the practice. We'll ride in together . . . I'm on the N-135. Head for the town of Iroz.' I ride through Zubrini and its massive magnesium smelting factory, and at Iroz I wait for Gary. He's rather flustered when I call.

'I'm lost. Couldn't find my way out of Pamplona. Sorry, I'll see you by the bullring . . .'

I enter the city of Pamplona along the fast-flowing, flooded River Arga. On this Sunday afternoon promenaders are oohing and aahing at the gushing floodwater. In places it's overflowed the banks; the towpath has partially disappeared, and there are detours around each bend. It's more dangerous than they realise. I come across soggy sorry Gerry the pilgrim in his late 60s from Northern Ireland, who missed his footing and fell in this torrent. The heavy backpack was dragging him underwater; anxious hands reached in and pulled his head above the waves. 'I thought I was going to drown. I couldn't get my head above the water. Without that help my wife would be a widow now.' He is utterly shaken, every bit of him is wet, and yet he is full of resolve. Accidents can happen in a split second.

Above me are the city walls and right in the centre of town are the bullring and the cathedral. I'm not sure which is more important: God or the stadium. Pamplona, the city of Hemingway, the mad running of the bulls. It's the capital of Navarre, home of Richard the Lionheart's lonely wife Berengaria, and the most beautiful first city to come across in Spain after the long haul over the Pyrenees.

Gary and I meet at the bullring and it's an emotional moment. I'm with my pal of 40 years, my great cycling inspiration, on this amazing adventure. I've gone up and over the Pyrenees, ridden into the heart of bullfighting country, and now I'm with my great friend.

'Let's head to Hemingway's bar for beer, tapas and dominoes. We've got something to celebrate.'

'Sorry. I forgot the dominoes . . .'

'Well, go home and get them!'

UWE

13

Hill of Forgiveness

PUENTE LA REINA

EUNATE

PAMPLONA

ALTO DEL PERDON

It's better not to think too much about what might have been. Regrets pull you back. Look for the positive in every encounter.

Gary and I have met and now we part. He's gone ahead, on his journey to Santiago, knowing where he'll be staying each night. I'm going my way, with no idea. Everyone's adventure is their own, and I am quite happy to have us riding 'together' a couple of days apart. We'll catch up each evening on the phone.

Now I'm in Pamplona alona. It will be good to have a day of rest to recover from several days' strenuous pedalling and to bask in my sense of achievement after climbing the Pyrenees on my Timmeee E-bike. Some culture and inspiration will be very welcome. There are expressive paintings of the region in the Navarre Museum that remind me to paint a watercolour of the summit of the Pyrenees. I use my sketches and photos to capture the bleakness in two-tone purples. I like painting angry squally expressive skies.

I head out to explore the narrow winding streets where the running of the bulls happens every summer. Martin and I would have run around with our fingers as horns, so it's essential to get into the bull heritage. This is April shower season and the rain showers are torrential. It's tricky trying to man-oeuvre around people along the narrow streets in a constant procession of umbrellas. My sketchbook – Pamplona section – is full of umbrellas. The tourist office team are very helpful, with Maddy giving me an ornate Pamplona civic city tie pin and city badge. I'm looking the part as the collection grows on my cycling tie. In exchange I give her a Martin name tag.

'Where's your favourite view in the city?' I want to know.

'The north-east corner of the walls with the view of the cathedral,' she offers without a moment's hesitation.

As the sun reappears and lights up the snow and storm clouds on the distant peaks, it is a perfect spot to paint. Strong sunshine, shadows and scurrying clouds bring the view into sharp relief. I want light and shade, especially on the cathedral towers, and I'm so absorbed in the piece that it's approaching teatime when I stop for lunch. I share the painting with Maddy and her team afterwards and there are excited exclamations. 'We know where that is!'

I can hear the voice of brother Martin in my head – 'I'm happy. You me' – and in the ancient church of St Nicholas, with the warm uneven timber floor, I am pleased to ask for a

Camino blessing from the priest on duty and place a Martin Mallett name tag behind an altarpiece in thanks.

Today there were not many miles, but plenty of smiles . . .

I'll need those smiles as I face the torrential rains and wind up next, on the forbidding mountain known as the Alto del Perdón – the Hill of Forgiveness. This is a special place on the Camino and pilgrims are heading there, heads down, huddled into the wind and rain. A Scotsman, in his kilt, trudges along with grimly gritted teeth, as his legs and knees get wetter. The track disappears into mud and rocks, and then a stream runs down the middle of it. I abandon it and take the long safer tarmac ten-kilometre detour up to the wind turbines and pilgrim statues on the exposed mountain top.

I know I am in a windy spot when there are rows of turbines gracefully turning in the breeze. Or whirring like demons in the freezing rain and gales, as they are today. Alongside is the fabulous set of iron pilgrim statues rocking and rattling in the wind and rain. It's one of the great sights along the Camino and hauntingly evocative. In reality, every pilgrim who comes past them today looks like the statues. Head bowed, footsteps trudging in despair across this wild expanse of lonely hilltop. Forgive me, this may normally be a favourite photo stop, but today people hurry past, because it feels like the end of the world. I attach a Martin name tag to the collection of ribbons on a nearby post – Martin's there blowing in the wind – and turn to head further into the gale. Gary has warned me not to risk the steep and treacherous muddy track – to take the tarmac – but with gusts this strong I need to pedal furiously to go downhill!

I feel as though I'm on the Road to Hell.

He was batting tennis balls to his dog when I came across Chris Rea again. Last time had been when he guested on one of my shows for 'Fool if You Think it's Over' or 'Driving Home for Christmas'. Mrs Mallett and I were house hunting and Chris invited us in for a cup of tea. 'If you don't find anything, you can always buy this one . . .' And that's how we came to be living in the home where he wrote 'Road to Hell'. I'm writing by the window where the words 'Scared beyond belief way down in the shadows' were penned. Chris used the shower to create the watery effects for 'On the Beach'. The fountain in the pond has a Chris Rea scar on it. He dropped the statue on his guitar fingers while assembling it. Look after those valuable creative fingers, Chris!

A two-hour hot chocolate break doesn't make much difference. I might have dried out in the steaming café of soggy pilgrims, or at least thawed? Hardly. What is the point of being out in these conditions? I suppose, so that I can appreciate the blue-sky days that will come. Light and shade, summer and winter, sunshine and gales. Got to have one to appreciate the other.

I could carry on. The map shows it isn't far to a dry, warm and welcoming place, but instead I go out of my way to visit the twelfth-century octagonal church at Eunate. My friend Freddie said it was one of his highlights and I know he'll ask me about it. Am I really going to tell him I didn't bother because it was raining?

The detour is only a few kilometres but when I get there I have a sense of déjà vu.

There's an octagonal church of similar vintage in the City of London's Lincoln's Inn fields. The London church has the tomb of William Marshall the great guardian of the Plantagenet kings and defender of Magna Carta. At Eunate I want to ask, 'Why here, in the middle of nowhere?' and 'Where's your historical hero?'

I'm ready to find somewhere to stop and get dry now. At the next town, Puente la Reina – translated, it's the Bridge of the Queen – there's the oldest *albergue* on the Camino, dating from around 1400 ('when I was young and you were even younger', as we'd have said on *Wacaday*). This sounds good and they offer me a sleeping bag but when it's unwrapped, it's a child's puffa jacket. Oops. Change of plan. Instead, I opt for a little family hotel with my own room; I'm soaked to the skin, and I want to dry out in comfort.

Over dinner I meet a couple of English women walking the Camino – in the whole two months I only ever encounter eight people from Britain, and two of them are friends of mine. These two want to talk but I'm not quite in the mood. Roma's amazing football comeback against Barcelona in the Champions League is somehow more appealing. And yet at breakfast they surprise me, and it brings a lump to my throat. 'We looked you up and read about your reasons for doing the Camino. We are so sorry to hear of your dear brother Martin. We bought you this.' They present me with a Camino bracelet, which I will wear every day. Such a little thing, and so thoughtful. I am disappointed with myself for having preferred my own company. Before leaving, I paint the Bridge of the Queen to remind myself to pay attention.

Regrets pull you back. I'm reminding myself to look for the positive in every encounter.

I had been standing by the side of the road at the entrance to the motorway outside Munich with my thumb in the air. It was a popular spot to hitch-hike this September day in 1975. There was someone else waiting for a lift. Etiquette means you wait beyond the first hitch-hiker to be picked up and don't nick his ride. I hitched lifts all over Europe in my university days. Simon Calder, the well-known travel expert, started the student Golden Thumb hitch-hiking club and he and I would compare notes on great places to get free rides and who could hitch the furthest.

Another hopeful approached, looking for a lift. The bearded bloke in his late twenties greeted me: '*Guten Tag. Wo gehen Sie?*'

'I'm hoping to get to Berlin,' I replied.

'Ah, English!'

There are three crossing points from West Germany to Berlin and I was looking for either the southern one or the central one near Hannover. A lift to either would be fine. If not, then I'd head somewhere else. That's the beauty of standing by the side of the road with your thumb in the air. You go to where the ride takes you.

'I live in Berlin,' said the bearded one. 'If you get there here is my number. And by the way, my name is Uwe . . . Uwe Radkte.' Our conversation lasted no more than two or three minutes, during which time two more hitch-hikers arrived and the line grew.

'So good luck, Timmy. I wait further up the road. Maybe see you in Berlin . . .'

Eventually, I was in luck when a businessman in a nice BMW offered me a lift to Hannover. It was a memorable journey. I was 19 years old, and we talked of all sorts of things. My university course, our families and what he had done in the war.

'I drove a tank in Russia. I was at Stalingrad.'

I looked at this man who had stopped in his nice car to offer me a lift, having seen more of Europe's turmoil than I will ever see – I hope.

We came off the motorway and took a quiet road through pine trees and the gently rolling hills of southern-central Germany. Then the road ended abruptly at barbed wire, lots of danger signs and several rows of tank traps, fences and ditches. On the other side, the road continued to a small town. It was as if a harsh scar had been scrawled across an otherwise lovely land-scape. Like a mournful Caspar David Friedrich painting from the early nineteenth century, with a twentieth-century twist.

'This is the border between the West and the DDR – the German Democratic Republic . . . See the birds fly over the border? For them it's easy. For us to get to that town is a long 200-kilometre journey through the border control. They speak the same language as us in the DDR. Take a photo and show it to your friends . . .'

We continued in quiet contemplation. The BMW-and-Panzer-tank-driving businessman and the questioning English student. It was dark as we arrived at the service area near Hanover. 'Good luck, Timmy. I hope you enjoy Berlin when you get there.'

A young German stopped next, in a French 2CV packed full of all his stuff. I sat with my rucksack on my knee. We didn't say much, just listened to the radio instead. Our common language was pop and as we approached the East German crossing Abba came on Radio Luxembourg singing 'SOS' across all the borders of the Continent. Every time I hear that song I picture this scene. Bright lights, grey concrete, barriers, queues and the armed border guard approaching in his dark green uniform and cap.

We turned the radio down. 'Passports!' ordered the guard as he peered in through the open window without a smile. For some reason I felt guilty.

'Stay on this road to Berlin. Do not leave it,' he instructed. We set off along the concrete road and the very first thing we passed was a big sign on the motorway bridge: 'The German Democratic Republik celebrates 30 years. Visit Poland.'

It seemed so bizarre, that welcome, celebrating three decades since the end of the Second World War and inviting/instructing travellers to visit Poland. Did it suggest we weren't welcome in East Germany?

An hour later we had crossed the featureless communist country on Hitler's motorway and gone through another border control into the bright lights of West Berlin. My generous lift-giver dropped me at a youth hostel. There was nobody on reception. I found a spare room and bedded down on a mattress.

Next day I rang Uwe. He lived in a block of flats in the northwest of the city, out by the Berlin Wall. He had a great view of the concrete wall and sandy barrier (known as the death strip) that snaked away across the city. 'That was my home,' he pointed eastwards, 'until they didn't like me any more.' He smiled. The story came out piece by piece. He was a teacher, with a wife and daughter, living in the East of the city. But some of his ideas didn't sit well with the Stasi secret police, so he'd found himself under surveillance and then arrested. They told him to leave. He kissed his family goodbye and was expelled. 'I had the wrong politics. Now I can look out of my window, see where my wife and daughter live. I can speak to them on the phone, but I can never see them . . . You are a Westerner, you can go into East Berlin, you can get a day visa, but I cannot. I suggest you go and visit. Oh and by the way, I am having a party when you return.'

Checkpoint Charlie in the centre of the city was the sole border crossing. I had to change money into Ost marks (good luck finding anything to spend them on) and the first thing I saw, when I was through the checkpoint, was war-damaged buildings, and bullet holes from the Russian siege in 1945. Alexanderplatz boasted the impressive new TV tower in the

East, but there was just nothing to watch on DDR TV. At lunchtime, I found my way to Humbolt University, on the palatial avenue Unter den Linden, built during the Enlightenment, and sat with some quiet students eating noodle soup and rye bread. They absorbed the sight of this Englishman in jeans covered in badges, a bright cheesecloth shirt – the usual distinctive Timmy clothes. They were from the port of Rostok and after glancing at each other said that no, they couldn't travel to the West – and that was the limit of our conversation.

Back with Uwe, there was the promised party of six people, all Osties, East Berliners who had either been expelled or had escaped. It was difficult to understand what they said and I regretted not spending more time learning my *Der, Die, Das* German lessons in school. One young couple with the biggest smiles could speak a little English . . .

'You look happy. Are you celebrating something special?'

'*Ja*, we have just come from East Berlin, this week . . .'

'That's amazing. How did you get here?'

'We escaped in, how do you say? . . . in ze boot of a car. There is a man who, for some money, could help us.' The car's suspension was rigged, the couple and their young daughter were hidden in the boot, and after handing over a year's salary they had escaped to the West.

'So, what now? Will you go on to West Germany? Cologne? Hamburg? Munich?'

'No, we are Berliners. We will stay here.'

At the end of the evening Uwe revealed that the party had been arranged especially for me, so I could meet some real Berliners. The thing he didn't say was, 'Don't take your freedom for granted.' But the evening and the kindness I was shown have always stayed with me . . . I have a photo of Uwe, a photo of the view from his high-rise flat, and two pictures I took at

the zoo. I don't have a photo of the people at the party. Nor any photos from East Berlin. I was too scared to take one in case I was arrested as a spy.

Years later, on 9 November 1989, the Berlin Wall came down. Within hours it was being chipped away and sold as souvenirs. The two halves of Germany were reunited peacefully in a brilliant example of what can happen when decades of repression are resolved without bloodshed. The following Easter we decided to film a *Wacaday* series in Blaahlin (the nickname we gave Berlin after the Blaah! catchphrase from Mallett's Mallet). Among our great tales was the story of Frederick the Great and the collection of giants he had in his army. Frederick of Prussia loved collecting tall soldiers and hated committing them to battle in case they got hurt. At the Charlottenburg Palace I dressed in an Enlightenment era uniform and stood on stilts to try to join his regiment. Hilarious.

Next up was a travelogue with the Berlin Bear, and a James Bond spy story at the Glienicke Bridge where, throughout the Cold War, spies had been routinely exchanged between East and West. Now the rush hour traffic whizzed across the bridge oblivious to its role in Cold War tensions. I dressed in instantly recognisable spy uniform – trilby hat, dark glasses, gaberdine mac – and held a newspaper with eye-holes cut out of the page.

That evening we were preparing for our highlight: the story of the Berlin Wall with a *Wacaday* twist. In the hotel I was telling Mrs Mallett about my last visit here and meeting Uwe, while idly flicking through the phone book in the room. Those were the days when every city had a telephone directory. Radtke . . . I remembered his surname: Uwe Radtke . . .

I looked down the Rs. Radtke Alex, B, J, M, T, U . . .

U. Radtke. I wonder I dialled the number . . .

Burr, Burr, Burr.

'*Ja.*'

'Er, hello, excuse me. Do you speak English by any chance?'

'*Ja.*'

'Well, I'm looking for Uwe Radtke . . .'

'*Ja.*'

'I met him in 1975 when I was hitch-hiking across Germany.'

'*Ja.*'

'He lived in West Berlin . . . He had come from the East.'

'*Ja.*'

'And he had been expelled for having the wrong politics.'

'*Ja.*'

'He had a party for me with his friends who were all Osties . . .'

'*Ja.*'

'Is this you? Uwe Radtke?'

'*Ja*, this is me.'

I couldn't believe it. The first number I had called and he was in; he remembered me, my visit and the party, and yes, he was absolutely ready to come over immediately to meet me.

Ben, the producer, was all for filming us together and having me tell the story, but first I wanted to have a chat with him and find out how his life was panning out and let him see what we were doing for children's TV. The evening progressed with big smiles and not enough common language. Uwe was now a teacher of politics, and he was still in Berlin. We invited him to come to the Brandenburg Gate and watch me tell the story of the fall of the Berlin Wall.

I was dressed as usual in bright clothes and wild specs and armed with Mallett's Mallet. There were guards; I hit them with the Mallet. I danced on top of the wall and bashed it beautifully. It was funny. It was colourful. It was hopeful. It took a long time. Uwe looked at us in bemusement.

'This is for children, *ja*?'

'Yes,' I said. 'We tell the stories of the world in a way that children will understand and laugh at.'

I gave him a Timmy pic.

After a while, Uwe said he had to be going; he shook our hands and left, and I had the feeling I'd missed the opportunity that Ben wanted, to tell Uwe's story. To bring something different to our *Wacaday* fun. We did reverse shots, wild shots and close-ups, and it took much of the day, but if we'd had more of the language, or a little bit of flexibility . . . But there's no point in 'what ifs'. Last year we went back to Berlin after Christmas. I related the story to the family and they all wanted to know . . . 'Well? Did you see him again?' I looked him up on Facebook while we were there. It was easy to recognise Uwe from his profile pic. He looked just as I remembered him from 30 years ago. But my reaching out to him produced nothing. Uwe Radtke, thank you for what you showed me. I'm so glad our paths crossed on the hitch-hikers' road and I hope my *Wacaday* humour wasn't misinterpreted in any way.

One of the important parts of these films was that we never did any voice-over back in the edit. All jokes were made on the spot to show that we were laughing with – never at – the people and places.

Because of this, *Wacaday* was able to deal with all sorts of world events. I'm glad we did the fall of the Berlin Wall, Glasnost and apartheid. Ludo the director suggested we describe Glasnost as moving out of the darkness into the light, by stepping from the shadows of a dark alley into a colourful, sunny, lively street. I'm glad I was body painted with the Aborigines for the corroboree; it was great re-enacting the Battle of Rorke's Drift with Zulu warriors, though I still feel a little sheepish at the part of the story where the injured British warrior took up the pickaxe and smashed a way out of the besieged hospital. I don't know what possessed me, when I told the story on camera, to do it for real with the pickaxe that I saw resting against the wall. I bashed a real hole in Rorke's Drift heritage camp to demonstrate. Oops.

The *Wacaday* story that has attracted the most attention is the one we made about apartheid. How do you describe something so alien, so utterly humiliating, so completely wrong? We spent some time thinking about it, then Ludo said, 'Play games with the children we meet.' Good idea. I did; and the simplicity of being able to play and talk to different races illustrated the story and the unfairness of the apartheid system. I'm proud that my work on children's TV touched on real current stories as well as historical and cultural tales. If you ever see any on the internet, tell me if any of these tales still work today.

So much happened because I stood by the side of the road with my thumb in the air.

Today I'm riding my Timmeee E-bike on my Camino.

No regrets.

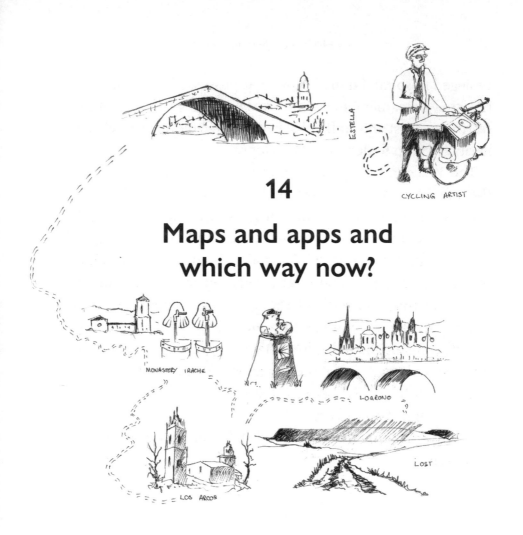

14

Maps and apps and which way now?

Where are we headed? Who knows the way? Ask someone with a map.

Preferably a real map, not just one in their head.

If it's a map in someone's head, you get this: 'Along here till you come to a big building, keep going, then you go along a bit and when you come to the shops you keep going – until – no, wait a minute, there's a bend and it's after the big tree or the traffic lights or the petrol station that's shut now.'

I love maps – especially old maps with relief settings showing hills and valleys. Looking at how we used to be. Finding out when your own home first appeared on a map. It's a family thing. My dad and brother Paul spent ages designing their own country with maps and towns, mountain ranges, deserts and marshland, principal railways, roads and canals. Son Billy loves maps and flags, and games where you fly around the world.

It's funny that when we are lost and need to ask someone the way, getting directions can be an effort. Be prepared for local habits. In Scandinavia I was looking for the art gallery in a well-known artist's town. There were no signs for it at all. I went into a shop.

'Do you know where the tourist information is? I'm looking for the artists' quarter.'

'No, but I have a map . . .'

'Great!'

'But it does not show the tourist information.'

'Oh!'

'But it does show the artists' quarter.'

'Perfect.'

'You can have it if you like!'

The house was spectacular – and shut on Mondays. I had to go back the next day.

In Ireland one green and growing May time we were on a horse-drawn caravan in the Ring of Kerry. Our horse, Georgie, knew two instructions.

'Wee, Georgie!' = Go.

'Woah, Georgie!' = Stop.

It stopped anyway, automatically, outside the pub. Asking directions in County Kerry is a serious business and there's a routine involved . . .

'That's a fine-looking caravan you have there.'

'Yes, we're enjoying it.'

'And a fine-looking horse too.'

'He's called Georgie.'

'The best name for a horse, indeed. Did you try a drop of the black stuff? Oh yes, that's the finest drop in all of Kerry. I've lived here all my life, you know.'

'So you know your way about these parts?'

'Indeed I do. I always take a walk every afternoon.'

'I bet it's lovely. Could you please tell us which way?'

'Ah, you'll be lost, will you?'

'No, it's just that we'd like to know if we go this way or that way to get to –'

'Ah, now then, to be sure to sure . . . If you're heading to Dingle, you say?'

'Yes. Yes?'

A sucking in of the teeth. 'Well, let me see now . . . If you're heading for Dingle now, I wouldn't be starting from here. Good day to you.'

Knowing where you are is reassuring, but not knowing where you are is so liberating.

I'm used to cycling with paper maps, but for this Camino I've got a Wahoo GPS that records my route. I can upload it each day to my social media accounts to show exactly where I've been, where I've stopped, the little detours I've made and where I've painted or had a Martin Mallett moment with his name tags.

Using a route planning app (Komoot) gives me something to aim for. Vaguely following the dotted line isn't a bad idea. You can choose to be solely on the tarmac, solely off road or a mixture of both. Each day I put in a 'hoped for' route that touches on stuff I know I might want to visit and then see how far I get along it. But there is still nothing like asking the local expert. And the local expert is always in the tourist office. I prefer consultation to looking at things online; having that personal interaction; the smiling bit of advice or the kind word of encouragement. And of course you need a person to give you the pilgrim passport stamp.

All travellers on the Way of St James carry their pilgrim passport; to prove they really are pilgrims and to collect stamps along the way. Back in the Middle Ages a passport was proof you'd done the trip. Sometimes, a wealthy landowner would even employ someone to undertake his pilgrimage for him. Come back with the stamped pilgrim passport in order to be paid. I ask everyone to write their name alongside their stamp, then every stop is a person I've met and engaged with. The stamp becomes the record of a meeting.

Straddling the river, the town of Estella captures my attention. The river is in full flood, and the ancient bridge twinned with the famous medieval one in Mostar, Bosnia, is a steep cobbled-stone challenge to cycle over. In one of the town's ancient churches there's an icon in the process of being restored – by someone with a limited palette and no art training. It's a complete disaster and will make the international news in a few days' time. At least they tried – though it would have been better if they hadn't!

Remember the story of Jesus turning water into wine? It was his first miracle, at a wedding reception. There's another miracle along the Way of St James . . .

Just outside Estella is a monastery with a famous winery attached. At the entrance, there are two taps. Take your choice. Water or wine, or both. Next to the taps is a sign: 'You must be 18 years old.' That's right – no miracles until you are old enough!

Which tap would you choose, to fill your water bottle?

Me too. I fill my spare bottle with the red stuff and attach the Mallett name tag to the statue alongside. I can hear him saying, 'Hmmm nice!' Martin always liked the church communion wine.

I am constantly thrilled to see the landscape changing over each hill. How could the world vary so much? As Navarre gives way to Castile, the big ring of mountains surrounds an enormous wine region. Tempranillo becomes Rioja and every field is given over to vineyards. These vineyards, at this time of year, are bare gnarled sticks with tiny green shoots that will race along the wires in a few weeks' time. The snow-capped mountains south of Logroño frame the bare vines, around which wild oilseed rape grows freely and apple blossom lends flakes of white to the vista. It's an artist's paradise – but challenging in these windy, gusty conditions to stop and paint *en plein air*.

Tonight I meet my first cycling pilgrim. Marianna, in her early 60s, is from Holland and like me has pedalled, on her own, from home. Her smiles are warmly encouraging. We will meet several times along the way, and I'm intrigued by her Dutch map and guidebook that give her plenty of opportunities and variations each day. She arrived at the *albergue* before me and bagged a room to herself by paying a little extra. No chance for me, all single options are taken, so I'm in one of those big dorms with 20-odd bunks and it reminds me of dormitories at boarding school. It's not my best sleep. Too many night-time noises, and in the morning everyone wants to be up and out before the sunrise.

I'm going to have breakfast and see the little town.

Under the impressive carved archway of the local church is the burial spot of Cesare Borgia, a sixteenth-century son of a pope. I'm surprised popes had kids, but the moral here is that what is normal today may be quite strange tomorrow. However, a smile, a kind word and a good turn will always be appreciated throughout the ages.

The sun finally comes out at midday and at last, on a quiet lane with the occasional vehicle and plenty of pilgrims for company, I am able to paint again from the back of the bike. My subject is the majestic entrance to the capital of Rioja – Logroño – with snow on the mountains along the horizon and oilseed rape lining the route in front of me in electric yellow. Guess what I'll be drinking tonight! I'm pleased to capture the spires and towers of the city matching the rows of dark cypress trees in the foreground. Pilgrims walking through the yellow fields and white hawthorn blossom. It's the promise of spring in the winter winds. A little van pulls up alongside me. I give the driver a smile and a wave. He winds down the window and berates me in Spanish to get out of the way!

Here's my favourite story along the Way of St James. In Santo Domingo Cathedral is an ornate hen house with two live roosters in it! The background to this story is sex, miracles and incredulity . . . Santo Domingo was a good-deeds monk in the Middle Ages. He built a bridge over the river and a refuge for poor pilgrims. A German family stopped here overnight and the inn-keeper's daughter fancied the hot teenage lad, Hugonell. When he turned her down, she was hopping mad. A woman scorned, type of thing. She hid a silver cup in his bag and reported him. The evidence was compelling and Hugonell didn't stand a chance – he was quickly tried, convicted and hanged. (A bit cut and dried in those days and not much room for an appeal.) When his parents got through the crowds they found their young man hanging there – still alive. 'Santo Domingo saved me,' he gasped. And they hurried to the mayor, who scoffed: 'Your lad is no more alive than my dinner.'

At which point, the roast chickens on his plate promptly jumped up and crowed! Yikes! Good tale. I wonder what happened to the inn-keeper's daughter. Hope she got her just deserts.

Meanwhile birds remain in the cathedral to this day – two roosters in their special hen house. It's a great tale. Forget Saint Domingo. Live roosters in the cathedral are much more exciting. This is exactly the sort of story we would have loved to recreate on *Wacaday*. Retelling famous legends was one of our favourite bits. 'It's a true story, Wideawakers – we made it up ourselves!'

It's important, of course, to give a story a *Wacaday* twist.

Thor the Norse God of Malletting!

King Arthur and Wac-scalibur!

Cape Wac-anaveral – that's one small step for a Mallett!

Timmdiana Jones and the fourth wise man! After the gifts of gold, frankincense and Blaah, the fourth wise man brought a T-shirt and a lollipop.

Someone in the crew would offer up a gag and we'd all start adding to it. Get a few props and run around a wonderful location with the crew joining in to play all the parts!

Things didn't always work out as well as we hoped. We were filming in Thailand and had several guides to help us with locations and permissions. Two of them had the best *Wacaday* names ever – Nit and Warranit. Everything was fine until we came to do the travelogue piece as the King of Siam, 'Yes I am, yes I am'. *The King and I* is glorious regular festive telly with lush costumes and Yul Brynner in the lead role.

So Timmy in a tuk-tuk – the rickshaw has a nice rhyme to it – going around dressed as Yul Brynner, wearing a load of ties. You get the idea. I was in my element. I was wearing the pointy Thai hat thing and being the king of all the ties, and suddenly Nit and Warranit got upset. 'You can't do that; it's disrespectful to the King of Thailand. You wouldn't do that about your own royal family, would you?'

There was a pause, because of course we would do all sorts

of gags about people in authority in Britain. It's an interesting cultural thing. Yet it was our guides who were upset, not the people who joined in my story. We waited until Nit and Warranit had left, and quietly finished it off without them, but with the locals who loved the sight of a funny Englishman in costume joining in the national dance.

All of life is a Camino, a journey in search of something. Hopefully to reach our potential. On the Camino de Santiago you follow the official (and homemade) yellow arrows to the destination of Santiago de Compostela. My career has been a Camino – it's just that I'm putting up the signposts as I go, instead of following them.

'After considering your performance in the first-year examinations, the board of examiners has resolved that you are required to withdraw from your course of study.'

Crikey, I can remember the exact words when I opened the letter from Warwick University that September morning. I apologised to my dad for letting him down. 'You didn't let me down. You let yourself down, son.' Ouch. What happened there, then? I hadn't done the work. Didn't revise properly, didn't take the exams seriously enough and believed other students who said, 'They won't chuck you out. They never do.'

On the first day back (hopefully) for my second year, other students were arriving and unpacking, happy and excited. I was in a suit and tie, preparing an apologetic appeal. I didn't have much of a leg to stand on, but I wanted to continue my course. It was a long wait for the appeal board's decision. One tutor argued strongly to make an example of me and get me out. Others saw something in my enthusiasm and determination. Eventually, I was allowed back in on a pass degree.

'What's that?'

'No honours degree for you, Mallett. But do the work that's required, hand in your assignments, attend the lectures, and we'll let you stay on. It's clear to all of us that you are going to go into broadcasting after here.'

How did they know? How did I not see the path that others could clearly spot? Thanks to the understanding of my university tutors (and doing the work required) I got my pass degree in History and History of Art and I did go into an entertaining and media career. But do the homework, follow the mapped-out route, and don't let yourself down.

Where's my map going to lead me now?

Fear. I wasn't expecting to be frightened. I knew I'd be vulnerable. Indeed, every day I'm knowingly vulnerable. Where will I stay? What will I eat? Which way will I go? By accepting vulnerability as part of the pilgrim's package you leave yourself open to potential. Potential meetings, potential acts of random kindness. We don't naturally feel very comfortable with this idea. We like to have things planned. Indeed, planning and prepping is an essential ingredient for a successful, rewarding adventure. Can you plan and prepare for vulnerability? It doesn't sound right, does it? Especially if vulnerability leads to fear.

The N120 road runs right across northern Spain, and the Camino comes into contact with it again and again over many days and weeks. There are speeding lorries and heavy traffic. I'm not going to risk those. I don't want to be knocked off my bike and killed by some impatient driver. The pilgrim's way, which runs vaguely parallel a kilometre or two away, is a sea of mud and I can't face it. My GPS is suggesting a route over a wide-open empty landscape with a single rocky track. There is no signpost. I instantly regret not having a paper map of the area. I check my phone. No signal. I'm relying on the GPS on the bike. I check the tyres, my water bottle and look around for an alternative route.

Nothing.

No sign of housing, no farm, no way of knowing how well used the track is. I set off with an ominous feeling and soon find I am talking to myself and the bike.

For some reason I've taken to referring to the bike as 'Martin'. I feel a bit daft talking to the bike, but it suddenly becomes reassuring. 'Well, Martin, let's go carefully. I don't want a puncture out here. I don't want to fall off and injure myself.' I am alone and the further up the hill I go, the worse my state of mind becomes. It is no better as I round the summit and see the track disappear into a ditch. This is hopeless. I don't want to have to go back and take the main road, as that could be dangerous. There has to be a village or something eventually. The only thing to do is to keep on going.

And going.

I come around a contour and see the big black storm cloud above the sharp escarpment on the other side of a wide valley. *I'm in for it now,* I think, and then suddenly a sunbeam lights up a distant field of yellow oilseed and beyond that is a tiny glinting church spire. I've never felt such relief. Immediately, I get out the acrylics and paint the view. Not content with that, I do a loose watercolour sketch too and wait for the storm to hit. Those two pieces of artwork represent me giving thanks for the appearance of safety. I laugh with relief as my wheels squelch through the muddy farmyard on to the country road. We are not used to emptiness. We always expect civilisation to be just a stone's throw away.

It isn't always nearby.

This was not the first time I'd been scared. Our honeymoon was terrifying. Not the being married bit; but having a machete waved threateningly in our faces. Mrs Mallett and I were on safari in Kenya in search of wild animals behaving naturally in the wild. There were perfect scenes for me to sketch, and others in our minibus party wanted to frame long, lingering close-up photos. Not our driver. He wanted to show us every wild animal and every local village in Kenya. 'Come on, we go now!' So we had a discussion between ourselves and decided that less is more. We wanted to spend longer in each spot and if that meant missing another watering hole, well so be it.

I'm not sure how it came out when we put it to him, but the next minute our driver reached under his seat and drew out an enormous machete and started shouting and waving it in our faces. Woo! We backed away from the massive blade, terrified, and another driver ran over to disarm him. Now there was a stand-off. We asked head office for another driver. 'You are 200 miles from Nairobi; we cannot get another driver to you.' We asked if we could swap drivers with another party. Naturally no other tourists wanted our knife-wielding chap. In the end there was an unhappy, awkward peace treaty brokered by other locals, and after the machete was safely removed from him and our minibus, we reluctantly got back on board. It was not a great success, that safari. It's much easier to see animals in the zoo.

15

The rain in Spain falls mainly on . . .

We always remember the place where someone did us a good turn, the place where we didn't connect and the place where something unexpected happened.

I cycle into the Castilian capital, Burgos, after a long, tiring day. I've enjoyed some afternoon sunshine along a muddy wooded track. Camino waymarkers have been popping up regularly, scallop shells and yellow arrows. The yellow arrows are almost all homemade. Legend has it that the original arrows came about because someone had a job lot of yellow paint left over from something else. He used it to put arrows on to trees, walls, sides of buildings and the occasional signpost. The homemade quality of the arrows is quite appealing and I chuckle at messages like 'free hugs' or a single boot atop a marker.

Burgos is one of the jewels of northern Spain, its cathedral choir stalls the perfect place for a Martin Mallett name tag. My brother Martin loved singing. He'd carefully look up the hymn number. This wasn't easy, as he didn't see numbers in sequence or as having any physical value. He just liked the shape of them and the fact that they meant something, even if it wasn't clear to him what that meaning was. Take hymn number 483. Martin would read the number on the hymn board and know to look for a four.

While the introduction is being played and the first verse begins, I stand next to him, watching him carefully turn the pages in case he's missed something. First, he needs to get the book the right way up, and he's left-handed so it is easier to start at the back and flick forwards . . . Once a four is found he glances at me hopefully, pointing at the page. 'Four!'

'That's good, Martin. OK, now you need an eight and a three . . .'

Mistake. Martin heard 'three', so now he's looking for any three. We are into the chorus and Martin is singing loudly and happily while still looking for the numbers. How much patience have I got? Without taking the book from him, I flick through to the pages beginning in the 480s and point at the page with 483 on – not the hymn number, just the page. 'OK, Martin, we want four eight three . . .'

Verse two is underway and Martin looks hopefully at the page. 'There!' he says confidently, pointing at 482. 'Four eight two.'

'Next one, Martin. We're on four eight three . . .' Second chorus of the three-verse hymn is under way. 'Ah, here it is . . .' as I discreetly point in the direction of 483.

Martin is delighted. He's found the right page, and he's holding the hymn book like everyone else and singing away. He can't read the words, but he wants them pointed out and likes a finger running along the lines. Then he gets to the chorus and he knows the tune. At the top of his voice he sings away. Doesn't matter what the words are; he's giving it volume and is happily part of the action.

Yes, Martin and singing are one and the same . . . Favourite Martin songs – from *The Sound of Music*: 'Edelweiss' and 'Do-Re-Mi'; from other film favourites: 'Chitty Chitty Bang Bang', 'Any Dream Will Do' and 'Yellow Submarine'. Martin loved music. He has to have a name tag in the Burgos Cathedral choir stalls and join in loud and proud, especially at Christmas when it's 'O Come, All Ye Faithful' and 'Hark! The Herald Angels Sing'.

Once I've found the spot to paint the view of Burgos, across the river, and done a couple of sketches, a weird sensation overtakes me. Apparently, it's quite common for many people on this pilgrimage. The urge to keep going, to be on the way. I didn't feel this in Pamplona or Bordeaux. But now, early afternoon, there's a sense that the wheels need to keep turning. Stopping for long seems to dissipate the momentum. Maybe it's a hunger to see more, to explore and to experience the business of journeying. By mid-afternoon I've left the city and headed out to the great plains of northern Spain – the Meseta.

Immediately, I'm more relaxed. I'm on the saddle. I feel different being a tourist on foot. Everything improves as soon as I'm on the bike. I'm moving, I'm observing. I'm looking at potential images to paint or draw. Funny how my spirits rise as I pedal.

You think the big city is the gem to aim for, but in fact it's the smaller villages that offer you the most.

There are some delightful climbs and big descents. I meet some South American mountain bikers on the way. Weeks later I'll see them again: 'Hello Peru!' 'Hello England!'

Two women are walking ahead of me. '*Buen Camino!*' I call out and ring my bell. An American accent jumps with a start.

'Whoops! Sorry, didn't mean to startle you. Are you OK?' I stop to check. One of them complains of aching feet and asks if I have any water. Of course I do and offer them my spare water bottle and a bar of chocolate. 'Oh my God, you're an angel!' I'm used to being called lots of things, but this is a surprise.

A few kilometres later, I stop at a village with the best *albergue* on the Camino. There's an après-ski-type beer bar to welcome me, there's a secure place to lock up the bike, heated floors, small dorms, clean bathrooms, good showers, individual power points by every bed, reliable Wifi, great restaurant and a good self-service kitchen.

I need somewhere to celebrate victory for both my football teams today, and this is the perfect place! Beer in hand, I take stock of where I'm staying. *Albergues* are springing up all along the route. Providing pilgrim accommodation is a fabulous business and gives a great return night after night during an ever-lengthening season. As one cynic pointed out, it's a cash-based operation, utterly dependable, you'll always have customers, and pilgrims don't vote. This particular *albergue* is in a medieval street and is proof the Camino has revitalised the village of Hontanas. Every family in the two or three streets has someone working in the Camino industry: housekeeping, supplies, taxi service, hospitality. The hours of work have changed too; there are customers all day long. Pilgrims are generally up and off first thing, so the place is cleaned and made ready by 10 a.m. The next customers arrive for refreshments by 11 and the rooms begin to fill by lunchtime. Evening meal is at 7; lights out by 10. More and more places offer smaller dorms or private facilities and most imperative of all is Wifi and connectivity.

This evening we are serenaded by the American women on guitar. I was puzzled by the guitar because they weren't carrying it earlier when I met them. Of course, it goes ahead in a taxi, along with their suitcases and laptops.

Next morning, a Martin Mallett name tag is placed across the street in the stone wall. I leave a Timmy gift with the manager's mother busy in the *albergue* kitchen: a little watercolour-painted postcard of their delightful place. Happy days and good luck with the business!

After yesterday's sunshine, it's cold and wet again, of course. (I can count the number of non-rainy days so far on one hand.) I'm on a track leading up a muddy, rough, 12 per cent hill with a terrifying 18 per cent concrete-path descent the other side. I check the disc brakes. What would you do here in the rain and wind? Would you cycle or walk down the hill? I agree. Thank heavens for the brilliant Timmeee E-bike. Such climbs are not an issue. At the bottom I meet another cycling pilgrim, a Hungarian lady on a fold-up city bike. She has walked it down.

Sometimes rough and muddy, sometimes smooth and wide, the Camino is constantly challenging, especially when I want to paint it.

Art has always been in the Mallett family. My dad was a painter all his life, and his gentle enthusiasm got us interested in galleries. Great Aunt Mabel Gear was a famous pet portrait painter and my big brother Paul paints lovely landscapes around where he lives in the West Country. Mum's comments could always be counted on to encourage us. 'Nice painting, dear – I love the frame!'

When my Mrs Mallett was expecting our son Billy we were in America and I was painting pictures of the Florida Keys. I've always attempted to document our travels in a sketchbook and paintings, such as along Australia's great East Coast Highway alongside the Great Barrier Reef; and the summer excursion across the Rocky Mountains and the western provinces of Canada. Our trip through the Red Centre of Australia traced the tragic trail of Burke and Wills. All of these I covered in watercolours and acrylics. Our house has some of these paintings on the walls, lots in sketchbooks and I'm lucky to be in galleries across the country. Every *Wacaday* filming trip would have a painting or two to feature in the stories on air. I realise I've been telling my stories in film and paintings ever since I can remember. This is just a continuation of that process.

At the ancient ruined monastery of St Anton, I'm determined to stop and paint. On fine days, there's an enterprising bar by the road and Gary sang its praises to me. On cold rainy days, like today, there are bedraggled pilgrims heading for the nearest café to get dry and thaw out. The ruin is monumental and has a road running right through the middle of it like a road through history, a passage through time. There are huge archways over the track, and the soaring walls of the ruins tower above my head. Throughout the centuries this has been an important place on the Way of St James and it'll be here long after I cease to be a memory.

Across the Meseta, the plains of Burgos, I'm in a wild, windy landscape with a thin line of muddy track to follow.

Featureless

Relentless

Stunningly lonely.

The figures in their ponchos trudging with heads bowed are

starting to resemble characters in a fifteenth-century painting by Breughel. I'm travelling through villages where storks make their untidy nests on top of each church tower. These streets might be pretty on a summer's day, but today they look grey, grim and in need of cheering up. It's people who make the villages dynamic. Pilgrims give them their energy and keep them alive. That's a strange thought. It's not the residents, but the curious passing visitors who vitalise these places.

I'm cycling along the Castile Canal and I'm reminded how much I like waterways. They follow the contours of the land and bring me into contact with unexpected scenes.

On one of the overnight bike rides a while back, coming merrily out of the pub very late, we came across fishermen in pyjamas pulling 'Quasimodo', the giant perch, out of the Grand Union Canal.

'Why do you call him Quasimodo?'

'Cos he's got a lump on his back.' Sure enough this enormous fish had a hunchback and was clearly used to being caught. But by men in pyjamas? That was a bit odd. We put it down to the weirdness of the overnight bike ride.

As a teenager, bikes were naturally our mode of transport. One evening, my school friends Steve and Jack called on me to bike down and join them on the Peak Forest Canal. I agreed, but not before I finished some school assignment (what a diligent pupil I was).

I found them by the canal bridge having an altercation with some other kids in a canoe. 'We're going to tell our dad on you!' the kids cried as we rode off to the dirt track to play.

Sometime later Steve looked up. 'Quick! That's their dad. Leg it!' he cried and the three of us cycled off as fast as possible. Except Jack's chain fell off. Not once, but twice. And the bloke caught up with him.

'You know what this is for!' he shouted as he threw Jack and his bike into the canal. When the bloke had gone past my hiding place, chasing after the fleeing Steve, I shakenly went to help Jack out and retrieve his soggy bike. We made a sorry pair heading back to my house, where my mum greeted us in surprise.

'What happened?'

Pause. We glanced at each other. 'Jack's – er – been in the canal,' I offered.

After a bath and changing into my clothes – 'I'm not wearing your undies,' scoffed Jack – we were cheering up. Then there was a knock at the door. The angry man was standing there with his two kids, having a go at my mum about us chucking stones at them.

Jack, now dry, defended himself. 'Did they tell you they were swearing at us? We told them off and as they got out, we splashed them. What you did to me is assault.' Jack always knew the right thing to say. The bloke backtracked and hurried away. He'd also seen my dad's large crucifix on the study wall and was possibly feeling embarrassed about his language. My mum and Jack's mum had a discussion, and the upshot was: leave it alone, lessons learned.

Years later Steve and I came back and marked the spot with a plaque on a tree: 'At this point in summer 1971, Jack was thrown in the canal!' I bet his bike still squeaks with rust.

I think of how far Martin, the bike and I have come from home and in the nearby town of Frómista there's a lovely brotherly moment in the church of St Martin. Carvings on the pillars of Adam and Eve in the garden of Eden having a frisky time. 'Rude,' Martin would say with a grin . . . I pop his name tag under the statue of St James by the altar. I'm tempted to stay in the town for the night, but the light is good, and as the afternoon warmth gives way to the early evening chill, I cycle into a small town with a long name of Carrión de los Condes. Here Freddie the American is single-handedly renovating an eleventh-century chapel. People have the strangest hobbies. Freddie is determined to make this derelict chapel a place for music and art, and he is organising activities to raise the occasional euro. Impressive. We arrange to have dinner together.

Before the meal, I pop into the church and in time for the speedy Catholic mass. No dessert, just the main course wafer. Hey, where's the wine? Why is the priest the only one to get that? Well, there's plenty of wine with the three-course pilgrim menu. The pilgrim meal is always the same. A salad to start, a piece of hake on the bone, with chips, for main course, and for dessert there's flan (crème brûlée), ice cream or a piece of fruit. And often a bottle of wine. More than a couple of glasses and I'll fall over.

What is the thing that connects us to a place? Shopping, a conversation, a meal, a painting? Today I need to smarten myself up. My ride doesn't begin this morning until I've had a haircut from a barber who won 50,000 euros on the lottery and kept on cutting. A winning haircut. What a treat. There's a lot of pleasure (and sometimes a risk) in having your hair cut somewhere new. How about a different country, where you don't speak the same language? This barber shop is next to my accommodation. I go in and watch as he takes great pride with his work. Then it's my turn. 'Hola! Haircut please.'

He begins with a tape around my shirt to stop the bits going down my neck. Clippers, followed by cut-throat razor. Keenly sharp and tidy. Scalp massage, scissors, combing, brushing, trimming, checking, grooming, tidying. Twenty minutes later and I'm feeling a smart man about the bike again, with a crisp haircut, great shave, smelling sweetly of moisturiser and hair cream. I'm the best-looking cyclist on the road today! It's a bargain at less than a tenner. I'll be coming back to this barber again!

What would my mum say? It's one of those 'rites of passage' things.

'You know the way to the barber's, dear. Here's one shilling and sixpence. Please bring back the change safely, because we need it.' I was just old enough to go on my own, crossing the road, down the ginnel, over the zebra crossing, to the shop with the red and white pole twirling around outside. There were two barbers in white coats, both busy snipping, and a long red leather bench to sit on while I waited with comics to read. I had *The Topper* each week at home, so I read *The Beano*. 'Everyone we know loves *The Beano*.' Strange to think that years later I would voice the adverts for *The Beano*, and during *Wacaday* I would have my own Timmy Mallett comic in the shops.

'Right you are then, sonny,' said the short, fat, bald barber, indicating the chair.

'I'll wait, thank you,' I said. I didn't like being called sonny.

When the boss was ready, he asked, 'Would you like me to cut your hair, young man?'

'Yes please. Short back and sides.' I much preferred being called young man.

It's strange how the barber appeared to practise every time he went snip snip snip, and the buzz of the shears was loud in my ears. Hair went up my nose. I tried blowing it away and wanted to brush the hair from my face, but wasn't sure whether I was allowed. At the end the boss rubbed Brylcreem on to my scalp and gave me a nice quiff like a pop star. 'That'll be one and thruppence, please.' Ting-a-ling went the doorbell as I left clutching my threepenny-bit change.

I felt fabulous and my neck itched only a bit. I looked at my reflection in all the shop windows as I headed home. On the corner was my favourite shop, with sweet jars in the window. The sweet jars looked even better than my reflection. I could get sweets to share with Paul and Martin, and it would be all right. But I wasn't very sure whether it would be. I clutched the paper bag of stripey sweets – three for a penny, three each.

Mum was delighted with the haircut. 'You look very smart. Well done. Have you got the change, dear?'

I didn't know what to say. I held up the bag of sweets and blushed.

'We needed that money, and I asked you to bring the change home.'

'I'll take them back,' I snivelled.

'No, they won't take them back. You had better eat those sweets and remember, if we haven't anything to eat later.'

Through my tears, I ate them. They didn't taste nearly as nice as they had looked because I didn't deserve them; the family would starve and it was my fault. And to this day, I always think twice before I buy a treat after getting my hair cut . . .

But today there's a different kind of treat after the barber. I've gone about 500 metres when there is a painting opportunity by the bridge. A row of stunning pink cherry blossom at its peak for the morning. I'm used to always stopping when I see the cherry in bloom and my mobile rings and DJ Tony Prince wants to chat on air about how the pilgrimage is going. He's fascinated by the journey and the daily paintings. There's a difference in the air today. It becomes more noticeable as the day progresses. I think I almost dare to believe that spring may finally be on the way . . .

My route follows an extraordinarily long straight Roman road that is always full of pilgrims. Row upon row of walkers disappearing into infinity. On the brow of a hill I turn around and look back 12 straight kilometres and ahead another 12 more. That dead straight line is so ancient and so unusual. All our roads of the last 2,000 years have had bends and kinks and detours. We aren't used to the direct route any more, especially when it's flat and seemingly featureless. Not entirely featureless, however.

On the outskirts of a town called Ledigos I come across a row of trees marked by pilgrims. I love trees. In our garden I've sculpted the oak tree into a bird's nest of branches through twisting and tying the new growth each season. Among the branches are the Snoopy telephone from the TV set, ancient keyboards and shoes through which the branches grow. Shoes in a tree look as hilarious as they sound. The branches have grown into and around each other like the famous 2008 Olympic Stadium in Beijing.

Then there's the tennis-ball tree. An apple one with clumps of old tennis balls attached together with cable ties, growing moss and algae in the boughs. Next to that is the frying-pan tree. Doesn't everyone have a frying-pan tree? Every time Mrs Mallett chucks out an old frying pan, it gets painted and hung from the branches of the beech tree. The eucalyptus I planted a generation ago is tied into and around itself every summer to create shade, with one huge branch to hang the hammock on. The yew shrub is cut into the shape of Bart Simpson with wild haircut, the box hedge is shaped into a castle. It wasn't meant to be a castle; it just became one as I cut and trimmed while listening to the football. 'Oooh! A save. Wow! What a goal!'

All of these trees are inspired by those we had at boarding school. The best summer games were building dens in the plantation – the planny. The dens got more and more elaborate, and up on the hill called the Knott, in Arnside, are the two ancient stumps from which the hill got its name. My mum would spend every walk tying little saplings together to make another pair of knotted trees.

We seem to be keen on art – and are taking and making it the art of the woodland. The fact that trees can become part of our art and creativity appeals to me and I like the way pilgrims leave their mark along their Camino.

16

Who let the dogs out?

Animals appear often in our conversation – nice weather for ducks; it's raining cats and dogs; mad dogs and Englishmen – and animals are all along the Camino.

Officially the halfway point of the Camino Francés is the ancient Roman city of Sahagún, with an age-old Roman gateway and a cat lying across the road sunbathing. But it's only half way if you start at St Jean at the foot of the Pyrenees. I'm well past that; I've already cycled 2,000 kilometres from home. The gateway has been here for a couple of millennia, and I'm quite confident a Martin Mallett name tag will last for some time. Let's see. I slide it into a gap between the ancient stones.

Late afternoon sunshine takes me to a little town with the Spaghetti Western sounding name of El Burgo Ranero, where I'm meeting little Angus the border terrier and my pal Stevie. It's my third country and his third visit with me. Stevie is driving home again – with Angus for company – from southern Spain, and he generously makes a detour of several hundred kilometres to come and find me in a little country hostel some way from the motorway. The evening is pleasantly warm and a donkey watches us while we eat, and we discuss my choice of Caminos to Santiago and my possible return route via Santander and the Bay of Biscay. I'm grateful for Stevie's company and toast him with the hip flask he gave me for the journey. His encouraging parting gifts include some more boards to paint on, the kind offer to take home around 25 completed canvases – 'You've been busy!' – and a lick from Angus the dog.

Hey, it hasn't rained today! This is so utterly unusual, it's worth celebrating.

I'm woken up by the tuneful braying of the donkey. Insistent and demanding and somehow very Spanish. Back in the 1980s there was a donkey called Blackie that was rescued in Spain by an English newspaper campaign. The name became a byword for anything Spanish. In fact, we honoured the story by inventing a game on *Wacaday*. Contestants on the phone had a Blackie the donkey creature that moved along the track when they got the question right . . .

First question: 'What name would you like for your Blackie the donkey?' And he would be named after a teacher or friend. 'Eeyore, Eeyore, ee always calls me that!' Occasionally Blackie the donkey would have a different coloured saddle. 'What colour would you like your Blackie the donkey to be?' And the green, red or blue Blackie the donkey would be moved along, trying not to end up in the gunge.

Cute.

This donkey has gone before I have time to go and pat him.

Blackie wasn't our only great animal star on *Wacaday*. The biggest star on the show was Magic the cockatiel, my pet bird. I got him from a magician, hence the name Magic. It was either that or Howard, cos he had a tuft of feathers that made him look like the pop star Howard Jones. Magic was a beautiful bird and very friendly and chirpy. He lived in the kitchen above the pinball machine, and whenever I opened his cage door he came out to fly around and chew the wallpaper. I'd coax him back to his cage with a piece of ribbon. That ribbon was very important to Magic. Sometimes he would get a little frisky on top of the cage and rub himself vigorously on the ribbon. The head would go down, and his tail would go up and there would be a ruffle of feathers that seemed to say, 'How was it for you?'

Magic was a natural TV star. The little crowd of loyal fans at the door to the studio would ooh and ah excitedly at him, and Magic would go into TV-am and wait for the show to begin. Now, amazing as it sounds, *Wacaday* never had its own studio; we shared the space with *Good Morning Britain*. In the three-minute ad break between the shows, the cameras would swing around to our little area and the lights would go up. Magic would squawk excitedly and then we'd begin. There was no studio audience, either. All the audience sounds came from the crew. They just responded naturally to my instructions to look at each other and go Blaah!

When I opened Magic's cage door on air, out would come the little star and he'd climb on top of his cage, where I'd leave his ribbon. It was his comfort blanket and it wasn't uncommon for him to start his little 'exercises' during the show. If he wasn't getting enough attention Magic would fly off to whichever camera had the red light on and sit on top of the lens. Sometimes you'd see a blur, his grey tail, hanging down in shot. A highlight for the participants was to have Magic land on their head or, better still, land on me and leave a little present. The unpredictability of a little bird flying around a TV studio was obvious. It was quite common to find Magic flying up into the lighting rig, where he could stay for ages after the show. There was the lighting team with their lighting rods, gently trying to encourage the feathered star to come back down to the ribbon on his cage.

He always let me know how he felt with a firm nip of the beak. When mini-cams came into the budget we called ours a 'Magi-cam' and installed one in Magic's cage. He had more presents and pieces of post than anyone else at TV-am. Unlike some TV stars, the one thing he hated was a mirror. That reflection of a competitor would send him into a pecking frenzy.

Magic's little cartoon strip was drawn by a friend of mine from Stockport, Ash Haynes. Ash only had a black and white TV – honestly! Colour took a while to make it to his house. So he didn't know about Magic's bright orange cheeks. All the drawings showed him grey; but the characteristic Ash got spot on was Magic's appetite for things you wouldn't expect a little bird to eat: anything and everything that he could get his beak into. As well as the wallpaper at home, he chewed the *Wacaday* set, and any stray fingers that wanted to stroke him. Magic was a one-person bird and I was the only one allowed to scratch his head and tickle his chin. I'm proud to have shared the stage with such a favourite for so many fans. Animals of any kind have a great resonance for most of us. We're lucky that they offer companionship and affection, and it's a delight to reciprocate.

Today is the proper start of warm spring weather – sunshine, sunglasses, shorts sort of weather. I go about 300 metres and come across the perfect spot to paint early morning reflections on the lake.

I love the very start of every day. Check the bike is in order. Tyres OK? Any squeaks? Bit of oil needed? How about cleaning away any muck and dust? Attach the panniers to the bike rack. Secure the art bag and GPS, put on helmet, cycle gloves, and wheel the bike to the kerb. Have a look around. Have I seen what I need to see in this town? To be more precise, have I seen what I need to see in this street? Often, there's something I failed to spot yesterday, or something that deserves a second look. It doesn't matter what the weather's like. I know I'm unlikely to ever come this way again, and it would be a shame to have missed something, wouldn't it?

Today I do what I always do: sniff the air, feel the temperature, notice my surroundings. The resting dog lying by the kerb panting slightly, the man sweeping the step, two ladies talking at the same time, shutters being raised, a car pulling out from the parking space. I glance behind and set off slowly. Always slowly. There's something delicious about the first few pedal turns. I'm listening to see if there's anything amiss – any rubbing? Does everything sound and feel OK? But I'm already ahead of myself. Just sitting on the saddle and turning the pedals gives me a thrill. I've got a grin on my face and the Bluebells hit 'Young at Heart' in my head. I'm out here, on my big adventure, only myself and my bike to rely on. 'Are we ready, Martin? You me, ma bubba.'

Already at the slowest speed I can go, I'm travelling too fast! The road is delightful. I pass the man with a wheelbarrow full of manure. *'Buen Camino!'* I call out and he waves his head, cos his hands are full. The road is almost empty of cars for 25 kilometres and the poplar trees give a lovely sense of scale. Purple lavender and heathers in abundance by the roadside. 'Buen Camino!' I call to the pilgrims I pass. Lots of them. Mostly walking singly, they raise their hands in greetings. The smiles are reciprocated. This is a personal adventure for all of us and, for some reason, you receive more when you're on your own.

There is a market in the first town, offering lots of opportunity to observe people and sketch. Old boys chatting while their wives buy essentials. I need a cuppa and a piece of tortilla. Standing at the bar are a group of friends putting the world to rights. People-watching while I refresh is one of life's great pleasures for me. What are they talking about? Football? Things they should be doing? The way they are standing tells me these are old friends at peace with one another and the day. There's a dog lying by an old man's foot, waiting to be petted. Get the sketchbook out, Mallett.

Bar Elvis is proud of its hand-painted signs: 'We spak Englis' and 'No pain, No glory'. Sitting outside are two Frenchmen, Anton and François, who are walking to Santiago, and with them is the donkey. We strike up a conversation.

The donkey's name is Salome and it's such a treat to meet a pilgrim on four hooves. Salome has an odour. The smell of a beast of burden. Head down, one leg resting, waiting while the men sip their drinks. I rub Salome's head and scratch the ears, which are dusty. There are two large canvas bags on either side of the donkey.

'What happens when you get to Santiago?'

'We go home . . .'

'What happens to Salome when you get to Santiago?'

Pause . . . They look at each other and smile.

'Sausages!'

I laugh and hope it's a joke.

I've been to the city of León before. I came with Gary five years ago, and enjoyed it as a starting point on what turned out to be a recce Camino. Then we stayed at a monastery around the corner from the world-class stained glass in the cathedral and we came across a Slovenian pilgrim, complete with medieval cloak, walking alone to Santiago and back to Slovenia. Now I'm pedalling my own journey from my home. Like most cities in Spain, León shuts from one till four, so I want to keep going, and follow alongside the N120 for the rest of the afternoon. I can't escape the traffic. There's a perfectly good motorway nearby, but the lorries won't use it as they don't like paying the tolls.

By my reckoning, I'll be in Santiago sometime next week, when I want to see the archbishop. I've written to him. Had no reply. I've got nothing planned and I've been on my bike for the last six weeks. I am just another pilgrim, and there's no reason for him to give me even five minutes. But let's not worry about what may or may not happen. Stick with this afternoon. It's a nice day, enjoy it.

Into the pretty village of Hospital de Órbigo, with storks on the roofs and the longest bridge on the Camino. A great monument deserves a great story and this one involves a knight in armour, a fair damsel and a scrap for love. Back in the day, some brave knight smitten with love for the girl of his dreams said he'd protect her virtue by challenging everyone who wanted to cross the bridge. Hundreds of challenges and fights later he's still standing! Every year they re-enact the story. I think this bridge deserves a modern-day guardian. Brother Martin and I used to play 'Knights and Warriors' and I have a recent photo of him running me through with an invisible sword. Time for a Martin Mallett moment . . . His name tag is now between the stones on the parapet of the bridge.

This is the town where I get a treat to eat – trout is on my pilgrim menu, which makes a nice change. When growing up, fish was a Friday thing. On Sunday we'd have a roast, and for the following days variations of the leftovers. Mum would mince things up and make a meatloaf. Dad was never very keen on meat and we would tease him about it. 'I don't like the texture of it,' he'd say. It was after my visit to the local library one day that I began noticing what I eat. In the entrance was an exhibition of black and white photos on breeding animals for slaughter and it didn't look very nice. I decided to give up meat for a week. The most amazing thing happened. I started tasting vegetables. Like many people, I was a little careless about feeding myself. I'd cook a meal and really enjoy the chop or whatever the protein was. Then I'd have a go at the potatoes and if I was still interested I might eat some of the vegetables. The day I gave up meat for a week, I started thinking, 'Wow, how enjoyable were those greens! How tasty that corn! How interesting cauliflower cheese is!' I still eat seafood, which didn't feature in the exhibition. I'm working on the assumption they still have a fighting chance of getting away. I suppose I'm a vegetarian/pescatarian for variety.

I wake up with a dodgy tummy. Ah! Spanish belly. Serves me right. I enjoyed too much of that red wine last night with my menu *peregrino*.

I am at an artist *albergue*, which is really nice and reflective, with paintings on every wall space. As usual, I begin the day slowly, letting the walkers hurry off at the crack of dawn. I'm going to paint from yesterday's images. I work up the 'blokes at the bar' and the cherry-blossom cityscape at the entrance to León. I'm also working on a painting of Salome the donkey. I want to place a beast and a pilgrim walking through that unkempt Spanish landscape. I'm thinking of Don Quixote and call my painting 'Donkey Hote'. The owners of the *albergue* are interested and do their own internet search on me. When they want a selfie by the sign, for their social media page, I'm happy to oblige.

Photos and autographs are what I do. It comes with the job of being well known. After every show, each personal appearance and panto performance, I make myself available to do a meet and greet, have a photo, sign an autograph. Autographs are still sometimes collected, but far more common is the request for a selfie. It's a bit like stamp collecting. Something to put on your social media – proof that you've been there, met that person. But you won't be able to find a selfie from 15 or 20 years ago unless you have a hard copy. Ah! The days of winding the film on, taking a picture of the dog to finish it off, and waiting for the prints to come back from the developers. Photos were valuable then. Especially the one of the dog. I'm used to people greeting me as if we know each other.

'Don't tell me! I know you.'

'OK then . . .'

'Oh, go on. Tell me.'

'But you said "Don't tell me"!'

'Didn't you used to be Timmy Mallett?'

'Yes, and I still am. That's my name!'

Sometimes it's TFM: 'Oh my God, it's Timmy F . . . ing Mallett!'

'Nice to meet you too.'

Yet even people who weren't born when Mallett's Mallet was on every morning seem to have an idea of who Timmy Mallett is. That bloke with the Mallet, the glasses, the bright clothes. Youngsters who weren't born during *Wacaday* see me come on stage and understand colour, comedy and chaos. Most days, I'm asked, 'Have you still got your Mallet?' Not on the Camino

I haven't, but you can still easily buy Pinky Punky online. It's a pleasure to bring a smile to people's faces. Aren't I lucky?

Throughout the noughties I took Mallett's Mallet and 'Itsy Bitsy' to student nights across Britain and I headed out of a Sheffield hotel late one night at the same time as someone was arriving. That 'Oi, Mallett!' was too loud to ignore. 'Behave,' I said and turned to face David Walliams, still on a high from his on-stage *Little Britain* performance, apologising. He was delightfully star struck and we arranged to meet again over breakfast before he went off for three hours' swimming – training for his marathon River Thames swimathon. Reaching his potential.

Arriving for breakfast in a Liverpool hotel, Hollywood actor Eddie Redmayne greeted me.

'Hello, Timmy. Last time I saw you I was on Singing in the Shower on the *Wide Awake Club*. I lost.'

At dinner in Bristol one time, Queen's Brian May stopped by our table. As he left, Mrs Mallett remarked, 'He was nice – whoever he was – but he needs a good haircut.'

I can make mistakes too. I was enjoying the piano music at a club with the keyboard player from Ian Dury's Blockheads. He and I were singing along together when I noticed a young woman wanting to join in. Except I didn't notice properly and was embarrassed when Chris Evans pointed out I'd blanked Kate Moss.

It's a slow ride in the sunshine around lots of pilgrims on the track. A school party is walking 20 kilometres to Astorga – a nice school trip! This is part of the route I've travelled before and some things are recognisable, others aren't. I remember the statues. Scarecrows dressed in pilgrim-discarded clothes – jackets, scarves and boots (it's always an odd shoe) that make them look quite overdressed. The road is suddenly a dual carriageway-sized track that's been graded and flattened and widened, and had drainage channels dug either side. Its red sandstone contrasts with the grey-green of the olive trees. I come around a corner to see a great spot to paint these against the ochre-coloured hills sweeping up to the snow-covered mountain range of León. The warm spring sunshine dries the acrylic paint quickly and I work fast to get the snaking road in with the detail of the lines of people and the Iberian blue sky. Some pilgrims stop to look and comment. Others hurry on.

I'm not sure what the rush is, because up ahead a herd of several hundred sheep blocks my way. A proper sheep-style traffic jam. The shepherd and his dogs are trying to herd them along the roadway, but they are all over the scrubland either side too. At one point, I'm surrounded by these dusty bleating sheep, and that transports me back to the golden age of woollen garments, when the best wool in the world came from England. The fleeces of East Anglia paid for the grand cathedrals and huge ornate churches that were far bigger than the villages ever warranted. Astorga boasts one of the finest cathedrals along the route.

Presumably paid for by the fleeces of Castile?

I'm aware of how the sheep always follow a leader. Are these never-ending lines of pilgrims doing the same, I wonder – following the backpack up ahead, occasionally falling alongside into conversation, then drifting apart again as everyone goes at their own pace?

Suddenly the savage barking of chained dogs sets me hurrying on my way sharpish. Chained dogs and pilgrims don't go together very well . . .

Better chained than unchained, though. Sheep dogs rounding up their flock are fine, but there's something terrifying about being chased by a snarling, gnashing dog. I'm just on my way through and I don't mean any harm. Why can't people have more docile pets? Take George and his pet Albert.

We met George and Albert in Australia's Northern Territory. George was a bit shy at first – which was hardly surprising, as keeping a pet crocodile is not strictly legal. In fact, it's absolutely against the law. But he'd had Albert for over three decades, after finding him as a tiddler in a creek somewhere and bringing him home to show the family.

We talked George into showing us Albert, the 30-foot saltwater crocodile that lived in a fenced enclosure in George's back yard. Albert lay in the shade of a bit of scrubby bush, in a shallow pond surrounded by a high wire fence.

'Do you ever take him for walks?' I asked.

'Hell no, mate! He's a croc!'

'Well, do you teach him tricks? You can't exactly cuddle him.'

'No, he just lies there.'

'What happens when you go away?'

'Nothing. I feed him once a week or so; he can go for ages without tucker. If I went away, he'd be fine for a good few weeks. Do you want to feed him?'

'Er, what do you feed him on?'

'Goldfish.'

They were great big barramundis, which he kept in the freezer in the garage.

George set up the A-frame stepladder alongside the fence. He sent the cameraman to the other side of the fence and told me to climb up the ladder. It was a tall ladder, not particularly stable – in fact 'rickety' is a word that springs to mind. At the top I had a grandstand view of this prehistoric creature. Albert hadn't moved a muscle since we'd arrived. His big crocodile eyes just stared at us unblinking from the top of his head. Nothing.

George joined me at the top of the ladder with a bucket, and brought out a frozen barramundi fish. It was a huge big thing and he banged it against the side of the fence, then held it over the edge. The next second I was staring into the jaws of hell as Albert opened his ginormous mouth and leapt out of the pool. BANG! His jaws snapped on to that frozen barramundi with a crash you could hear the other side of the continent. I screamed and the cameraman went white. George had let go of the fish a split second before the croc had bitten through the bone.

We were stunned and shaking. 'Wanna feed him one yourself, Timmy?' asked George.

'Happy to watch,' I said, climbing down the ladder with my legs quivering.

'Couple of those fish will last him for a week or so. Sometimes I give him a chook from the chook raffle, or if we get a bit of roadkill I might feed him that.'

It's the weirdest pet story I've ever come across, and here's the postscript from last summer. At Henley vintage boat parade, a very English affair, a chap in his boat steered up to me. 'G'day, Timmy. I'm Phil from Australia. You won't remember me; we met years ago.' The thing is, as his story unfolded, I did remember him. He had briefly been a deep-sea fisherman off the coast of Kenya, and we'd come across each other during a *Wacaday* shoot while trying to catch a spectacular marlin on camera (instead we caught a shoe). Afterwards, we shared a beer and a laugh together. Then, he had been on a gap year, from the far north of Oz, and now he lived a few miles from me.

'Do you remember when I told you about George and Albert?'

'Oh yes,' he said. 'I know One-armed George.'

'No,' said I, 'he had two arms.'

'Not any more he doesn't.'

ASTORGA

17

The Iron Cross

JOSE

E BIKE!

IRON CROSS

GAUDI STATUE

FENCE OF CROSSES

EL GANSO

Counting your blessings. It's a good habit to get into – I hope.

The Camino encourages enterprising people to try things that are different, colourful and authentic. There's a refreshment stand on top of a hill nowhere near a village. Here the bloke in charge is handing out fresh fruit and drink. 'No charge,' he says. 'I enjoy helping pilgrims. If you want to, you can leave whatever gift you like.' And that encourages more generous donations than a fixed price. It's very lucrative. A refreshment stall in the middle of nowhere. How welcoming. How obvious!

Every person on the Camino calls out as you pass: '*Buen Camino!*' Which translates as 'good trip'. It's an encouraging greeting, but being serenaded by a musical local is even better. José and his guitar are entertaining people on their way into town. It's a funny, uplifting moment and I join in with his cheerful song and hear him all the way down the hill.

Astorga is one of my favourite towns along the Camino. It's perched on top of a steep rocky incline that catches everyone unawares. The famous architect Gaudí has left his mark on the palace and the gothic cathedral, which have his extensive carvings and decorations. In the museum I find wonderfully gruesome illuminated-manuscript images; those ancient artists had lurid imaginations about devils and temptations. I find a space in the rood screen of the chancel to place my brother's name tag and imagine him rebuking those wicked-looking characters with a wagging finger. 'Be nice . . .'

In the afternoon sun, I set off gently up the road on a big climb through pretty, sleepy villages, and as the way gets steeper the temperature climbs too. It's bizarre to find myself in hot weather. Two days ago it was bitterly cold and wet – now it's 26 degrees. After unrelenting arctic conditions it's summer. What happened there?

It's a 20-kilometre panting climb, up 1,500 metres through the mountains of León – higher than Ben Nevis – to the Iron Cross, one of the most significant places on the whole Camino. 'Come on, Martin,' I mutter to my steed. 'Nearly there! You me, reach our potential.' It's a strange mantra, which changes as I pass a group of other cyclists. 'E-bike, E-bike,' I call out cheerfully, and that faint hint of superiority beams across my face. I'm practised at this after pedalling over the Pyrenees, and though these peaks may be just as high, the weather's better and I'm getting fitter and stronger every day.

There's a patchwork of spiritual tributes woven all along the roadside fences. Through the years, people have marked their journeys with crosses made from sticks and twigs, and decorated their plaited work with ribbons and strings. Onwards and upwards, and as I reach the summit a car pulls up and an elderly lady with a stick gets out to walk the 100 metres she can manage. She is determined to do her Camino, however modest it may appear. A group of German pilgrims are celebrating an open-air mass on the grass. I listen to the familiar rhythm with the unfamiliar words – picking out the parts I recognise. There's a gentle solemnity about the makeshift setting.

All around, there are views across to the other mountains in the range, stretching out west into the dipping sun. I can feel the late afternoon breeze, smell the pine trees; it's lovely to stop and catch my breath. It may be the hottest day of the year so far but there are snowdrifts up here to bury my face in. The snow catches and crunches as I stick my face into its icy mounds. I'm going to spend some time here.

Above me is a vast mound of stones surrounding a tall wooden pillar with an iron cross on the top. Since the early days of the pilgrimage people have carried a stone from home and laid it at the foot of the cross as an atonement for sins. The pile is made up of stones from every corner of the globe and there are thousands upon thousands of them. Fitting easily into my hand, my stone is painted with a Union Jack. I've carried it from my garden on the front bar bag. Next to it is a piece of Aberdeen granite that sparkles in the sunshine. Martin lived for more than half his life in a Camphill community at Newton Dee, gently doing his best every day. I picked up this large pebble at his funeral and now here we are together for ever on top of the world.

Rather than as an atonement for past wrongs, I prefer to use my stone from home as an opportunity to count my blessings.

Here's what I'm thankful for. Family, friends and health. I've got great friends and today they feel more important than ever.

I have friends with whom I cycle, play sport, watch football, have a good discussion; there are those I tease and am teased by; those I run an idea by. I have work friends, family friends, phone friends, Christmas friends, lunch friends, club friends, long distance friends, email friends, and friends who are encouraging me on my Camino.

I like the friends who drop in unannounced and want to share a bit of news. I'm delighted that I'm worth dropping in on. Other friendships have run their course. That's OK; it was good while it lasted.

I often make catch-up calls when I'm painting alone in my studio. I like the company of a 'watcha-up-to?' chat. Don't be surprised if the phone rings and I'm just saying 'hiya'.

I went to one of those reunions where you wonder if you'll recognise anyone. It's the mannerisms that we keep for ever and are intriguing to rediscover. The way someone looks down at their feet when they laugh; the phrase they always used to use; their laughter. I enjoyed the event until someone came up to me, saying, 'Great to see you again, Timmy. Do you remember when we . . .' and reeled off a host of things they remembered, while I smiled, trying to recall them. But then I bumped into someone I was eager to speak to. 'How good to see you again,' I said, and could see in his eyes that I didn't figure in his recollections at all. Ho hum! We can never be certain how we fit into someone else's life. To be on the safe side, it's better to offer a kind word and a smile when we greet a stranger. It might just make their day.

I'm feeling fit and healthy and I'm doing as my mum advised. She used to say, 'You only have one body, son; make sure you look after it.' It seems to be that when our appliances go wrong we don't think twice about fixing or replacing them. But we um and ah about seeing the doctor. For fitness I like sport. I love cycling, I swim for an hour every morning in summer, play five-a-side (five-goal Timmy) and I love my tennis. All these things are activities for the better months. In winter I go into hibernation and enjoy the brain stimulation of puzzles.

I have a great family: my lovely friend and wife, Mrs Mallett; hard-working son, Billy the Gardener; and bigger brother Paul, who always makes me laugh. I carry my mum and dad in my heart with dear Martin. A friend commented that Martin was elegant and seemed to float into the room, almost like a dancer. Our parents, Michael and Nan, met at amateur dramatics in Marple – no wonder being a performer is in my blood. I've got two delightful aged aunts, Anne and Jay, who are full of mischief and chatter, and my dad's brother John, who was just like them with a cheeky smile. He passed away two days ago, just before his ninety-second birthday. There are lots of crazy cousins and then there's Mrs Mallett's mob gathering in Melbourne.

The day you become a parent is one of the biggest days of your life. I was in the middle of a tour and had arranged to have two weeks off to be there for his arrival. But Billy was in a hurry and arrived on the day I was due to do two afternoon shows. Mrs Mallett woke up early and said, 'We should get to the hospital; my waters have broken.'

I'd made a birthing tape of nice calming music. All of it was the wrong choice. 'I need an epidural!' gasped Mrs M. The gynaecologist came in from playing tennis, still in his shorts, and remarked, 'That may slow things down.' I wiped my dear wife's brow, held her hand and gave helpful useless advice: 'Breathe, darling . . .'

'I bloody well am!'

At 12:17, out came this alien with a pointy head. I was handed the scissors to cut the cord. Crikey, it's a tough thing to cut. Then I held little Billy, kissed him and felt how all new parents feel. Emotional and weepy. Ten minutes later I was in the car being driven 100 miles to Bristol Hippodrome for the two o'clock show. I made a couple of calls. 'There may have to be a little delay to the start of the show . . .' And to Billy's grandparents: 'I'm on the motorway heading to my Bristol shows, and just to let you know: Billy has arrived.'

'What? On the motorway???'

He was baptised by his grandad and named William Theodore, to be known as Billy. The two names come from one of our favourite bodacious films at the time, *Bill & Ted's Excellent Adventure*.

'I'm Bill S. Preston.'

'I'm Ted Theodore Logan.'

'Bill & Ted.'

Being a July-born boy, birthday parties were always busy with outdoor games. 'What's the time, Mr Wolf?', 'Round the garden' – on to the trampoline before being caught; and watery fun, like 'Shark attack'. Billy and I would invent games on the way to school. We played 'Gridball' – there's no ball, but the winner is the first to run across the car park and jump on the grid; 'Finger on the button' – stand on the platform with your finger opposite where you think the train door button will be when it stops, and 'Make sure the weeds don't jump out' – where you put the little fella in the wheelbarrow on top of the garden debris and run around the garden being loud. One day, Billy announced, 'When I grow up, I want to climb up the ladder and sweep the leaves off the roof.'

He found his niche when he started mowing people's lawns. The result? It looked good, smelled good, he was complimented, got paid, and it needed doing again in two weeks. The horticulture course at college was brilliant. Now he's Billy the Gardener, and after a couple of years looking after Chris Evans's estate, he's running his own garden maintenance and design business and knows the Latin name, nickname and common name of most garden plants and shrubs in the country. He also knows the nickname, the colour of strip and the ground of every football team in England, and how to get there, because he's been to them all – 92 Premier and English football league grounds and many more in lots of other leagues.

Right now, Mrs Mallett is in Melbourne with mum Maisie for her hundredth birthday in a couple of weeks. Maisie is the youngest of seven (they'd run out of names when she arrived early May during the last year of the First World War). I send her a little loving video message from here, to go alongside her other messages of congratulations: the embossed cards from the Queen, the Governor General of Australia and Malcolm Turnbull the Prime Minister; the video message from Theresa May; greetings from the Mayor of Woking, where she was born, and from the Mayor of Glen Eira, where she lives now, and a letter from the wonderful Dame Vera Lynn. Bluebirds are over the white cliffs of Dover.

During the Second World War Maisie worked in a munitions factory, and once peace was won she was a pastry chef at St Stephen's Club on Westminster Square opposite Big Ben. (It's a lively bar, still frequented by MPs between the division bells.) After their shifts, she and the other young hopeful workers would sit up on the roof looking out across the River Thames and the bomb-damaged landscape of London. Dreaming dreams, they discussed what they wanted to make of their lives. Hughie and Maisie were sweet on each other and envisaged emigrating to Canada and making a life together in the

New World. All the dominions were advertising for migrants and there were great deals for those willing to make the journey. Hughie went ahead to Nova Scotia to find somewhere for them to live and work, and sent back glowing letters with gifts of stockings and delicious sweets (still rationed in Britain).

Then a week before her departure Maisie received a letter: 'Dear Maisie, don't come. I've found someone else. Have a nice life. Sorry . . .' Her mother consoled her, 'Never mind, dear. You'll find a nice Woking chap . . .' But Maisie wasn't about to be put off so quickly. She decided to go and visit her sister Grace and her husband in Sydney. She could get a ten-pound passage as long as she stayed two years. 'I'll try that and see how it goes . . .' Her parents saw her off at Woking station, and through the smoke and steam came the words, 'Goodbye, Mother. I'll be back in a couple of years . . .' They would never see each other again.

In Glasgow, an old troop ship, the *SS Cameronia*, had been hastily converted for migrants. One deck for men and boys, another deck for women, girls and babes. Maisie shared a cabin with half a dozen strangers for the six-week journey. No men were allowed on the women's decks after dark. Food and the entertainment were limited. You had what you were given, and if you wanted some singing or a laugh you made it all up yourself. There was an old, barely tuned piano in one corner of the lounge. A young man, David, played and sang songs and entertained anyone who wanted to join in. Maisie and David's eyes met across the piano.

Their friendship grew into something a little more. At some stage before the ship docked in Australia, David revealed he was heading to patch up a shaky relationship and would be getting off in Melbourne to see his young son and the boy's mother. Twice in a matter of weeks Maisie had been unlucky in love.

It was not an easy parting. David left the ship in confusion, lost his belongings at the docks and discovered that his family was not pleased to see him. In desperation, he headed for the only friendly face he knew in Australia – Maisie's.

As the ship docked at Sydney's Circular Quay, Maisie looked out at the waiting crowds, trying to spot her sister Grace. That's when she saw David waiting for her.

'I thought you were in Melbourne?'

'I was, but it didn't work out. I want to be with you.'

'Welcome to Australia, Maisie. Who's this chap?' asked big sister Grace.

You can imagine the awkwardness, the hasty exchange. 'Where are you staying? When will I see you?' So many things to sort out. Grace quickly took Maisie off to their migrant hostel in a Sydney suburb and David found himself a bedsit in the city centre.

Life at the migrant camp was a challenge. A bullying commandant sparked a rebellion when he wouldn't allow young families to have their own family mealtimes. In desperation, 20 families clubbed together to buy cheap land and build homes, away from his control. There was a reason the land was cheap. It was very poor soil, and several landslips in foul weather washed away the road they had to build.

Working on their homes in their own time, needing jobs to support themselves, Maisie continued as a chef, baking the Australian speciality the coconut lamington cake, and every second weekend she got time out from helping on the building site to see her boyfriend, David. They courted on Sydney trains, Bondi Beach and underneath the iconic Harbour Bridge, where young lovers would meet for time alone.

Grace's family still live in that house that Maisie helped to build in the early 1950s. It's a testament to the hard work and homebuilding determination that I've so admired in her.

David got the sort of job that hasn't existed for many years now, becoming a travelling salesman across New South Wales and Victoria, selling self-help books for public speakers. He and Maisie had a year-long adventure in a caravan, visiting country towns, demonstrating the art of eloquent delivery – perfect for anyone who wants to sell something.

Arriving in Melbourne they moved on to selling second-hand pianos and boats. Then the stork brought along three little children – the future Mrs Mallett, Davina and Steve.

I think of Maisie as a great pioneering spirit: the one who kept the home fires burning, the lamingtons rising and food on the table. Maisie had the courage to make something of her life. She wasn't afraid to get out there and explore what it had to offer. Setbacks and disappointments were part of life's rich tapestry.

We had locked ourselves out one day, and at the age of 75 she wouldn't hear of us climbing up to the bedroom window to let ourselves in. To our delighted laughter she exclaimed, 'Let me do that!'

Here I am at the Iron Cross, thinking of Maisie and the lovely comment she would make if she were here: 'That's a silly place to leave all those stones lying around like that. Someone could fall over.'

There's a warning sign about the wind (I think), saying, 'Attention cyclists. Outstanding strong circulate with caution.' That sounds like a Maisie message.

Yes, I'm counting my blessings. Health, family and friends. Wouldn't life be different without them?

18

The Winter Camino

'Hey, chuck a U-ey!' It's a favourite phrase in the Mallett household and makes us stop and reconsider. Sometimes, you spot the obvious if you turn around and go back again.

There are dozens of different Camino de Santiago routes to the fabled destination of Santiago de Compostela. On this adventure so far, I've cycled the Pilgrims' Way, the Way of the Plantagenets, the Way of Tours, the Way of Vezelay/Le Puy, and through Spain on the Camino Francés. But now at the ancient Knights Templar city of Ponferrada there's a choice. The Camino Invierno, or Winter Camino, winds a little further south through Galicia and was traditionally used when the steep pass over the mountains to the small stone town of O Cebreiro was blocked with snow. Since 2016 the Winter Camino has been officially recognised and signed, and I'm keen to try something different. I cycled the O Cebreiro route last time I came this way and we had a boiling hot ascent and a zero-visibility, torrential descent.

I ask at the Ponferrada tourist office about this new route and their faces light up. They get very few travellers along this strange new option and I'm one of the first this year. The tourist office team and I swap badges on my tie collection and I plan to set off just as soon as I've visited the castle. The Knights Templars were a religious warrior group who wore their faith as obviously as their armour and are the epitome of Onward Christian Soldiers fighting the good fight. Most proud of defending Christendom from other faiths, if they couldn't do that by persuasion they were just as happy to use force. Their castle at Ponferrada is one of the finest examples in Europe of a Christian stronghold, and the exhibition room has beautifully illuminated manuscripts showing different Christian warrior attire and heraldry. I can't help but think they look like medieval football strips.

There are detailed maps, which attract my attention, and even sheet music for a Knights Templar marching song. Please tell me they had a version of 'Itsy Bitsy'!

On the edge of town by an old bridge are a pair of Camino pillars, one pointing the popular way to the Camino Francés and a new one with an arrow southwards – the Camino Invierno. I'm in for a shock and a treat. The road immediately begins with a climb on a rough track that is a lot harder, more rugged and less maintained than anything I've come across recently on the Camino Francés. *Watch out, Mallett. You don't want a puncture on this bumpy lumpy route.* But the attraction is that I'm all alone on a road in spring on the Winter Camino – enjoying apple blossom, wild flowers, real villages and being a tourist attraction for the locals. The Camino is always a very personal journey and even on busy sections with lots of other travellers you are in your own world. But this is strikingly different. I don't see a single pilgrim and I won't for the next few days.

The Romans were the first to discover the attractions of this route, as it follows the valley of the River Sil and there are spectacular rock formations, which makes it feel like another planet. I enjoy painting the striking orange cliffs of Las Médulas, the largest open-pit gold mine in the entire Roman Empire. There are plenty of different subjects to inspire me to paint.

Including the man sharpening a massive blade, some sort of machete or scythe. What strikes me is how he's sitting on a log in his yard, with the blade on his lap, wearing his slippers! I am absolutely fascinated by his absorption in the job, with no obvious thought for health and safety. And why doesn't he just get a whipper snipper? Surely that would be quicker and more efficient! I engage the man in conversation and sketch him as we chat. I say 'chat'. He speaks Spanish or Galician (I wouldn't know the difference) and he has no idea what I am talking about. But for a few moments we smile and converse and make a connection. And now here he is in paint. Hard at work – in his indoor footwear. I can't figure out why anyone would sit outdoors in their slippers, until I see the locals in their wooden clogs that their slippered feet fit inside so much more comfortably. Sometimes you just have to watch . . . and learn.

So unusual is the sight of pilgrims on these little-used roads that the usual greeting, *'Buen Camino'*, is replaced by the simple *'Buen Viaje'* (Good trip), with a look of astonishment at a fully laden cyclist coming past. It's a delightful ride, stunning scenery: stork nests on the telegraph poles and in the villages strange redundant steps that lead up to the first-floor balconies that have long disappeared. Steps to nowhere . . . Now isn't that a song? We're on the road to nowhere . . .

There are very few places to stay. All this will change in years to come as the route gets busier and better known. Right now, I feel like a pioneer. In the medium-sized town on the border with Galicia (Domingo) there is the choice of one, very plain hostel. That's where I'm staying. The regulars look at me, intrigued, as if I'm a bit out of their usual experience. Everyone is buying a lottery ticket and I buy one too, remembering that at home son Billy is always getting lucky with a scratch card. My prize turns out to be the next day's cycle ride through a heavenly landscape.

In the bright morning I head up the steep track, following the new signage. There's a Martin Mallett moment, when his name tag sits in a new wooden seat as I paint the view overlooking the lakes. Later I come across a convenient slate table and benches which act as my outdoor office and I make some calls to the archbishop's office in Santiago and to Chaplain Mat in Winchester. Santiago Cathedral people are aware of me and I'm feeling more hopeful now about some sort of meeting in due course.

The Galician spring has come to life in two days and it's a thrill to cycle a never-ending valley on this brand new Camino. Eventually I meet something familiar – the N120 – now almost completely empty. It's followed me for 500 kilometres from Logroño and it helps that it feels as if at least 60 kilometres of it is downhill! I'm able to freewheel mile after glorious mile as it weaves its way, criss-crossing the river again and again.

Gosh, it's hot! Not just pleasantly warm. So I cool off by sticking my head and hat in the village water trough beneath the fountain. I set up my phone on the tripod to take a photo, and as it goes click the mobile gently topples into the water. Er, nice one, Mallett. I'm amazed it still works. I take a long cooling drink and count my blessings; and as I wipe the phone dry, Paula comes out of the café with a delicious homemade snack – a slice of local delicacy. Thank you. A little act of random kindness that means so much and it gives me the energy to carry on in the late afternoon heat. Uphill and around the mountain for over 20 kilometres to a lonely hostel in an empty town, where naturally I'm the only guest.

I like this *albergue* family. Bruno, the son, runs it with his mum and dad, who cook me a delicious meal and offer to do my laundry. They have had five pilgrims in the past month, which isn't enough to keep the business afloat. They'll be closing and selling up in a fortnight. Shame, but nothing lasts for ever. I paint a postcard watercolour pen and ink sketch for them as a thank-you memento. Their back garden is a mixture of small vineyard, apple orchard and oilseed rape crop. The colours and smells are delightful and it's easy to spend the morning painting there.

Maybe new people will keep the hostel going. Maybe they won't. I'm just glad that it's here today.

On the rolling road ahead of me an old man pushes a wheelbarrow laden with olive branches. It's a captivating image and I take a few photos of his back bent under the weight of the olive branches. I'll start with a sketch, and then a painting will emerge set in this wild-flower and yellow meadow. Olive trees bent and twisted with age, the elderly man with his comfortable hat, baggy trousers and familiar jumper, at peace with his work. I'm reminded that there can be dignity in good labour. Whatever we set our minds to, and do with the best of our ability, has worth and value.

There's a climb through villages and an opportunity for a

Martin moment at a roadside well in the shade and again at an ancient chapel with the bell-pull outside the locked doors. Great! I wrap a name tag around the bell-pull and when I ring it the sound echoes across the valley for eternity.

Martin was the bell-ringer at his church in Aberdeen. Perfect. He and I learned to ring rounds and call changes as teenagers in Hyde. One of our favourite times together was climbing up the spiral stone steps of the church tower to the ringing chamber. I'd stand with him and be a guiding hand on the sally with the handstroke and Martin, alone, would pull the rope tail – the backstroke. 'Four to five,' calls the ringing master, and Martin and I turn to face the next ringer. Martin and I liked doing our bit for our church and our community.

Being part of a band, ringing those bells full circle, is a peculiarly British thing. There are over 5,000 church towers in England where bells are rung like this, along with a handful in Canada, the USA, Australia, New Zealand and South Africa. On our travels it's one of those things we aim to tick off, a bit like the visit to a football ground. But be warned, bell-ringing is not much of a spectator sport. Don't imagine you're going to see something energetic, athletic, logical or remotely comprehensible! You rarely see bell-ringers smile. There's too much concentration involved. Making sure you lead or follow correctly. The ropes are dancing up and down; it looks like studious chaos in the ringing chamber of a bell tower. Change ringers don't ring tunes as such; it's more a matter of following mathematical formulas that are impossible to explain but have impressive names like Grandsire Caters, Stedman Triples, Reverse Canterbury Pleasure Place Doubles! Church bells are the soundtrack of Sunday mornings and it's a gentle reminder of a Christian tradition that dates back hundreds of years. Just remember to let go of the rope if you pull too hard and break the stay. No one wants to end up cracking their head on the ceiling.

In the café on Saturday afternoon there are several dozen blokes playing cards and drinking coffee. Football is on the TV, horse racing is on the radio. It's a familiar Saturday afternoon anywhere. Look around the bar, all the blokes are wearing their coats and caps indoors; hear the chatter, timeless and comfortable. There'll be a little smile if someone backs a winner. Long periods of muttering as the cards are considered. They'll get home – eventually – and their wives will ask, 'How was your day?'

'Good.'

'How are so and so's family?'

'Don't know; never asked.'

'What about so and so's health?'

'Dunno. Not a subject we ever mention.'

'So what did you talk about?'

'Stuff. It was fine.'

Husbands and wives have such different concepts of a good chat. When the men meet each Friday for football, and afterwards for beers in the pub, we talk and laugh all evening and have a great time, but the subjects are never ever what our wives would talk about. This Saturday afternoon painting of the men in the café playing cards is titled 'Wisdom'.

At the town of Chantada, the rain strikes and I cut short the ride; I'm 100 kilometres from Santiago. Traditionally, most pilgrims aim to spend their last night on the road just outside Santiago, then journey in fresh to arrive in time for the midday mass. It's not a bad plan. So tomorrow I think I'll have an easy ride and arrive comfortably the day after – Monday.

Things happen and plans change. I'm into a rhythm now of between 60 and 75 kilometres a day. That gives me time to explore, paint and be absorbed in each day. Make sure there are No Regrets. I'm enjoying this adventure so much, I'm not quite ready for it to reach a climax. Anticipation can be better than realisation. We put so much thought and energy into how good our lives will be when we've achieved the little goals we set ourselves . . .

Going to get fit, going to feel better in these new clothes, going to climb this hill, going to learn something new, going to aim for promotion, going to do a good turn. (Shame that last one isn't on the list every day.)

'Are we nearly there yet?!' That's a phrase from *Wacaday* I still use when I'm heading on a journey. I'm saying it now in this hilly region of Galicia, and I'm faced with some big steep climbs. 'I think I can, I know I can . . .' I decide to give the Timmeee E-bike battery an extra charge over lunch. I will be glad I did. I don't realise how important that charge will be.

I'm in Lalín, considering how far to aim for today, when it happens. I am about to pedal away. I look the wrong way and a big truck misses me by a millimetre. It's so easy to do. I let my concentration waver for just a split second. I feel the wind whistle past my face as the lorry speeds by.

Straight away I get off the saddle, put the bike on its stand and have a few words with myself. I am 50 kilometres from Santiago, I've pedalled across Europe, but all of that counts for nothing if I go home in a body bag or end up in hospital with smashed limbs. I think of what my family would say and how annoyed they'd be. I take a drink of water, look around – tell myself to be more aware. There's nobody else here I can rely on. It's just me and my bike.

Accidents, when they happen, go into slow motion. One summer night I was driving down to Oxford on a quiet M6.

It's hard to imagine these days, but I've driven down the motorway on New Year's Eve and seen only five vehicles between Knutsford and Cannock services. This particular night it was warm and I was desperately tired. I stopped at Hilton Park services for a short nap.

I wake again after 2 a.m. and want to get going. But I'm fighting utter weariness. The window is down, the radio is on and I'm torn between going slowly to stay awake and going faster just to get there. The A46 is a winding road and I know I need to stop. 'I'll pull over at the next layby,' I say to myself, but the next layby comes upon me too quickly and I'm sailing past it. 'Right, the next one then.' And a moment later I've hit the kerb. I'm flying through the air, the car and I are as light as a feather and I'm heading for something. 'I'm alive, I'm alive,' I shout to myself as I know I'm going to hit a tree. And then crunch! Pause. Breathe. Is there anything trapped or broken? I'm at an angle, right-hand side down, my glasses have fallen off, and it's that early cold twilight before dawn when everything is just a blurred shape. I open the door and fall into the muddy field or ditch. The car has hit a telegraph pole and ploughed through a farmer's hedge. It's on its side and my heart is racing. I know I could have been dead. I know I should have stopped and slept. I'm just days away from starting my new TV career at TV-am and all of that could have ended before it began.

Minutes later a car pulled up to see if I was all right. I was driven to Banbury, where my girlfriend met me in tears. I became aware that someone cared for me and my crash had terrified her. The car was a write-off, of course, but it saved my life. I thank the Lord I was driving that not-very-Timmy, beige coloured Fiat Miafiori, because it was built like a tank. Anything else and I'd have been dead that night.

So now I need a cuppa.

I also know I need to stop about 25 kilometres from Santiago to give myself a full day's ride and a nice rest before cycling into the city tomorrow. I must be more shaken than I realise. Strangely there's an issue with the promised accommodation along this Camino. I keep seeing signs for pilgrim hostels and *albergues*, but they're either not open or easily missed.

'Not to worry,' I keep saying to myself. 'There'll be another one in a couple of kilometres.'

I spend the rest of the day constantly searching. That's when the battery level drops and my energy too. Without realising it, I've got myself into a pickle again. I want to stay somewhere nice. Then I want to stay anywhere. I seem to be missing the *albergues* – I'm sure they are all around me; but now I end up cycling over a hundred kilometres. My bike battery runs down to 1 per cent, but the GPS has to be charged from the bike, and my phone is hovering on the red.

Hmmm. Not a great technology day.

I end up in Santiago this evening, far more stressed than I would have liked. I'm tired, crabby, anxious and annoyed at myself. This is not how it's supposed to be. I should be fulfilling my challenge with a sense of achievement. But I'm just another man on the road, thinking that my trip matters. It only matters to me, and nothing is worth getting so stressed about. I find a place to stay on a busy central Santiago street. I tell myself to have a shower, a little food, a good sleep. Refreshment will make things look a lot better tomorrow.

I fall asleep thinking, *Have I really cycled over 2,350 kilometres from home?*

ARCHBISHOP'S PALACE

PILGRIM OFFICE

PILGRIM PASSPORT

TOMB OF ST JAMES

DEAN JOSÉ

BOTAFUMEIRO

19

Santiago de Compostela

This is the moment. This is the day. Everything fast tracks to the outcome of the next few hours. Am I going to judge the success or failure of this adventure on what happens now?

I've arrived in Santiago de Compostela and there's a meeting I want to happen. I intend to share the goodwill messages from Britain's and France's political and spiritual leaders, and a future head of state, with the archbishop and cathedral of Santiago. I've been given the task of somehow reuniting the Hand of St James, in picture form, with the rest of the body, and there's an invitation to extend.

Trouble is, I've had no reply to my emails and letters to Archbishop Julian Barrio Barrio.

Hmmmm.

Let's see what happens when I knock on the door.

The archbishop's office is across the square from the cathedral, and I need to speak first with the vice chancellor, Manuel Jesus, Julian's diary keeper and personal assistant. The chap on the desk by the door downstairs makes a call. 'He's not in. Try again in an hour.'

An hour later it's no better: 'You must send an email to Manuel Jesus.' I'm frustrated. The doors are shut and this feels like an utter failure. Words of encouragement in Britain appear to count for nothing in Spain.

I need to think things through again.

First, I'll take my three signed pilgrim passports to the pilgrim office and collect my Compostela – the Latin certificate that's supposed to signify my accomplishment. I'm only partially interested in this, because my journey isn't complete. But I understand the significance: this same certificate has been presented to millions of pilgrims over the centuries.

I head to the pilgrim office. It's moved. Last time I was here, there was a funny little place up a flight of stairs where pilgrims waited and chatted with each other and shared their stories before heading into a modest room. There they answered questions and collected their final stamp and the Latin certificate in a scroll.

Now the office is a block away in a huge pilgrim complex where there are dozens of counters and a number system like at the post office. 'Cashier number six, please!' Youngsters on their gap year sit filling in the forms in their poor handwriting. There are so many pilgrims coming into town every day, it's become a conveyor belt.

'Name? Where did you start? On what date? Which Camino did you take?'

I feel as if I'm trying to get through the ID process at a call centre: 'Last three direct debits? Your inside leg measurement? Second letter of your memorable date? Your uncle's pet's favourite food?'

For what's meant to be the celebration of an achievement, this feels a little disappointing. I don't want a Latin translation of my name (Timotheus Mallettum?). I'd like my name spelt correctly, please. I do want the distance noted, and I have ridden half a dozen Camino routes.

'Then you'll want the larger certificate and cardboard tube. Buy over there and come back with the receipt.'

When my mobile rings, with a radio station wanting to celebrate my arrival at Santiago, I laugh. 'I've got this certificate,' I say. 'It's in Latin, so will be very useful at the chemist as a prescription for calm-down pills!'

I head into the cathedral for the pilgrim mass. Nobody knows if the famous piece of drama will occur – there's always a question mark. Has a wealthy pilgrim given a donation? Does it depend on the tides? The cycle of the moon? Or does it happen every day and they just don't want to tell you that? I've been given a top tip. Sit north or south in the cathedral transept to get the best view of it.

The 'It' is what everyone has come to see. The enormous incense holder being swung over my head – the *Botafumeiro* – is so big, it takes eight men pulling on the ropes to swing it from aisle to aisle and it almost touches the ceiling. Of course, most of the audience/congregation are staring at it through their mobiles, filming, because the Cathedral Police tell us not to. It's a fabulous piece of theatre that takes my breath away. Originally, the *Botafumeiro* was designed to fumigate smelly pilgrims – we all shower a little more these days – but the two-minute display at the end of the mass, with musical accompaniment from a singing nun, is without a doubt one of the finest spectacles and soaring moments I've witnessed in any public building. Even my friend Gary, who is wonderfully 'bah humbug' with regard to organised religion, declared, 'Now that's why you come here. That's what you come to see.' The ornately decorated censer, the size of an incinerator, swoops and flies over our heads with billowing sweet incense flowing from it. The nun's singing rises and falls in perfect rhythm; the congregation gasp and want to applaud in awe. It really is a 'don't miss it' moment.

After the service the crowds head to the statue of St James. It's traditional to lean over and hug the saint. It sounds odd, but I'm in the queue, and everyone else does it, so I just join in. Down the stairs in the crypt is the place I've come to see: the Tomb of St James the Apostle – covered in solid silver and gleaming in the light behind the metal grille. The lighting focuses my attention. This is the final resting place of the saint, companion of Christ and early leader of the fledgling Christians. He's gloriously untouchable and this experience is surprisingly moving. My friend Andrew had made an intriguing suggestion: take your photo of the Hand of St James from Marlow and place it as close as possible to the tomb, then take a photo of the two. It's the nearest I may get to reuniting the Hand with the other bits of him – assuming, of course, that they are all in there. So I take the handy selfie!

Now, to mark the occasion I leave a Martin Mallett name tag in a special place in view of the shrine. 'I'm happy. You me.'

What about meeting the archbishop?

In my email from Chaplain Mat in Winchester, all those weeks and another country ago, there was mention that, if needed, I could contact the English-speaking archivist in the cathedral,

Francisco Javier Buide, member of the Diocesan Committee for Ecumenism, Director of the cathedral archive and lecturer at the Compostela Theological Institute. Crikey, that's a title and a half. I wonder if it will be any easier than trying to see Don Manuel Jesus or Archbishop Julian?

At the cathedral door, security lead me to the sacristy. The Singing Nun walks past, and I thank her for her wonderful contribution to the *Botafumeiro* spectacle. She beams and gives the slightest of bows. Minutes later, I'm sitting in the library office of Francisco, who comes in with a broad smile, excited to see me. The archivist, in his 30s, is a cheerful, enthusiastic academic whose passion is collecting saints. Brilliant. I collect different spectacle frames and he collects saints. I think he wins on points.

'Within five years of the murder of Thomas à Becket, in Canterbury Cathedral,' he tells me, 'there were chapels dedicated to him all along the Way of St James in Spain.' Francisco studied in Oxford and is fascinated by Becket and really intrigued by the story of the Hand of St James and its connections to Santiago. I tell him about my encounters with the bishops and how I'd like to meet the archbishop and invite him to the UK.

'Let me ring the archbishop's office,' he says and I hear the words '*Peregrino, bicicleta,* Timmy Mallett, *famoso, Inglese,* television, *artista,* Oxford, Winchester, Prince William, Macron, Theresa May . . . *Sí*'. Manuel Jesus has been expecting me and is terribly sorry but Archbishop Julian Barrio Barrio is not here this week; please would I see the dean of the cathedral at 5 p.m.?

The dean must be one of the hardest working people in the cathedral. He's the one who oversees everything, the CEO of a massive, multi-million Euro organisation. He's the top dog responsible for the clergy, staff, buildings, fixtures, fittings, workmen, visitors, worshippers, tourists, pilgrims, cathedral school, stone yard, finances, health and safety, museum, artefacts, reliquary . . . everything. Not forgetting that the cathedral is the final resting place of St James the Apostle, companion of Christ.

The dean is a busy man.

I'm expecting a *mañana* moment. 'Sorry, he's got a full day – you'd better come back another time, please.'

At five o'clock, Dean José Fernández Lago is in the foyer of the sacristy, waiting for me, smiling. We head into a wonderful baroque reception room upstairs that has welcomed kings and princes, popes and cardinals, knights and bishops, and today – a cycling pilgrim.

We sit at an impressive leather-covered table. José and Francisco want to know about the Hand of St James – the missing piece of the saint in the cathedral. And I begin . . .

'In the early twelfth century . . .'

The dean and archivist are listening closely as I go through 900 years of the journey of an ancient relic.

'. . . and that's where it is today.'

'But how do we know the mummified hand came from here?' asked José. 'And how did it get to Mainz in 1114?'

Ah, that old line about provenance. I'd asked the priest at Marlow why the Hand wasn't on public show and he had told me, 'We've been asked not to display it. There's no provenance.'

Provenance. Origin. How much proof is there that something is what we think it is? We like things to mean something. We all have possessions that have sentimental value for us. At no time did the dean, archivist or I pose the question, 'Shall we just open up the silver tomb and see what's inside? Maybe there's a missing left hand as well as a separated head.' Of course, that might be revealing, but really the point of all this is faith. For faith to work, we just need to believe. We don't necessarily require things to be tested and DNA'd and checked for carbon dating. A positive sample could perhaps pose more questions than answers, and anyway the cathedral at Santiago would gain nothing from going down that route and I have no intention of asking them to.

In the Middle Ages everyone had a piece of the true cross, or a knuckle of St what's-her-name. It was easy to make a living selling religious relics, and the faithful lapped it up. There's a pardoner in Chaucer's *Canterbury Tales* who tells how he sells indulgences and in his bag has pigs' bones masquerading as those of saints.

These days we are a little more circumspect. We tend to be less keen on icons and religious relics. We demand proof of everything. It's why we have so many CCTV cameras everywhere. But we can still respond subjectively with regard to 'evidence'.

I like the way people have thought differently in different times. But some things stay the same. To be human means everyone who has ever lived has felt the same emotions: love, hope, laughter (when someone slips on a banana skin), despair and happiness (when their team loses or wins) and curiosity. Curiosity about the way the world works is a great thing. We're always questioning and examining, and so we should be.

We sit quietly for a moment . . . and then Francisco speaks. 'There is a record of the eleventh-century Archbishop of Santiago giving a gift to a Patriarch of the Orthodox Church. The meeting is believed to have happened in northern Italy. It would have been a very important gift; something of immense value. The Great Schism of the Western and Orthodox churches happened in the middle of the century and this may have been an attempt at reconciliation or making an alliance . . . I wonder if it could have been this Hand?'

He could be right. Recently, in Mainz, they uncovered the wealthy remains of an early archbishop in the grand eleventh-century cathedral. Mainz was considered a Holy See, on a par with Rome, Santiago and Jerusalem. It's a connection that could benefit from more study.

The fact remains that for nine centuries the mummified Hand of St James has been in the Thames Valley in England. Is it from the body of St James? It bears the marks of a brutal removal from the arm. The sinews have been ripped. It's not a clean cut. Did this occur before or after death? If this is getting uncomfortable, does it matter if it is the Hand of St James? It's still a hand, a very old hand, and handshakes are what we usually use to greet each other. I'm satisfied that this hand is an ancient relic. I don't need proof of its provenance to be reminded that it's had a profoundly long journey and was once the left hand of someone. Maybe a saint? Maybe a sinner? But definitely a person with hopes and fears, who experienced all the joys and terrors of being human.

'I brought these photos of the Hand with me,' I tell them. 'Would you like to see them?'

They both lean forward excitedly. I show them the photographs, the letters of greetings and goodwill from my bishops and religious and political leaders. They respond, impressed. I reveal the photos of brother Martin, and hand over the collection for them to examine. I extend the Bishop of Oxford's invitation to come and visit, and to see the Hand of St James themselves.

'Thank you so much, Timmy. And now we would like to ask you to do something for us . . .'

What could this be?

'Tell Theresa May that when she has finished with Brexit to come and visit us when she walks her Camino.'

Back in the heyday of pilgrimage, when Chaucer was writing his wonderful *Canterbury Tales*, all sorts of people – kings, princes, rulers and dukes – would trek across the Continent along with the commoners to Santiago and back every single year. There's every reason to suppose the Prime Minister may become one of their band.

'Last year over three hundred thousand people completed their Camino in Santiago,' said José. 'This year it will be three hundred and thirty thousand. In a few years it will be half a million people, and maybe more in a Holy Year when the Feast of St James falls on a Sunday. Your Camino, these photographs, letters and your story, with your permission, we would like to keep in the cathedral archives for ever. Yours is a special story and we are so pleased that you have shared it with us.'

I love this; they'll recognise my little trip if, in exchange, I spread the word to the Prime Minister. José and Francisco stamp and autograph my pilgrim passport and sign my bike pannier with a flourish. I leave the letters and photographs with them, and after an hour's discussion with these busy, good people I head to a quiet nearby café for a little refreshment and contemplation.

That's when a voice exclaims, 'Oh my God, it's Timmy Mallett! Can me and my mate get a selfie and buy you a drink?' Two blokes have just finished their walk from the coast along the Camino Inglese and this is their moment. Our two journeys are intersecting at this point and I listen while they try to make sense of what they've done.

It's been a big day, and tomorrow another thousand pilgrims will arrive – in the peak season over 3,500 people – for their big day. The scale is enormous, but everyone has an individual, personal tale. There's a delicious parallel with St Peter at the Pearly Gates and the never-ending stream of hopefuls: 'Been a big day today. It will be another big day tomorrow, and another after that!'

Get your Compostela, see the sights, buy a souvenir, have a farewell meal and say your goodbyes.

Most people head home at this stage with a warm sense of achievement and some tales. I'm imagining how medieval pilgrims might have felt. What did St Francis of Assisi do in 1212 when he arrived in Santiago? Have a chat with some animals perhaps and then turn around again and start walking home? The reality is that pilgrims through the centuries have come here, perhaps in the hope of absolution for some wrongs, maybe hopeful of a cure for their condition. Today's pilgrims may take a budget flight home and be back in the office on Monday. Is that it? Just something to tick off your bucket list? Been there, done that. 'Did you have a nice holiday? Got any blisters?' 'My mate went on that walk once and met his wife.'

I'm ready to wend my weary way homewards too, but first I need to visit the end of the world and work out just how I'm going to get back.

20

The end of the world

FINISTERRE

COSTA DA MORTE   MUXIA

Meeting very old friends and colleagues in the last place we'd expect makes us realise we are all on a big trip together. That fork in the road leads us down widely differing paths, so it's revealing when we compare notes of how we got here.

The Romans called it Finisterre, or the coast of death – Costa da Morte. It was as far as one could travel in western Europe. After that nothing but the sea and the land of the dead. Nice thought. I have an idea about this place, but it needs a couple of days to form.

I'm in search of the best view of Santiago de Compostela. I

remember my friends at the tourist office, who would welcome a change from the usual 'Where is the cathedral?'; 'How do I get to the airport?'; 'Where is the toilet?'; 'Where can I leave my kids while I go to . . .' I love their reaction when I say, 'Your town is gorgeous. I'm an artist and I want to know your personal favourite view of the city.'

The reply is that the skyline from the park is the easiest to reach, but the little gem is by the gardens next to the museum of Galicia. In the spring sunshine the rooftops glisten and the spires of the city soar. It is great to make a day of it, absorb the messages of congratulations on reaching Santiago and then explore and paint. I return to show the tourist team what I've done and a voice behind me says, 'OK, Timmy?' It's Marianna, the Dutch cyclist in her 60s, without an E-bike, arriving into Santiago two days after me. We share a meal together to celebrate and discuss plans for our journeys home. Marianna wants to put the bike on a bus to Bilbao and catch a train from Bordeaux to Holland. I'm still cycling. The bike is being serviced at a Santiago bike shop by Fernando who guarantees everything – for ten minutes! He also has a good tip for the route to the end of the world. 'Head to the sea, it's only thirty kilometres away, and follow the coast line.' Good call.

My old boss at Piccadilly Radio, Tony Ingham, walks into Santiago at midday. Michael, our colleague, put us in touch with each other when he realised that we were both on this adventure at the same time. Tony and I haven't seen each other in over three decades and yet his smile is instantly recognisable as we embrace on the steps of the cathedral. We feel like long lost brothers. 'Hey, kiddah!' He always greets me like this. Then Tony puts his feet up, to rest them, while we share a beer and a Manchester catch-up. The dusty well-worn boots stir something.

'Remember when Neil from *The Young Ones* had a hit with "Hole in My Shoe"?'

We both start laughing. "'Hello, shoes,"' I say. "'I'm sorry, but I'm gonna have to stand on you again . . ."' I'd put out a plea on air for listeners to send in to the radio station a shoe for Neil (played by the great actor Nigel Planer). Just one shoe, either foot, definitely not a pair. They arrived by their hundreds. Shoes covered reception, they filled up the presenters' office. We stacked them in the on-air studio and Tony went bonkers. 'The phones are blocked, demanding you stop. Kids are sending in one each of their parents' best shoes!'

First, I apologised. It's always a good plan to say sorry; say it will never happen again and tell your bosses what they want to hear.

Then make a big fuss about it on air and give away free records to anyone who wants their shoe back and manages to find it in the pile!

Now I'm wondering . . . 'Were our days on Piccadilly Radio really unique, or does every generation feel they have the best memories? Were Queen right when they sang about radio's time, power and finest hour on "Radio Ga Ga"?'

'Well, kiddah,' says Tony, '*Timmy on the Tranny* certainly did what I asked for and more . . . and look at the industry awards you picked up.' We'd sat down in his office in autumn 1982, me in multicoloured knitted tank top, purple trousers, red glasses. Did I ever wear something that matched? Never have; never will. 'I want you to do what you did on Radio Luxembourg: play pop hits and blow the competition away.' We discussed the sound of big radio. Be loud, outrageous, funny, give away huge prizes, play the same song over and over if it's needed and be important. Make the kids of the north-west talk about Piccadilly Radio all day every day. With those simple instructions I began my night-time pop show in early October with the biggest name of the day – Adam Ant. 'Goody Two Shoes' was the opening song, and every 15 minutes I played it again. It set the benchmark for breaking the rules. Think of a rule, then break it. Every link would have a jingle, a competition, a caller, a sketch/gag and sometimes they would all happen at once. Talk fast, make the show urgent, and insist everyone listens faster. Tony found helpers to answer the phones, come up with material and sort out the post. Andy Big Bird (named after Big Bird on *Sesame Street*), a student from Macclesfield, became Radio Diggle, the pirate radio DJ breaking in over my links; Karen Walsh, now a great TV director, was Aunty Boney Kneecaps, giving pointless advice to kids: 'I suggest the best thing to do with history homework is to lightly grill it with a slice of cheese, then throw it in the bin'; 'If you have spots, try standing in front of the mirror for fifteen hours a day and fiddling with them'; 'If you are concerned about your looks, put a paper bag on your head; no one will notice.'

A 17-year-old kid from Warrington came to interview me with his brother's borrowed reel-to-reel tape recorder, saying he was from the hospital radio. His questions were intriguing – 'Which are better: newts or frogs?' I gave him a character to play, with the catchphrase 'What I don't know – I don't know'. His on-air name was Nobby Nolevel. Which is how Chris Evans and I still greet each other: 'Hey, Nobby,' I say. 'Hey, Boss,' replies Chris.

I'd get the *Timmy on the Tranny* team together before each show and we would rewrite the words to the hits. Altogether now . . . do you know the tune to these?

There was something in my hair that night, gave me a fright, like Rambo!

240

Here in my pocket I've got a ball of string and glue.

Green green slime, goes on my head.

This to the tune of the hit TV show *WKRP*:

Hey there, if you've ever wondered
Wondered, where is that creep Timmy?
I'm living on the air at Piccadilly;
Piccadilly that's the one for me!

The speed of the team is the speed of the boss, and I was very fast. Everything had to be prepped, practised, crystalised and perfect by the time it got to air. There's no point in a link that doesn't deliver. Every night we worked and created and experimented, and tried to make the show better and funnier and faster and more important than ever. I sent Nobby Nolevel in the radio car down to the Apollo Theatre to review the pop concerts. Tina Turner was getting changed when Nobby walked into her dressing room and began a live interview, and then he got the kids outside afterwards to scream about how great it all was and sing her hits. A gangly goth-type 17-year-old came in to write and sing jingles on his keyboards about Wing Commander Timmy. 'Join Timmy's airforce!' That was Brian Cox before his D:Ream and 'wonderful professor of the stars and planets' days. A young Nick Robinson – back when being a political editor and hosting Radio 4's *Today* programme were a distant dream – was proud to play a colourful pimple zit in a Timmy sketch at Piccadilly. Listeners would offer up their own homemade jingles, and if they were any good, they'd be invited in to take part: they had nicknames like the Piccadilly Posers, Atherton Armpits, Bury Bozos, Worsley Worms.

TOTT spells Timmy on the Tranny,
build a shed, lock up your granny!

Tears for Fears, Captain Sensible, George Michael, Duran
Duran, Paul Weller, Toyah Wilcox, INXS, Spandau Ballet,
Culture Club, H2O, Tracey Ullman, Big Country, Eurythmics,
Kajagoogoo, Thompson Twins, Frankie Goes to Hollywood,
Howard Jones and Paul Young all made the journey up to
Manchester each time they had a record out, to be on the
show. 'If you're having trouble with your schoolwork we've
got someone who can help . . .' Nobby took Simon le Bon
round to someone's house in Levenshume and he had a go at
the girl's maths assignment, while her slightly bemused mum
and dad offered him a cuppa. Competition time: Win Boy
George's mascara; win Howard Jones's sock, and win your
height in records *NOW!* 'What's the name of Nik Kershaw's
wife?' (Answer turned out to be Mrs Kershaw.) 'Who wants a
full-size breeze block, a thermalite brick?!' This was prompted
by Wing Commander Timmy speaking to his airforce: 'Over!
Kkrr. Time to "thermalise" cred or troppo hits'; we gave away a
crate load of thermalite bricks from the manufacturer, who was
delighted with the bizarre publicity!

Pop stars wanted our help. Madonna was in town with her
first record, 'Holiday'. She was playing at the wrong venue,
the Hacienda, which was full of older fans of New Order, and
needed some screaming kids to show up. Could I help, please?
We packed the place with *Timmy on the Tranny* listeners and
the volume was extraordinary. She gave us her phone number.
A couple of weeks later, when she was number one, I rang her –
the number had changed. It didn't matter: we got Aunty Boney
to do an American voice and pretend to be her mum saying
she'd gone to the shops.

Lots of things combined to make *TOTT* an addictive pop show with an infectious energy. There was the exuberance of 80s pop and its stars; roll up to Timmy's merry-go-round . . . I play a micro selection of song snippets, and the lucky caller shouts stop on their favourite, gets to introduce it, wins a signed copy and a message from the star. We took chart toppers out on summer Funday Sunday roadshows: a double-decker bus bedecked with Piccadilly Radio banners, and a two-hour extravaganza followed that would be exhilarating, chaotic and ever so slightly confusing. There were pop stars live, in person, in the local park, messy games with masses of foam and constant screaming; was this a visual spectacle or a radio show? Combining the two always seemed to be a challenge, but a lot of fun. Maybe it was all practice for my next step – TV.

On this ride I'm savouring the pungent aroma of eucalyptus forests, the cash crop of Galicia. This crisp grey-green fragrance is all around me as I cycle the glorious scallop-shaped coast, bathed in sunshine, looking at potential painting images opening up through the dappled light – secret chapels, extensive shorelines, exotic flora, locals working.

Around each headland Finisterre becomes clearer and nearer. The water is like a magnet, drawing me closer to my destination. Last time I saw the sea was weeks ago – the cold grey windswept English Channel at Mont St Michel. This feels worlds away – like countries crossed, destination reached.

For those on the Camino, Finisterre is a must. I want to head as far west as I can go, and see what happens. I'm looking out at the sea, where the shellfish pots are visible. It's along this coast that the body of St James was supposedly brought ashore in his stone boat, surrounded by the distinctive scallop shells, the symbol of the pilgrim, that appear all around me.

I'm about to reach my furthest point, which I need to mark somehow. The large recycling bin between the bus stop and the shore gives me an idea. There are squillions of empty glass bottles in the bottle bank and one in particular, a beautiful blue gin bottle with a star on it and a bright orange cap, catches my attention.

Riding into Finisterre, I do a phone interview with Debbie McGee on BBC local radio. I like Debbie and she wants to tell me about a TV show she's been on with a bunch of celebrities walking bits of the Camino. 'Cyclists got in the way of us walkers! Finisterre was a let-down when we got there.' It isn't really what I want to hear when I've pedalled from home and had nothing but happy exchanges with other pilgrims.

The municipal *albergue* near the harbour is where I go to get the Finisterre Compostela certificate. There's a tiny office with a pleasant lady on the phone. Without finishing her chat she slides the glass window open, pulls out a certificate from the desk drawer and holds out her hand. 'Name please?' she asks, putting the receiver on the desk. The pilgrim passport is alongside photos of the bishop, the Prime Minister and Martin, and I begin to explain about my brother with Down's syndrome, reaching my potential, the blessing from the bishop and letter from the PM. She interrupts, picks up the phone again: '*Momento!*'

Then she stamps my pilgrim passport, puts my name on the certificate and pulls out a second one. Adjusting her specs, she looks at Martin's photograph, smiles, makes a little comment and hands me a certificate in Martin Mallett's name. 'Well done, Martin. *Buen Camino*, both of you,' she says.

I'm taken aback. I had been certain she wasn't listening to a word. There's a lump in my throat and my eyes begin blinking. We shake hands, smile and she shuts the glass with a wave and picks up the phone to carry on her conversation.

So much more meaningful and enjoyable than the Compostela occasion in Santiago.

I pedal up the last three kilometres and arrive by the lighthouse at the end of the world. Here's the last waymarker, signifying I've reached my destination. For some reason it's a powerful, emotional moment. I've seen hundreds of these waymarkers every day, usually covered in stones.

But this one . . .

Bare, marked with the kilometres: 0.00. The end and the beginning – the alpha and the omega. You can understand why I'm at the lighthouse the whole afternoon. I know I must paint this scene. The clear, bright blue sky, the azure sea, the waymarker, my bike and red panniers, the yellow spring flowers all around, and my backpack and a boot on the pillar to signify 'ma bubba' on his journey with me.

Nearby is a statue of a boot, where pilgrims traditionally burn their smelly pilgrimage clothes, and the signpost 'Let peace prevail everywhere'. A name tag goes on the lighthouse fence.

I have this blue glass bottle. It can't be plastic – I don't want to pollute the oceans. A glass bottle – well, even if it doesn't float, it can't get into the food chain. This looks like the perfect place to leave a message in a bottle in the sea, with a photo of brother Martin, his name tag, a map, a piece of Aberdeen granite, a Timmy pic of the cycling artist and a message. In fact, far too much! I can't get half of it through the neck of the bottle. Hilarious! A poignant message in a bottle, but it doesn't fit. The contents become much more modest, and then it's launch time.

There's a little beach with crashing waves, but when it comes to casting it into the sea, this is a boomerang bottle. Half a dozen times I throw it into the waves and back it comes, every time. This is not meant to be. There is something meaningful about the effort of finding a suitable bottle, filling it and locating the launch spot. And then the sea rejecting it. Sometimes, the best laid plans . . . I wonder if this is a story with a part two. I can imagine Martin laughing and shrugging his shoulders. 'No go!' he'd say. 'Never mind!'

I've got my own room at a lovely *albergue* at the entrance to Finisterre, where Rosa and her daughter look after pilgrims from across the world. A smiling bearded German man, Jan, and I have a spirited chat over a beer about his hometown of Berlin, and Brexit.

'Does Britain not like us?' he asks.

'Of course we do!'

It's an evening of talk, paint and beer, and before I set off next day I leave a watercolour piece for the *albergue* and an illustrated page in the visitors' book.

The weather now is more like I am used to. April showers, spring sunshine, cloud cover. We Brits are defined by our weather – I suppose because it changes all the time. When someone asks you about a trip it always begins with, 'How was the weather?' The climate today is a reminder that sooner or later I need to turn for home. A short stop to sketch the weird Galician storage barns is interrupted by a goat that comes across to nibble me and the picture, and the painting experience is abruptly cut even shorter by a rain shower.

At Muxía, 40 kilometres from Finisterre, is the special chapel by the sea that pilgrims head to. At this symbolic place, I'm finding myself tickled by funny moments. I've already chuckled at the boomerang bottle. Nearby, there's the football stadium and a stray ball that I can kick into the water for a 'wash-in'. By the chapel there's a weird curved rock to crawl through. It apparently brings you good luck if you manage it nine times and is reputed to fix any back problems. That's according to Herbert, the Austrian pilgrim I meet. I manage, just, to crawl through the rock. It's a struggle, and very funny. Herbert says, 'Good luck. I think, for you, once is enough.'

This is the spot that features in the film *The Way*, where the main character, Tom Avery, played by Martin Sheen, comes to spread the remaining ashes of his dead son as the culmination of his Camino. My Martin also has what feels like a particularly apt ceremony in the small wall surrounding the chapel. He got his certificate at Finisterre to mark his journey with me and this little moment with the never-ending sound of the sea is nicely symbolic.

Then I do a thoughtful watercolour, delaying the inevitable. At some stage I have to turn around and leave the sea, the Atlantic wind, the crashing waves, the salty smell and the pounding surf. I have to turn for home, if only to collect some different clothes and fresh underwear.

But there's more than that. I've got commitments at home: there are show dates, obligations to entertain, and my family are rightly asking for my attention. Come on, face the other way.

Try it.

I'm expecting that it will be a little bit of an anticlimax now. I've done it, right? Just head the other way and all will be well.

Don't be too sure, Mallett. My journey will lead over the mountains, in storms, with the clock ticking . . .

21

The long and winding road

Sometimes the best way to see where we are going is to look in the other direction at where we've been. It's surprising what the route back reveals about the course ahead, and what it is that makes us say yes to an offer we might otherwise have overlooked. These are true stories, Wideawakers . . .

Home is still a long way away, almost a thousand kilometres along the quickest and shortest route available, and will take several weeks via Santander, a ferry that runs only on particular days, and the notorious Bay of Biscay.

But now I've turned around towards Santiago and beyond.

The waymarkers have split.

One sign points to Muxía.

The other to Finisterre.

I've been to both.

It's time to head for a new, very ancient, route.

In the dorm at Olveiroa there's a perpetual traveller, Jonathan from Newark, who is now on his hundred and fourth country. That sounds impressive and somewhat obsessive. I don't need to visit every country in the world, just as long as I can remember something about each one I do see.

For instance, standing on the equator and watching the water going straight down the drain. Ten paces north and it swirls clockwise, ten paces south and it's anticlockwise – 'Kenya believe it?' Of course you can! Standing on the North Cape in the land of the midnight sun – revealing I'm closer to Canada over the North Pole than to London – 'Nor-way!'; in Russia, meeting mad, wild-haired RaspuTimmy (who looks a lot like me) in Leningrad; being in Italy, the home of cousin Spaghetti Malletti (who also looks a lot like me!), where I actually swam in the Grand Canal in Venice (am I mad?); touring Morocco on a magic carpet! – and joining the Foreign Legion armed, of course, with Mallett's Mallet to take on the fierce marauding Berbers; WAC like an Egyptian with Queen Hatchetsoup in the Valley of the Kings; and in Malaysia, meeting giant leatherback turtles on the beach in the hour they were born.

Wacaday was one of those shows that happened by chance, for which I am eternally grateful. Roland Rat left TV-am on the Friday to join the BBC – 'Rat leaves sinking ship' was the headline – and my new show began the following Monday morning, with some cartoons, a wacky 'make' from cardboard tubes and egg cartons ('Here's how to build the 8:15 from Paddington') and me presenting with a puppet called Terry. *Wacaday* got its name as a variation on WAC – the *Wide Awake Club*, the Saturday morning show. At this extraordinary time, I was doing four nights a week of *Timmy on the Tranny* on the radio in Manchester and then travelling down to London for Timmy on the Telly and the *Wide Awake Club* at the weekends. I wasn't sure at this stage that TV would become a comfortable home for me; and breakfast telly was just so new anyway, would anybody watch it? It turned out, in a very short time, everyone watched.

TV-am began in February 1983 and I was invited to do a pilot cooking programme that came to nothing. Then I was asked to host the Saturday morning kids' show *Summer Run*, an end-of-the-pier Blue Screen links show (where the pier was projected over the blue background). One of our first guests was a very young magician called Richard Cadell. You can see him today keeping the magic of Sooty and Sweep alive on *The Sooty Show*. Well done, Richard.

This morning I'm seeing Galicia in thick morning mist and it's a stunning gift to paint. Immediately I set to work capturing the storage *hórreos*, strange looking huts on mushroom-shaped posts that are a prominent feature of north-western Spain. They're shelters for grain, crops and household stuff, and the inverted posts stop vermin climbing inside. They make magnificent architectural structures to portray as the morning sun burns away the haze.

I ride through the hills, engrossed in the landscape, and take a wrong turn. I need to do a huge detour. I don't mind. Detours are an opportunity, and on a nice day I'm happy to see where they lead. I come across Marco the Frenchman, who's been walking the Camino from his home in Picardy since last October . . . Poor fella is starving, so I give him my lunch of fruit and chocolate.

There's an odd smell and the bike starts squealing. It's an urgent issue with my front brake pads. This is a surprise, because a week ago the service hadn't flagged anything up. Now the disc brakes are burning hot and they scream and stink when I apply them. Not good. But it's Saturday afternoon in Santiago, and everyone is at siesta. I'm stuck. Back at my favourite help point, Tourist Information, they send me to the out-of-town shopping centre and the big sports superstore, where I'm relieved they are able to get me going again, safely. I don't ever want to cycle without brakes.

But now the afternoon is dominated by angry storm clouds, and I'm caught in a torrential hailstorm on the outskirts of the city at Monte do Gozo, alongside the statue of two huge metal pilgrims with their arms aloft at the magical sight of the promised land – the gleaming spires of Santiago Cathedral. This is usually the first sight of Santiago for pilgrims; a view to lift the spirits because you've made it. For me it is the goodbye view, and the weather is a metaphor for this part of my trip. Exceptional cataclysmic conditions.

A dripping wet Martin name tag is pinned to a tree overlooking the city. I say my fond farewells and head eastwards into the storm, very relieved my brakes work.

About a month ago I had an email from someone I've never met, who knows son Billy from the football, and is a friend of a friend. Andy Fernandez introduced himself as an English Spaniard whose family lives along the Camino Francés and would be very happy to welcome me to their home. It's a little strange to accept the hospitality of someone you don't know, but I think of the other acts of random kindness that have been offered to me, and feel it might be good to accept. Andy and I have introduced ourselves on the phone in different time zones.

He is at the last game of the season this afternoon – Maidenhead winning a thrilling 5-2 game against Bromley – and throughout the second half, he gives me directions to his mum and dad's place, nearly 30 kilometres away. With the bike issues and wet weather, I am at the end of battery life on bike and phone, so he sends his mum out with an umbrella to look out for me! There is his poor mother standing in the rain, waiting for someone she has never met, on a bike and likely to be wet and muddy. It's an unusual dripping sodden introduction.

Carmen and Jesus are kindness itself. Having retired from Berkshire they headed to their family home in Galicia, where they live on the outskirts of their little town. Neither of them drives, and it's a daily walk of a couple of kilometres to O Pedrouzo for supplies. Jesus has acute arthritis, which limits many of his movements. After years of work at Eton College kitchens he can now barely lift a spoon. But his smile, and the warm embrace of the moment, is lovely. He spends each morning watching the daily church service on TV. Rich in colour, music, ceremony and familiarity, I can easily understand why it's so appealing. Carmen, in her housecoat apron, is happiest being a generous hostess. The couple's English is good, their smiles are even better. We talk of their son Andy (whom I've only met on the phone), families around the world, why they prefer Galician rain to English drizzle and how it's a shame I don't eat meat, because Galician meat is the best in the world.

Conversation is one of life's great pleasures. My mum loved a good chat. For her it was like a good meal. It needed to be enjoyed slowly and savoured. Then she would come back for more . . . Now that's a Mallett thing. 'What do you think about such and such?' My mum would often reply, 'I'm going to think about that for a few days and come back to you.' Sometime later, when you'd forgotten all about it, she'd say, 'I've got something to add to what we were discussing a week ago!' Her best exchanges were in her letters. Mum always wrote as if we were having a chat. 'You'll never guess what happened to me when . . .' What a story-teller she was. Unlike my dad, who couldn't tell a story to save his life. 'What did you do in the war, Dad? Did you kill anyone?'

'Er, no. I was in India in the Pay Corps and only held a gun once, guarding paperwork on a train. We weren't shown how to use the gun and we weren't given any ammunition. I just did deskwork.'

Boring. (But you'll see later what he did do in India and why it was so important to him . . .)

'What about you, Mum? Tell us a story.'

Then Mum would relate how she'd been born in early November in the first winter of the First World War. Her dad arrived at the hospital in uniform to check on his new-born daughter and her mother. 'Why are you in uniform, Will? They won't want you; you're far too old, nearly 40, and anyway it'll be over by Christmas.'

'No, it won't be over by then, and they are going to need everybody,' said my grandfather, who went on to win the Military Cross and became a lieutenant colonel in his regiment, commanding his battalion. While leading an assault on the Hindenburg Line in September 1918, German shells smashed him out of the front line and into an officers' hospital back in Blighty. His wife wrote to the family, 'Will's coming home, safely wounded!' When finally the war ended and the country rejoiced, little Nancy, aged four, burst into tears. She didn't want her father returning home and taking all the attention from her mum!

It's after lunch, when the rain eases slightly, that I leave a little painted watercolour for Carmen and Jesus's fridge door. I can't go before the incense and bells of the morning service from the TV have echoed around the house. We're sorry to leave one another, but I've got an exceptional distance to cover. My dear hosts, thank you for the biscuits, the fruit, the pasta, the chocolate and the little bottle of wine you stashed in my bag!

And this is where the Camino changes brilliantly. Because I'm now going the other way – backwards – I meet more people. Instead of people's backpacks and stooped shoulders I'm seeing faces. Hundreds of them. In a couple of hours this afternoon I count over 700 pilgrims rushing westwards, most walking, some on horseback, several in wheelchairs. It's a never-ending torrent of people covered from head to toe in enormous ponchos that make them look like trolls bowed under the weight of their covered backpacks. I'm on what feels like the M1 motorway of pilgrims, and everyone is heading in the opposite direction.

Two highlights this afternoon. First is finding the exact spot where Gary's bike chain snapped over five years ago. We'd walked five kilometres (in the rain, obviously) into town and luckily found a bike repair place. It's still there, only it's shut today, on Sunday, so don't break your chain again, Mallett.

The other is the well-placed bus stop in a field between town and village offering shelter from the hailstorm. There's no obvious reason why it would be there, but I'm glad someone thought of it, because it's very welcome.

I like public transport. We grew up waiting for the bus to Stockport, always sitting on the top deck by the front windows so that we felt the turns around every corner. Each town would have its own coloured municipal buses – green for the SHMD (Stalybridge, Hyde, Mossley, Dukinfield), blue for Ashton, purple for Oldham, red and white for Stockport. We tried bus-spotting for a brief time, but it was never as much fun as train-spotting. Brother Paul was the expert; he knew every type of locomotive, which region it ran on and why it was important. Dad tried sending him numbers when he went anywhere, but unless you see them yourself, said Paul, it doesn't count.

At boarding school, we watched the steam trains run across the viaduct from Arnside to Barrow-in-Furness. They were steam-hauled right until the end came in the summer of 1968. Paul was one of the lucky ones who went on the final British Rail steam train from Manchester Victoria to Carlisle Citadel and back. It was late, of course, and filthy, and teenage Paul joined the throngs of souvenir rail enthusiasts who rushed up to the steam engine and handed their tickets to the driver and fireman to sign. In the crush my brother lost his ticket. Several weeks later it turned up in the post with a letter from the engine driver. 'Paul, we found your ticket in the cab and traced it through the souvenir serial number. Hope you enjoyed the trip. We did.' What a memorable gesture.

All our holidays were reached by train – Llanfairfechan in North Wales, Skipton, the Lake District, the south coast, London and Edinburgh – and when Martin went to Aberdeen we complained, 'That's at the other end of the world!'

'Nonsense! It's only four trains away,' said Dad. 'To Manchester, change station, to Preston, change train, to Glasgow, change station, to Aberdeen . . . and taxi.'

We didn't take many taxis. They were a luxury. Until, that is, I bought my first car. It was shortly after passing my driving test that I went out one day with a shopping list – coffee, comb, car. At the supermarket I bought coffee and a comb. On the way home, there was a car for sale in the street. It was a black London taxi – an Austin FX4. I bought it and took the shopping home in it. My brilliant first car! Once, at the traffic lights on a rainy day, a lady got in with all her shopping and sopping wet umbrella. It didn't matter that I had a couple of friends with me. She sat in the back chatting away and giving me directions. We dropped her at her house and told her the trip was free cos it was raining.

I loved that taxi, except without a headrest it wasn't very comfortable on long trips, but at least, if I was feeling mischievous, I could get away with driving in the bus and taxi lanes.

It's so wet I call an end to the day at Melide, a grey town that has the feeling of a stopover to somewhere, anywhere, much more exciting.

This evening, I'm looking at the daunting map with all those hills between here and Oviedo . . . Is this a good idea to take the Camino Primitivo? It's strange how decisions can become more and more difficult, almost like mountains in themselves to climb. In this case they are real mountains and I'm not exactly confident.

Back in the dim and distant past, even before black and white TV – around AD 700 – the King of Castile began the tradition of pilgrimage to Santiago from his home in Oviedo. His route, the one I'm on, is known as the Camino Primitivo, and it feels a little primitive. Big mountain ranges, deep valleys, wild weather. I get lots of shaking heads and sucking in of breath and looks of sympathy. *Be kind to yourself,* I say over breakfast. *Take things easy and just try it.* It's the last day of April, the sky is grey and wet, wind blows the stinging rain into my face. It couldn't be more foreboding. Everyone else is heading the other way, but I've got a lunch date to keep.

I climb the hilly lanes, rattle over the cattle grids, weave through the pleading, bleating sheep and come across poor George, a lone pilgrim from Marbella, who's waving at me cos he's suffering from a stomach complaint. I have something at the bottom of my medical kit and give him enough for four days, together with a banana and a swig of whisky from my little hip flask.

George is a very happy pilgrim after that . . .

Being in the right place at the right time feels good. As a way of giving thanks, when I get to the next village I leave a Martin name tag on the tree beside the church and ring the bell for him. Along the road, a farmer is bringing home his herd of cattle. It's a domestic scene as old as the hills, the cows leading the way because they know that home means comfort and security, and it prompts me to call Mrs Mallett.

Dear Mrs M is in Melbourne at the hospital with her mum. Maisie is to be 100 years old in two days' time, and yesterday she fell off the loo and broke her neck. She's in a neck brace, poorly but more concerned about everyone else. 'Hello, Timmy dear. How are you getting on?' Maisie always checks on everyone else first. Before I can ask about her, she says, 'Are you all right all on your own on that bike? I'm worried about you. All that way by yourself; I'm very proud.' We are both impressed with each other, and she's concerned and I'm anxious. I'm also aware that this could be the last time I ever get to speak to her. 'I love you, Maisie.'

'I love you too, Timmy. Bye bye, Timmy. Bye bye.' Maisie is always the one to end the call, as it might be costing a lot.

Home. The cows and the farmer are heading there. I'm on the way home too. Billy calls me. 'Just checking you're OK. Have you heard about Granny?' Here we are across the globe, keeping in touch and thinking of one another.

I come over the hill out of the downpour into the stunning walled Roman city of Lugo for my lunch date. Five weeks ago in France, I met my first pilgrim, Gretel, who is walking from Ghent, and here we are with our paths crossing again. Gretel will be in Santiago in a few days and will be flying home on Monday. She's been an inspiration and an encouragement all the way, so it's lovely to share a lunch together and I give her a little watercolour to remember our Camino. In exchange Gretel tells me she's organised the best place for me to stay tonight, in a little town called Castroverde (it's probably the only place to stay). By the end of the year Gretel will be unable to walk, because of a debilitating muscle condition. This Camino will be her sixth and final.

In the centre of Lugo is the football stadium. The team are in Spanish league two (rivals Oviedo) and they kindly give me a couple of souvenir pins for my tie. Stepping out on to the pitch I can see the rows of empty stands and I'm instantly wondering how long it would take to sit on each one.

In autumn 1985 I sat on every seat at Manchester City and Manchester United raising money for Live Aid, non-stop for three days. We called it Seat Aid. It went like this.

Down at pitch side next to the dugouts, pull down a plastic seat and sit on it, pull down the one next to it and slide across to sit on that. Now do it again and again, until I get to the end of the row. Stand up, go up one step and start again going the other way. And so on for as long I can. 'Ha ha!' laughs everyone. 'Bet your bum will be sore doing that!' I have padding down my trousers and look a sight with an enormous behind. But it's not my backside; it's my wrists and knees that start to let me know about it. My knees, because I'm sitting all the time until I change rows and then they ache as I stand up. My wrists are involved in constantly pulling down each plastic seat, which springs up again automatically after I've moved on. Hour after hour after hour.

My friend Cari was in charge of keeping my spirits up, checking off the rows on her map of the stadiums and keeping me fed and watered. The lady with the food stall outside Maine Road gave us giant pies. 'Take a break,' Cari said after every hour. Manchester City's stadium was massive, and I was aware that Old Trafford would be bigger. The food and drink kept me energised until 11 p.m. when it was time to stop for the night and bed down in a sleeping bag on the blue carpet of the directors' box lounge. We were up again and sitting down very early and under pressure. It didn't help that someone had opened the wrong door and an alarm went off. There was a home match that afternoon and it was the big derby game against Manchester United. People would be coming and taking their seats early afternoon.

But there was good news. Maine Road had rows of wooden seats at the home end. I could just slide along these and they were suddenly much quicker. But they needed to be. I finished sitting on Manchester City's 25,000 seats barely half an hour before kick-off; and I finished a bit too quickly. Ouch! Splinter in the wrong place and I couldn't stay to watch the game. 'Come on, Timmy; we've got to get over to Old Trafford and the groundsmen are letting us in . . .'

It was such an effort to start again at the dugouts and slide along the red seats of United's ground. We listened to the game on the radio that September afternoon as the reds ran riot and beat City 3-nil. Cari was a massive United fan and very happy, doing little jumps in the air as each goal went in. The energy of the day kept me going and by midnight I was well on my way around the ground. The two of us in the massive empty stadium; Cari, so excited, with the keys to her beloved Old Trafford. 'Here you go, Cari; you're in charge tonight,' said the groundsman.

We rested in the away dressing room, one of us in the bath. Sunday morning it was cold and gloomy, and I needed to wrap up as my limbs started aching more and more. But then we were joined by well-wishers. Pop stars came to cheer us along – Captain Sensible ('Hey Timmy, that's not very sensible!'), the Belle Stars and Strawberry Switchblade came along and sang their encouragement. My friend Michele brought tuna sand-wiches and a kiss for good luck, and Piccadilly Radio brought along an outside broadcast unit and big crowd for an emotional finish. A total of 55,000 seats were sat on. I am very proud of it.

And which was my favourite seat?

The last one!

I spend the final day of April pedalling in frequent heavy hail and rain showers. Is this weather ever going to be kind to me? I'm steaming, and in Castroverde there's Anna coming out of a modest hostel to greet me. 'Hello, you must be Timmy. We are expecting you . . .'

To be expected, welcomed and embraced is lovely. I'm the only person staying here tonight. So ends my first eventful day on the Primitivo.

22

The puncture

Ever felt as though you need some sympathy? No chance! When things go wrong, let's make it worse!

It's May Day morning – crisp, cold, minus three degrees, with bright blue skies. In Oxford, they'll be singing from the top of Magdalen Tower at 6 a.m. Students will start the day drinking, and as always there'll be someone who thinks it's a good idea to jump off the bridge into the shallow River Cherwell. When I lived in my rented house in James Street, east Oxford (still rented out to lots of students), I could hear the singing from my kitchen.

I'm steadily working my way up the long mountain climbs on the reliable, dependable Timmeee E-bike; through the clouds to the top, by the wind farm in the snow, listening to the turbines turning in the breeze. It's my favourite month of May, and there's snow. I feel today will be a painting and pedalling day.

Each morning I plot a start and a possible finish point on my GPS, with a few places to explore, and on this occasion it delivers winding empty lanes along soft green folds of the hills, where I don't see a soul for many hours. I'm absorbed in the arrival of spring in the mountains, and the few locals I meet comment in awe on the bike. They don't get many cyclists here.

I stop to sketch old farm buildings and then draw long-horned bulls in the fields.

This kilometre or two takes ages because, as I cycle into the woods, a watery scene tempts me to set up the acrylics and examine water, woods and an old shack. It's not an easy scene to capture until I remember the maxim 'Paint what you see, not what you know'. The light flickers through the brand new lime green foliage. Tall trees show off orange and yellow ochre lichen covering trunks and limbs. Rocks and stones in the cascading stream create a delicious cooling tinkling sound and there's the contrast of white foam and dark, burnt umber water holes. Ferns, with a DNA stretching back hundreds of millions of years, are unravelling in the light and shade patchwork of my paintbrushes. There's the mysterious deep shadow of the shack entrance where Martin's name tag rests in the old oak lintel. I've a limited palette of colours and this is deliberate. I want to establish the mood of what I'm seeing in the simplest way possible. It helps that blue sky and sunshine come through the new leaves and fill the whole image with a kaleidoscope of shades. I paint blobs of light and shade that eyes will transcribe into forms of the trees, shack and stream.

Painting what I see, not what I know, is my way to be completely and totally engrossed in this scene for an hour or so. Any longer and the shadows will change, the highlights will move. I wash my brushes and realise that I am doing what I had hoped I would do every day. Cycle a bit and paint a lot.

Onwards and upwards.

Downwards and onwards . . . the afternoon continues to deliver – the drawing of farmers with barrows and scythe; ladies chatting on a bench: slippers, clogs, shawls and aprons.

At a modest town improbably named Grandas I stop for the day. There is the promise of some stunning views to enjoy tomorrow and I want to be fresh and ready to paint if I'm inspired . . .

Trusting that nothing will happen to the bike.

Next day is without a doubt the most scenic and spectacular day on the Camino Primitivo. The lake is sublime, the mountains encompassing and dramatic as I freewheel down seven kilometres. A highlight of my Camino. But with every high comes an equal and opposite low . . .

Because there's the weather. After the sunshine comes the rain – deliberate, relentless, with temperatures in single figures all day and a climb that goes up and up and up . . . for 14 twisting, turning, never-ending, ever-steeper kilometres, along the road, without a break.

This is tougher than the Iron Cross climb or the ascent from St Jean up the Pyrenees.

Pssssst. The back wheel feels wrong. I've got a puncture. Bikes are always getting punctures. Except this bike. In seven weeks and nearly 3,000 kilometres of cycling across Europe, I have had no tyre issues at all. Not even needed to pump them up. Today, up a mountain, in the rain, it happens. There's a sinking feeling . . . Off with the panniers, turn the bike upside down. Remove the back wheel and take out the inner tube. I call Rich, the bike man in Beaconsfield, for some reassurance as the clouds close in and the rain goes pitter patter on my poncho. It's not that I can't fix a puncture. Everyone who has a bike knows how to do it. It's just that I want to make sure I haven't missed anything. On your own in these conditions, weary, wet and alone, it would be easy to forget the basics.

Rich answers the phone. 'Hello, Timmy. What have you done?!' he laughs.

'How did you know? I've got a puncture.'

'It's the back tyre, isn't it? It always is . . .'

I follow his instructions and I've got a little emergency pump that pushes the pressure up to 50 psi. 'Yeah, that should do until you get to the next garage and use a pressure tyre filler to get it up closer to eighty psi.'

I must have done something right because I never had to pump up the tyres again. That Timmeee E-bike is amazing.

Over the pass at 1,150 metres I can't see a thing. The rain cloud is all around me, visibility has gone, my specs have misted up and are covered in raindrops. I start to laugh. It's one of those days when the rain will never end and the only thing I can do is keep going with a grin until I reach a café where I can thaw out and drip dry. I've only been to two other places that have been as wet. Cape Town in June when the Antarctic brought in 48 hours of never-ending rain and we only had a couple of days to film our *Wacaday* adventures; and Far North Queensland in March, the rainy season (known as 'the wet'), where we learned to play backgammon during a solid week of monsoon. 'Don't ever ask me to live here full time,' said Mrs Mallett, and she meant it. I don't know why she's so surprised by weather. On her first day in England in April 1988 she had looked out of the window at the white stuff coming down. 'Is that blossom falling?' she asked.

'No, that's snow.'

By late afternoon the rain has stumped me. Time to stop at a pilgrim hostel in a four-star palatial hotel. This sounds different. Believe me, it is.

The pilgrim hostel is attached to an upmarket hotel in a medieval monastery in Tineo, with a steam room and some comfort, and I take the opportunity to set up a little studio in the bar and paint the puncture scene. Then there's the best food on my travels. Fish stew followed by a mountain of fruit salad. I love this meal. It's wholesome, tasty, and I understand it. This evening I learn not to be taken in by appearances.

I haven't met many Brits on this trip, only eight in total, including Gary and Tony whom I already knew. A couple of walkers tonight at dinner are from the UK and the table appears dismissive of my cycle ride. There is a definite air of me not being a 'true pilgrim'. They quickly turn their attention elsewhere in the way people do when they feel that someone is not one of them. Maybe cyclists offend? It's a shame really; we're all just making an extremely long journey. Mrs Mallett has a maxim from her father, who used to say, 'If you find yourself with people you don't easily gel with, make an effort to find out what makes them tick.' Easier said than done. There are six of us in an otherwise empty restaurant, and we're all together because we are the pilgrims. Weirdly it reminds me of my time in the jungle for TV.

Nearly two years before *I'm a Celebrity . . . Get Me Out of Here!* I was in an ITV reality show about a courtroom jury, which never went to air. The first thing they wanted us to do was elect a jury foreman. Then we spent a whole week listening to evidence of a fictitious murder and had to decide whether the accused was guilty or not. The case itself was completely flawed. The scriptwriters seemed to be making it up as they went along.

The jury room was the centre of attention. They put together an interesting cast – comedian Julian Clary, medium Derek Acorah, Lee Ryan from Blue, art critic Brian Sewell, Nancy Dell'Olio, lawyer and one-time girlfriend of England football manager Sven Goran Eriksson, actress Wendy Richard, TV presenter June Sarpong, and TV host and ex-politician Robert Kilroy-Silk, our elected jury foreman. The arguments went around the room day after day and we ended up being more interested in what was for lunch, so the producers decided to put a bit of spice into the show. By having a vote for a new jury foreman. To see what would happen, I threw my hat into the ring and I narrowly won. And then something extraordinary happened. Kilroy talked the room out of their decision. 'Well, of course I can change, if you want me to do it differently. I can do this or that . . .' and after ten minutes of this, he announced, 'So let's have another vote – do you really want someone untried like Timmy, or me?'

It was amazing. He kept going until he'd done just enough to get someone, just one person, to change their vote and give him another chance. A master politician at work. We took a break for the producers to consider what to do next. I was standing at the urinal (with my mic unplugged) when Robert Kilroy-Silk walked in and stood right next to me. 'I know what you are doing, and I won't have it,' he said. I'm there with my zip down having a personal moment. Everyone knows the rule: if you can, always leave an empty space in a row of urinals.

'I can see what you are up to and I will not be beaten by you,' declared the politician.

Amazing. This man really needs it. It's a TV show, for good-ness' sake, I thought. I found Julian Clary and said to him, 'Our beloved leader has just gone off on one . . .'

'Don't give it any attention, Timmy. It'll all blow over; stay true to yourself . . .'

As I said, the show never even made it to air. It cost them a fortune to make, too.

But . . .

Over 18 months later, I was approached to be on *I'm a Celebrity . . . Get Me Out of Here!* 'We can't tell you who else is in the jungle; we want you to be a late entrant.' In the photo ses-sion for the title sequence the producer started acting strangely, and I became suspicious. I guessed they had a conflict up their sleeve, and I reckoned they might have someone particularly difficult. They did. I guessed correctly, and what a conflict it turned out to be.

In this series I came in late, with a huge character, ex-Dollar singer David Van Day. Captured in an enormous cargo net and imprisoned for a night in the tropical rain, we had to join ten other big characters all jostling for position. There were some vicious tongues in that camp and some desperately insecure people. It made for deeply unpleasant interactions and gripping TV. Camp commandant was (no surprise) Robert Kilroy-Silk, determined to make our lives hell. 'I've had history with Mallett,' he confided to the others, 'and he's not to be trusted.' The camp's moral compass came unexpectedly from cheeky cockney actor Joe Swash. Everyone loved him and he was a joy. Martina Navratilova gave sound advice before the tasks: 'If I was serving for the match and a nuclear bomb was about to go off, I'd hit that ball first. Focus,' she said. I was impressed with Martina. George Takei from *Star Trek* had a rich laugh, like liquid honey, that rolled around the camp and everyone else tried to keep up.

Brian Paddick, the ex-policeman turned politician, tried too hard, while model Nicola McLean had a tongue as sharp as razor blades. David Van Day had a plan and, wonderfully, amazingly, executed it to perfection.

In the live jungle trial, Kilroy had a series of ridiculous tasks to complete while being covered in slime and critters. It was hilarious, and I laughed. We were aware of what we had signed up for with the trials. You know you'll be asked to eat and drink disgusting things; you know you'll be covered in smelly horrible stuff. The bugs and challenges are part of the joy for the public watching. It was glorious. I loved it. Kilroy, covered in every conceivable bit of humiliating mess, went ballistic. He went to confront me as the titles rolled, and someone stepped in to protect me before things went too far. But the producers wanted more. They set me apart in a fibreglass cave, encouraged an 'us and him' mentality, and there was nothing I could do but grin and get on with it.

The producers of the show have little tactics they use. The crew are not allowed to speak to the contestants. They wear no watches, so you can't know the time; they constantly pull people out of camp and get them to stand and wait. Instil division. Make people nervous. Put them under pressure and wait for them to crack. There are over 100 cameras around the place and David Van Day worked them all. He took me down to the rock pool. 'Right, there's my close-up camera in that tree,' he said. 'I'm well lit by that sunbeam. Test, test, is my mic working OK? . . . If you're all ready in the gallery, then let's begin . . .' And he launched into an opinion about the women's bitching, bullies and the plot to get us. It was extraordinary, and I watched carefully. Mrs Mallett's advice before the show was clear: 'Don't pick your nose, don't weep, and don't stoop to gossiping behind someone's back.'

Kilroy was first out, of course, and others quickly fell by the wayside. I was buried in a coffin and covered with 50,000 meal-worms and cockroaches. (I can still smell them now.) They stood us in the tank of freezing cold water and fish guts for over an hour while I happily sang 'Itsy Bitsy' and told gags; I chased a herd of sheep and sheared them for a treat; all good fun and exactly what I expected. Next up I did a head-to-head drinking and eating contest with Brian, the tall, overbearing policeman, trying to be one of the gang. Metre-long sand worms, penis colada with bits in and a rather disagreeable piece of garnish. He beat me to revealing an empty mouth in the final challenge, but ruined his triumph by claiming I'd cheated.

I hadn't.

I left happily, with my head held high. Never voted out. Beaten in a tie break by an intimidating adversary.

There's a huge amount of ego and insecurity in that jungle environment. I've met other contestants over the years who have had a similar range of experiences, among them Yvette Fielding, the host of *Blue Peter* and *Most Haunted*, who said to me, 'We loved your performance in the jungle and couldn't believe the way they treated you . . .'

Lots of participants see *I'm a Celebrity* as a way of helping to build their career. Indeed, it's done wonders for all sorts of entertaining people – Joe Swash, Mylene Klass, Mark Wright, Stacey Solomon, Scarlett Moffatt from *Gogglebox*, Harry Redknapp, and most famously Peter Andre and Katie Price. But for many others it's a flash in the pan; over and done with before the credits have finished rolling.

For me, it was supposed to be a bit of fun. I collected the paper bark our camp food was wrapped in each evening and used it in my paintings of the jungle when I got home. I'm used to the great outdoors, happy in my own space, so I was ready to have a go at the trials, the cooking, the jungle encampment life. I didn't relate to the sharp swords of jealousy, desperation and bitter words of hatred. I'm secure in who I am and what I can do. I've never needed fame for reassurance of my worth. I have a happy family, a comfortable life. Fame is part of my job. It has no worth beyond what it is – offering the opening for a pleasant word and the possibility of bringing a smile into the world. Fame for fame's sake can be dangerous. There needs to be a reason for it and hopefully that reason is something worthwhile.

Weirdly, the discomforting impact of *I'm a Celebrity* lasted longer than it should. Each year, as the new series came around, I'd get anxious, fearing that somehow, unbeknown to me, I was going to be asked to go through all the unpleasant bits with some difficult people all over again. I am disappointed that the producers pre-fit people into recognised slots – the funny one, the annoying one, the weedy one, the one we love to hate – and then use this pegging mercilessly. But hey, they're human too and the concept, though unsettling, sometimes works. Until it doesn't, and you have a complete blow-up.

They gave me the series on DVD. I've never watched it back.

Next day I ride out of the tiny town of Tineo on my Timmeee E-bike with a smile and some pleasant exchanges. I'm following the Camino signs down the other side of the mountain pass into the region of Asturias, with its rolling hills, pretty villages and the most photogenic motorway I've ever seen. Almost immediately, the signposts send me down a swampy mud track . . . Hmmm. I quickly decide to stick to the road instead and it winds around for ages beneath the motorway, studded with stunning monumental viaducts, which stylishly graces these hills. Sweeping sky-high roadways that weave in and out around the valleys. There's gracefulness in infrastructure and monuments such as Stonehenge and the ancient stone circles, the Pyramids, Roman amphitheatres and Roman roads, cathedrals and great temples; and since the Industrial Revolution, unexpected beauty in roads, railways, ships and high rises. This motorway on stilts has freed up the old way and I can freewheel down the empty tarmac admiring the elegant pillars as I go. The moral is: don't dismiss it just because it's a road. There's nothing wrong with a magnificent highway.

I'm picking up the fragrance of springtime from the country lanes, which are full of wild flowers, including giant heath spotted orchids definitely worthy of a painting. I set up the easel on the back of the bike and as I'm engrossed in the moment, pilgrim Sabrina, walking on her own from Paris, stops to chat. (This is a route with far fewer people, so there's greater willingness to stop and greet one another.) Our conversation covers the scenery, the route, accommodation, fear and pleasure in being alone, and reaching our potential. All in just a few minutes.

The last big city before Santander, Oviedo, is the capital of the region, an artist's city with a glorious gallery and a stunning cathedral. At the entrance desk they stamp and sign my pilgrim passport and I join the throng of people from all over the world who have come to see the relics.

In the Middle Ages, every church or monastery of any importance had a relic – a fragment of the true cross, a bone of a saint – and people would travel far and wide to see them, paying, of course, for the privilege. These days we are more sceptical. A piece of the true cross? There must be enough fragments to build a forest.

Or maybe it's just our Protestant upbringing. Oviedo Cathedral in northern Spain houses a holy chamber of relics brought back from the Crusades nearly a thousand years ago.

The most important and impressive of these is the shroud that covered Christ's body in the grave – the same cloth Mary Magdalene and the other women found when they discovered the empty tomb early on Easter morning. This piece of material has blood marks on it and there is a detailed interactive display highlighting what you can see. It's impressive. I view the shroud from behind a grille, inside the holy chamber – it's among a group of other ornate relics that shout out trying to overshadow it.

I stand there mildly interested. And then some nuns come in with their knowledgeable, priestly guide. They all kneel before the shroud in silence. And this is the moment. Forget the audio guide full of dull facts and dates. A tour party of nuns on their knees before a blood-stained shroud. Now I see the power of reliquary, and it's mesmerising. Faith is all about confidence in what you believe. Why should we need any physical confirmation?

Catholic churches and cathedrals are full of great works of art, powerful images of the suffering that goes with the faith. But an actual relic. To this day, it has a power to impress. It's difficult to understand with our modern urge for proof. We expect to see DNA matches or the sort of investigation that gave us the 'king in the car park'. King Richard III had lain under a Leicester city car park for 500 years (the first two hours were free!). He was found just a few feet down and the tell-tale skeleton and subsequent study revealed the story. These nuns in awe at the Oviedo shroud don't need proof. However differently we think of relics in different cultures, it calls for a little understanding.

I'm musing on the mummified Hand of St James that is kept in a cupboard at St Peter's Church, Marlow. Altogether, this has been an unexpectedly thought-provoking day.

The Oviedo altarpiece is one of the treasures of Spain, and I like the idea of a Martin Mallett name tag finding its way beside one of the gems of medieval European art. I stare at the gilt and gold. 'You me, ma bubba.' Now, alongside the sixteenth-century carving, Martin can say every day, 'Nice church!'

When we grew up, we were a two-church family. Each church preferred a different type of service, and confusingly, St Martin's, down the hill, was the High church, and All Saints, up on Marple Ridge, was the Low church. We took it in turns which we'd visit each week. Mum's family liked All Saints, where we sang Sunday school hymns with actions – 'Wide, wide as the ocean . . .' – and Dad's family liked the smells and bells of St Martin's, where Uncle Lucas is remembered on the war memorial. I can see the appeal of both types of service, but St Martin's has unique Mallett family ornaments. We will never know, but I suspect that brother Martin was named after this saint and the large St Christopher frieze that adorns the side chapel. He was baptised here Christopher Martin, though he was always known by his second name. As a child with wanderlust it was not surprising that Martin would find his way into the church, once lighting all the candles and singing his way through the hymn book.

Everything has a beginning and an ending. Our family's connection of 40 years with St Martin's ended when we moved from Marple in 1969. Then nearly five decades later I went back for a special Sunday gathering and was able to offer thanks for what it had taught us about spirituality.

The churchwarden staves have ornate silver tops dedicated to my grandfather, William Newman Mallett (see, it's another William Mallett), who was a churchwarden between the wars. They were a gift in his memory when he died, the year after I was born. Sadly, the silver tops were stolen and St Martin's began locking its doors in the daytime. But then, seven years after the incident, Ed the vicar had a knock at the door from the repentant thief, who had kept the silver tops in a plastic bag under his bed for all that time and wanted to return them. It was a privilege to attend their rededication and I wouldn't have missed it for anything.

Things can come full circle. Endings such as these are immensely special and restore our faith in human nature. Sometimes we just have to be patient. Here's a little prayer from the heart: 'Lord, give me patience, and give it to me NOW!'

23

As I stepped out one sunny morning . . .

If I ever find myself unexpectedly thinking of someone or somewhere or some time, there's usually a reason, a connection. I wonder if the more we aspire to, the more we can accomplish. Joseph in his amazing technicolor dreamcoat said that any dream will do, but not every hope is fulfilled in the way we expect.

This isn't about how fast or how far you can go. It's more about how much you can see, paint and absorb. I want to go slower, please, travel less and paint more . . . Towards the end of each country, each border, each Camino route, even each day, I find

I'm asking myself, 'Did I miss anything?' It's part of the 'reach my potential' theme that is running through me. There's a great big world out there and the one who sees and does the most wins.

So, Mallett, don't leave Oviedo until you've enjoyed what it has to offer.

I visited the cathedral last night and now there's the other cathedral to see – the theatre of dreams, as football fans call it. I go on the pitch at Oviedo FC, which is about to host a big game; I like stadiums. They are built to impress. Performing in a stadium is magical. At the Diamond Music Awards in Antwerp, my band Bombalurina were on the same stadium bill as Kylie Minogue, Duran Duran, Jimmy Somerville, Kim Wilde and the Human League, among others. At the airport, we were whisked through the VIP route and even had outriders as we were driven straight through the city to the stadium. There we performed an 'Itsy Bitsy' set to 18,000 people. What an atmosphere! What a thrill! What a noise! When people started fainting in front of us, I was really impressed. Until Holly Johnson, of Frankie Goes to Hollywood, said, 'Don't big yourself up, Timmy. Those girls aren't fainting over you. It's because it's so hot and the air conditioning isn't working!' Humiliation continued at the airport. I lost my ticket and couldn't find my wallet. Someone had to bail me out and buy me a flight home. Whoops.

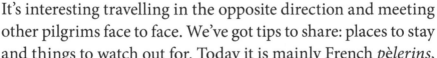

It's interesting travelling in the opposite direction and meeting other pilgrims face to face. We've got tips to share: places to stay and things to watch out for. Today it is mainly French *pèlerins*, many unsure whether to take the route over the mountains from where I've just come, or continue further along the coast and into Santiago via the northern route. I'm the advert for the Primitivo and sing its praises all the way.

Remembering the paintings I've seen this morning in the art gallery, I stop by one of the *hórreos* – the many storage huts on stilts – and consider the subject. These are different from the stone barns across the mountains in Galicia – square instead of long and narrow, with flatter roofs and consisting of more timber than stone in their construction. I'm painting blocks of simple colour, a mixture of Prussian blue and burnt umber for the deep shadows against the burning white of the village on the hill. New green meadows need a little emerald and yellow, and the sky is vivid azure/cobalt blue. I'm painting it because the weather is on my side. Cycle slowly, work fast. I've got more to see and I want to capture the spring flowers and the king of trees – the horse chestnut – in bloom. I remember the artist David Hockney talking about early May being the week of spring explosion and the painter's urge to capture it – *now*.

Sadly, the painting doesn't set me alight; it feels like a duty. Maybe because there's so much to do, so much to see, so much to paint and I want to do it all immediately. But then later, in the stillness of my room, I'll look at the painting again and it will be much better than I originally imagined. It will have something of the effort needed to get the perspective right, to convey the solidity of the structure, and I'll hear the little dog barking at me, and notice the marigolds growing wild by my feet.

At the end of the afternoon I'm running out of energy, battery power and time. I stop at a *Fawlty Towers* sort of hostel with a view that reminds me of something . . .

It's April 1985 and I'm heading Down Under to see friends in Melbourne. My Ukrainian friend Ola wants to wave me off but arrives late at the airport and jumps out of the car.

'Oi! You can't park here, love,' says the attendant as she throws her keys at him.

'Put it where you like then.' She runs inside the terminal and up to security and demands, 'I have to see him.'

'Too late.'

'You don't understand. He's leaving me and I'm pregnant!' And the tears start.

There's confusion and the person behind Ola says, 'I'll take your gift and give it to him. What does he look like?'

Honestly, you couldn't make this up. And just before the plane pulls away from the gate a complete stranger comes up to my seat and asks, 'Are you Timmy Mallett? Your girlfriend was a bit upset and this is for you. Good luck with – er – the baby and everything.' It's the oddest moment, and I open a carrier bag to find a selection of rye-bread snacks, Ukrainian delicacies that take a little while to grow accustomed to.

Ola wasn't pregnant, of course, and she sweet-talked her way out of a parking ticket too. Can't say I've had too many send-offs like that, but I've always admired the ballsiness of it.

I didn't realise it at the time, but this was a pivotal trip that would have consequences for years. I met famous Aussie people in the TV and radio stations in Melbourne and Sydney: Molly Meldrum, Bert Newton, Jason and Kylie, Jonathan Coleman, and a bunch of Aussie rock stars – Mental as Anything, Midnight Oil, Michael Hutchence and INXS, and I fell in love with the place. They call Australia the lucky country and it is. The humour is easy, the lifestyle is social, the smiles are broad and it's easy to feel at home there.

I wanted to see the Great Barrier Reef, Cairns and Green Island. These places had starred in the powerful Nevil Shute TV mini-series *A Town Like Alice*, starring Bryan Brown, Helen Morse and Gordon Jackson. Long cold winter nights in the early 1980s had been set alight by this favourite TV series and I wanted to see where it had been filmed. I stepped out into the warm tropical breeze and smelled the jungle growing. The man who had been in the airline seat next to me was up on business and offered to drive me around the Atherton Tablelands for the day. It was a great introduction to an outback region where people lived and worked as well as went on holiday. 'Good luck, Timmy,' he said at the end of the day. 'It really is a Town Like Alice.'

There's a song I love, from the original 1950s film:

A town like Alice is just the place for me,
With my own piece of ground, the mountains around,
That's where I'll be.
And when I settle down, it must be a town like Alice for me.

I hummed it to myself. I had a week's scuba diving course with a dive school before a day trip to the outer barrier reef to see the multitudes of colourful fish, giant clams and corals. Then a white-water rafting adventure in warm rain. This reef and rainforest experience exploded the senses. I was a busy action man.

My final day, I rented a Mini Moke and drove up the Cook Highway past the giant statue of the great Captain Cook, along what has become one of my favourite coastlines in the world. The signposts pointed to exotic sounding locations – Port Douglas, Daintree, Cape Tribulation, Yorkeys Knob. There's a war memorial at the Trinity Beach junction and I wanted to see one of these famed tropical beaches. Along the esplanade, where in the Second World War troops trained for the battle of the Coral Sea and the landings on Japanese islands, palms waved in the breeze, the surf crashed on to the beach, and on the grass, at a desk, sat a tall, casually dressed, elderly, smiling man in shorts by a sign saying 'Trinity Real Estate'.

'How do you like my office, then? Bet it beats yours!' Jon Wolff was right; it was the best looking office I'd ever seen, ten metres from the beach. 'Come on, Timmy, I'll show you the neighbourhood . . . That's Inge's café, she moved here from Sweden . . . here's the new school, the Catholic church owns this end of the village . . . a Lufthansa pilot has that plot of land, and here's a nice plot for building on one road back from the beach that can be yours for a bargain. Imagine owning that . . .'

It all sounded so simple. 'Just a minute! I'm on a holiday and I've just bought a house in Manchester. I live in England.' But it did sound nice. My own piece of land in Australia. The sun would never set on my property – it would always be daytime here or there. 'Sorry, I'm leaving later,' I said reluctantly.

'Not to worry; when's your flight?' And lo and behold there was Jon Wolff at the airport with the paperwork. 'Have a look; if you fancy it, just sign the papers and fax them back to me. I'll sort the solicitor and you can own your very own piece of tropical Far North Queensland. The value is only going one direction: UP. If it's not for you, no worries! Chuck it in the bin, have a nice life. I'm off back to my office by the sea. G'day!'

The plane peeled away over the glorious Trinity Bay, discovered and named by that man of adventure, Captain Cook, back on Trinity Sunday in June 1770. It was, is and always will be for me a view of heaven. You can often see Trinity Beach on TV; it's regularly featured as the spectacular setting for Nikki Chapman's links in *Wanted Down Under*.

I bought that plot on Connemara Close, with the help of a new young Greek Australian solicitor, Terry Karydas, from the big law firm in Cairns. Three years later I was back and went to inspect it. It looked dreadful. Someone had fly-tipped and I was woefully disappointed. 'Don't worry,' said Jon Wolff, 'I'll swap it for you. There's another lovely plot up on the hill with views of the ocean and the rainforest. For just a few extra dollars I'll get you the dream plot.'

Wolff did exactly that. Terry was busy doing the paperwork as I became the proud owner of the best piece of land in Australia. And that's where my dreams started growing. Imagine – six months here and six months there. I loved the idea of living on both sides of the world. In the next street was a Scottish architect, Gordon McCymont, and his Liverpudlian wife, Coralee. He worked for the World Bank and was often travelling through London. We met at a Heathrow hotel and designed the most thrilling house in the world. As I got more and more excited about how this traditional Queenslander wooden home would look, Gordon, suffering from jetlag, tried to stop himself falling asleep in his soup. This was before Kevin McCloud and *Grand Designs* on TV, but my project would have made a terrific show. I wanted a house on stilts, like the old homesteads in Queensland, where the airflow would keep the house cool. The land sloped away into a gully and I wanted to make use of all the height so I could enjoy the views. There would be lots of windows, a veranda or deck, an atrium with a palm tree and tree fern growing up through the central area. Down below, a secret pool, kept partly shaded to keep the water cool.

Sounds great, doesn't it? It's better than that. Gordon found me a builder who specialised in timber pole homes and work began during our honeymoon, when the first of 52 poles went into the ground, bashed in with Mallett's Mallet. In the wonderful months of 'Itsy Bitsy' going around the world, Mrs Mallett chose the fixtures and fittings, and then the pole house was ready for us to move into.

Except – it wasn't that easy to spend six months here and six months there. Especially when little Billy came along.

Instead, my dream pole house with Tasmanian oak floors, cathedral ceilings, triangular windows, 20-foot tree fern in the atrium, goanna in the mango tree and views out over two World Heritage sites (the Great Barrier Reef and the tropical rainforest) was rented out. This glorious home was where other people made their mark and dreamed their dreams. In *A Town Like Alice*, Gordon Jackson's character speaks of living in his London flat, thinking of a life in Australia, making his dreams come true. This resonates with me. Always has, always will.

Making dreams come true. Let's explore that dream of the pole house in Far North Queensland. Somewhere to live? Somewhere to make friends and connections? Terry my solicitor, with his love of sport and music, became my great friend. Together our families have explored the World Heritage rainforests and wild landscapes, the outback races at Oak Park, and the islands of the Great Barrier Reef, and we've often commented on how the warm rain of the tropics makes the mountains steam; they breathe as if alive. Terry's daughter, Eves, is a brilliant singer–songwriter, and her songs, including 'You Me' written for Martin during a Christmas together, pulse with the magic of dreams dreamed and the joy of fulfilling them.

Terry made an interesting observation a few years ago when Jon Wolff's prediction of values going through the roof didn't seem to be living up to much. 'Look at what the pole house has given you; the people you've met, the friends you've made and the experiences you've had. Value isn't always measured in monetary terms.' The easiest part of this pole house dream was all the hard stuff: buying the land, designing the home, building it. The hardest part has been living in it for any length of time.

We were talking, Mrs Mallett and I, about the dream of us

living in the pole house. How it might be a good idea one day, now that Billy was older. But I was surprised to find the dream was actually mine – not ours. It was forged before we were together as a family. I had a bit of considering to do. Dreams are important. They motivate us every day. Ambition is a good thing; it drives us to fulfil something in every 24 hours. If this dream was very nearly, but not absolutely, fulfilled, then it was time to consider what dreams could and should be achieved. 'Don't ever find yourself with regrets' is another phrase I hear a good friend use often. OK, so how do I let go of that unfulfilled dream without disappointment?

Perhaps I need to look at another dream and see it through. Could the dream of cycling and painting the Camino de Santiago be realised instead?

I'm trying to work things out. I'm in an odd sort of place and I'm not entirely convinced I've made a wise choice. But I arrive late in Colunga, hot and bothered, with little energy left in me, my bike or my phone, so I decide to stay and make the most of things. The bike storage is on the hostel balcony. The view from my window is like the mountains of the Great Dividing Range, and I think of Terry on the other side of the world and how this view reminds me of friends around the planet. There is even a swirl of warm clouds on the distant peaks that makes the mountains look as if they're breathing.

Come the morning, I pack up and go to check out. I'm careful not to let the front door bang shut, because there's no key to get back in. But, er, there's no one there. There are bars on the front door.

I buzz the buzzer. Nothing. So I go somewhere else for breakfast and return after 10 a.m. Still nothing. How odd. I know the Spanish are late risers, but even so. I squeeze my hand through the bars and leave my room key, the cash and a Timmy card with a *gracias* by the front door and think, *How great is this? The world is so trusting.*

Guess what is my favourite bit of the stay. Well, that's easy. The checkout!

My route hugs the Dinosaur Coast. And what a coastline. I'm admiring the flora, especially my favourite – those ferns – ancient and dating back to before the world knew grass, when dinosaurs stomped the Camino.

Around each corner the views open out and I expect to see prehistoric beasts prowling. Instead the road takes me down to the beach and within ten minutes I paint a view that I might see in Far North Queensland along the road from Trinity Beach to Port Douglas: the mountains running right down to the sea and occasionally wreathed in warm misty clouds.

Thomas and Gita from Germany seek my help. Gita wants my bike oil for the joints on her walking stick and Thomas has a great homemade contraption on wheels, with a harness around his shoulders and waist, that also needs attention. I like the way we are always striving to make new kit. Remember life before suitcases had wheels? Surely it's only a matter of time before backpacks all come with them too. I'm ahead of that with a pair of panniers and dry bag on the bike rack!

There's more inspiration in the warm sunshine. I portray the carcasses of old fishing boats that are exposed each low tide on this skeleton coast; coastlines always deliver secrets. I am following the narrow-gauge railway line that will be my lifeline if I by chance need it for a dash to my ferry. My full soundtrack today includes the crashing waves, the booming surf hitting the rock caves; a herd of cattle moo-ving slowly and noisily down my lane, blocking the way; and the joyful local music festival in town.

Music is universal and always stops me in my tracks. I like watching people perform, and I love joining in. (Wonder why that is!)

I sit down to dinner in the *albergue* in the tiny village of Buelna, with four French people, a couple of German women and at the other end of the table a lone Australian by the musical-sounding name of Luetta, who says, 'I'm from a little place way up north you won't have heard of.'

'Try me,' I said.

'Ravenshoe?'

'I know that little town. It boasts the highest pub in Queensland. It's got a heritage railway, the Millstream Falls, and the next stop is the Innot Hot Springs Motel.'

Luetta is astonished. All day I've been aware of the similarities between the two coastlines, so I'm not amazed when it turns out her brother and my friend Terry were once classmates in school. It's a small world.

Neither am I in the slightest bit surprised when an old friend calls my mobile later that evening. I make my apology and step outside for a chat with my lovely friend Geraldine (known for years as Germy Gerry), now a newsreader at BBC Oxford, who suddenly felt the passage of time deserved a little thank you. I'm away from home, from other distractions, so it grows into quite a chat. We talk of the *Timmy on the Tranny* team that had built up at Piccadilly Radio over those short but exciting years. 'Thank you,' says Geraldine, 'for giving us the freedom to fail, and the confidence to be extroverts. It was an act of kindness to let people have a go.'

The call lasts so long, I find the door to the *albergue* locked. I knock and bang on various windows and doors and wait. Someone will come and let me in, won't they?

We've all been in this kind of situation. Remember Maisie

wanting to go up the ladder and climb through our bedroom window? I'm waiting for someone to hear my calls and come and let me in, and while I wait, I drift back 40 years to another night at Piccadilly Radio. I'm on a couple of weeks' trial as a young hopeful doing the solitary overnight shift. Around half-four each morning the newspapers are dropped at the top of the escalator in Piccadilly Plaza. I stick on a record and pop outside the newsroom door to collect them. The door clicks shut. Oops. Hmmm, what to do? I go up to the plaza security booth and rouse the guard.

'Can you let me in, please? I'm on air and I'm locked out!'

He doesn't have a key: 'Piccadilly won't trust us with one.'

I can hear the station output. My album is playing on through the whole of side one . . .

Bedunk, bedunk, bedunk. The needle is clicking on the end of the record and I can feel my career slipping away. I'll never be allowed on air again. Where's the engineer? There are two of us in Piccadilly Radio overnight: the DJ on air and the engineer, somewhere around the back pretending to fix things and probably asleep.

On the reception desk is a phone. I ring every internal number in the book . . . *bedunk, bedunk, bedunk.*

Eventually: 'Hello?'

'Hurry! I'm locked outside. Put a record on and let me in!' (See. I thought of my listeners first . . .)

The engineer with sheepish face and dishevelled hair opens the door and I dash in. *Quick, cover your steps, read some news, any news, even if it's late. Pretend it never happened and hope nobody notices.* It's an uncomfortable hour until the breakfast show team arrive and take over. When the boss arrives, I confess the cock-up. 'Hmm,' he says. 'Next time, prop the newsroom door open or put it on the latch!'

The following day I get my first Piccadilly fan letter. 'Loved the show last night, especially the quiet bit!'

Now here I am again, on a warm and starry night in northern Spain, unable to get anyone to let me in.

I'm sorry to say, I force the poorly locked door open (please don't tell anyone).

Next morning, I leave the hostel a little watercolour as a gift. And very nearly tell them what happened.

24

Titanic

If an 'Itsy Bitsy' opportunity comes knocking on your door, it's a good idea to remember your manners . . .

My favourite Christmas present is always a jigsaw. I love hibernating on winter evenings with a 1,000-piece puzzle to work through. As soon as it's done, there'll be another one from the charity shop. When we were kids, we once got all the pieces of all the jigsaw puzzles in Dad's collection and stacked them up into one big pile. We quite fancied making a bonfire on the carpet. Mum managed to divert us to the kitchen table before we put a match to the pile. Amazingly, my dad spent the next few weeks making all the puzzles to get the pieces back into their correct boxes! This year I got a *Titanic* puzzle, without a picture to follow, but instead with a whodunnit mystery booklet as the clue. It was easy.

Titanic was always Martin's favourite film. He loved the scene where Leo and Kate stand on the front of the ship with their arms outstretched. It was always in our game of charades and Martin would take one of the women in the group and say, 'Soft lady, ma darling,' as he stroked her cheek with the back of his hand. The two would stand with arms right out and we'd make a point of being slow to get it, just so we could see his delight when we eventually did.

It's a pleasantly warm and sunny morning in Cantabria and I follow the track to a stile and footpath. Over the fence and around the corner I come face to face with huge long-horned cows and their guardian bull. They stare at me. I stare back. Any sensible person would back away immediately. As I'm not sensible, I choose to paint them instead. From a safe distance I begin and they patiently sit or stand for me, staring with great big eyes and even bigger horns, silhouetted against the vivid sky.

Behind me, I barely notice the ocean crashing against rocks, but when I turn around I am greeted by the drama of waves against the black forbidding cliffs. One spot, looking in two directions, provides completely contrasting images. The perfect pair of subjects to fill my morning. Such moments aren't common. They are consequently joyous.

As I pedal slowly up the hill out of the village, I exchange a friendly wave with a local woman. Then seeing the scallop shells on my panniers she calls out to me, concerned, as I pass by. '*Señor!* Santiago!' She stops me, because she thinks I am heading the wrong way to Santiago!

There's nothing like a different perspective to give you a sense of the distance you've travelled. Weeks ago, coming out of Burgos, I stood and stared at the snow-capped mountains away to the north. Today those same white-topped mountains are deep to the south.

In between I've cycled westwards as far as it's possible to go on this great continent, turned around and made my way back over the mountains. Now, with the Bay of Biscay on the other side of me, I stop and allow myself to be touched by the vastness of this journey I've been making with my brother in my heart. It feels like a special Martin Mallett moment. The Camino signpost is the spot – the distance marker: close to 500 kilometres from Santiago, that distant glistening city. Martin has been with me all the way and I say a little prayer of 'you me' for us both.

I spend my final night in Spain in an ancient converted monastery in the pretty tourist town of Santillana del Mar. It still has little monks' cells with a set of bunks in each. I'm sharing with an Italian bloke who has distinctive feet aromas. There's a comfortable lounge for us all and the cloisters have been made into the dining room for breakfast. It's a slow stroll down the cobbled street to the bars and restaurants, and a pleasant place to share with people all heading the other way to Santiago. Hello, goodbye . . .

I wake to a beautiful fragrant Spanish May morning, the ochre stone colours soft in the heat haze, wild flowers thick in the meadows, and riding into the sunshine is heavenly. I find a good place for my last painting in Spain, which may be an analogy that encapsulates my Camino experience.

The foreground is full of a multitude of wild flowers – I paint them in thickly and quickly. A glorious dazzling range of colours and textures, they're like the detail and range of each and every day. Usually, we look at our days in overall terms. Was it a good day? A challenging day? But within each and every span of hours there are the highlights and disappointments of a kaleidoscope of experiences. Meetings, contacts, an unexpected happening, the energy of colleagues, thoughtfulness of wondering.

Beyond this range of colours and growing grasses in the meadow is the silhouette of the distant church. I'm reminded of the spiritual connection we have to our cradle of beliefs and to be thankful for family, friends and health. In the distance a hazy sky reaching down to the challenging contours of the blueish-purple mountains suggests our flickering dreams and aspirations on this mysterious, intriguing earth. All encompassed in a painting of a colourful wild-flower meadow. Spain seems to hold its breath in this gentle light.

I reach the Santander waterfront with an hour or two to spare before my ferry ride home. All the things I want to see are within a few metres.

The cathedral treats me to images of nuns chatting. What do nuns chat about? What would nuns' gossip be about, I wonder?

Mass is coming to an end with three ladies of the congregation singing beautifully, their voices echoing around the ancient stonework. I make a point of thanking them and they are delighted that someone has noticed.

The piece of cathedral art that catches my attention is about the Road to Emmaus, but it seems to be just as relevant to the Way of St James. In the story of the Road to Emmaus, two pals were walking, and talking about the events of the first Easter weekend, when someone joined them. According to the story, the stranger they were talking to was recognised in the unexpected and domestic manner of breaking up a loaf and saying a blessing. I find myself wondering whether undertaking this Camino will reveal something I've already recognised.

There's my Martin Mallett stone to deal with. I've brought it from his Aberdeen home in my bag and carried it for two months. I found it by accident yesterday. (Shows how much I tidy the bag.) It's a flat piece of Grampian granite and I can't decide whether to leave it on a waymarker or skim it across the sea.

The waymarker for the Camino del Norte is outside the cathedral. It's a signpost set too high for me to reach, but instead in front of the cathedral there's a water fountain and I try skimming the stone here. I'm an expert stone skimmer (and modest), but it sinks to the bottom without a single bounce, just like a stone should. Hopeless! If at first I can't skim my stone, take my shoes and socks off, climb into the fountain and try again! And this time it's a perfect skim. A fine and funny way to finish marking my route on land.

Along the waterfront is the bank of Santander. I think of the man, a century ago, who hated carrying change. Whenever he had a pocket full of cash, he'd get rid of it by stepping into a bank and opening a savings account. He had hundreds of accounts, and of course forgot where all his cash was kept, so when he died the accounts just kept on growing. Banks all over the world have millions in unclaimed dormant accounts. Enough to keep a small country afloat. I wanted to test out the process, so in the 1980s I went around town with a handful of change, opening accounts in different banks in more and more ridiculous names.

In the first I had 'Gosh Golly Gosh'. Next I was Mr 'Jumpina Puddle'; and then I was 'Hugh Mitconcerns'. I was finally refused an account when I applied under 'Sir Winges Blunt'.

It was good fun and proved that saving money could raise a smile.

Santander is surrounded by city beaches, and one of them, the Playa de los Bikinis, brings the special song in my life to my lips.

It was a lovely May evening in 1990 when I took a call from my agent, John Miles. 'I've been speaking to Brian Burge, the marketing man at Polydor, and the upshot is, Andrew Lloyd Webber would like you to come to tea to discuss an idea for a record . . .' There was a bemused look on Mrs Mallett's face as I tried to explain. But then, so many Mallett projects and proposals are weird and wonderful.

Andrew Lloyd Webber has an outstanding collection of pre-Raphaelite art. It's the largest private collection in the world. We talked of things we both love and artists we both admire. The conversation was going well until I went to the loo.

It's not unusual to have interesting photos in the downstairs loo and Andrew's collection featured Leyton Orient. That was a surprise. After all, my team, Oxford United, were still basking in a recent 3-nil League Cup victory over Queens Park Rangers at Wembley and I made the comment, 'Who's the fan of Orient, then?'

'I am actually. I'm on the board.'

Hmm, try not to put your foot in your mouth, Timmy. I was glad when the subject moved on to music. As an award-winning radio DJ my experience was in pop music, so when he mentioned Michael Ball as someone he enjoyed working with, I offered an opinion I would have been better keeping to myself.

'Don't think much of him,' I remarked.

I still can't believe I said that. Here was someone Lloyd Webber had known and worked with for many years – a man with the voice and range of the very best in the world – and

I was comparing him to some piece of ephemeral throwaway pop.

Andrew looked at me.

Brian from Polydor looked at me.

My agent, John, looked at me. 'But you like him and Andrew's musicals, don't you, Timmy?'

'He's all right. They just aren't really my thing . . .' The hole was getting deeper and I had no idea how rude I was being.

They all looked at one another.

'I have this idea,' said Lloyd Webber, 'to recreate one of those great old pop hits from the past and give it a new slant. We want to re-record "Itsy Bitsy Teeny Weeny Yellow Polka Dot Bikini" and I wondered if you would like to sing it? I could ask Michael Ball, but . . .'

It started to dawn on me that perhaps I ought to pick my words a little more carefully. I needed to dig my way out of my own hole. Maybe a joke would help?

Er, maybe it wouldn't.

'Look, I'm on the telly,' I said. 'I have a mallet and hit people on the head and go Blaah!'

'Why don't you have a go? If it doesn't work, it doesn't matter. But you could have a go with our musical director.'

I had no idea what a musical director was and I threw another reason not to do it into the mix: 'The trouble is, on Friday we are off filming for a month . . .'

'OK, well, it's Monday today. How about I see if the studio is available on Wednesday? And if it works, then we can go ahead. We'll put it out under a pseudonym, so people will try and work out who it is. We'll call the band Bombalurina.'

??

'One of the characters from my West End show *Cats*,' volunteered Andrew.

As we were leaving and shaking hands at the door Andrew casually asked me, 'I presume you can sing?'

I said nothing and looked at my agent.

'Of course he can,' said John. 'Timmy's a great singer . . .'

And so, despite my dreadful, embarrassing behaviour, that is how on Wednesday morning I came to be driving down to Scratch Studios in Chertsey to work with the best musical producer in the world, Nigel Wright. Less than a week earlier, one of those dinner conversations between Andrew and Brian from Polydor had stirred Andrew into having his own record label and to launch it with something fun like a summer hit. Nigel Wright had a demo of 'Itsy Bitsy' made within 24 hours and my name came up to front it.

It was a brilliant session. Line after line, phrase after phrase, we went through the song. Nigel, and his assistant Robin Sellars, chose the best take of each note, and as the day progressed and the laughter grew we started to make something utterly magical. 'Be more Timmy!' they said and we chuckled away. Towards the end of the afternoon, Nigel suggested I give them a few Timmy-Isms: 'Some "Utterly Utterly Brilliants" and a "Blaah!" or two and a bit of "Pinky Punky" too.'

'What are they for?'

'The B side. We've sampled some bits from *Wacaday*.' Amazing. The whole thing was put together in a joyful happy day, and I took a cassette away with me. That cassette went on the *Wacaday* tour to Russia, Norway and Crete, and we played it all through our filming adventures. A month later it was released to the world, and three weeks after that it was storming up the charts as the summer series of *Wacaday* began.

To make the summer holidays special a record-breaking heatwave arrived. The year 1990 set the benchmark for great summers, and the soundtrack to that one was 'Itsy Bitsy'.

Collectors of pop trivia should note that the longest song title ever to get to number one is 'Itsy Bitsy Teeny Weeny Yellow Polka Dot Bikini (that she wore for the first time today) Oh Yeah!'

One newspaper did us a massive favour with a fabulous front-page photo of Princess Diana in an 'Itsy Bitsy' bikini and the headline: 'Itsy Bitsy, Teeny Weeny, Di's a Dream in Her Bikini!'

Never before have I ever been so clearly and obviously in the right place at the right time. John Miles was delighted and relieved. Relieved, because despite what I'd said to Andrew that night he'd still gone ahead with the project; delighted, because this was John's second number one. Some 16 years previously he'd topped the charts managing the Wurzels with 'Combine Harvester'. Then he'd put a load of hay bales outside the studios of Radio 1 and with his brother, Smiley Miley, got them on to the Roadshow around the country.

This summer of 1990, the roadshows featured 'Itsy Bitsy' performances at Southsea, Minehead and Weston-super-Blaah! I flew straight to where I needed to be in a helicopter after coming off air on TV-am. Far more appealing than I were the two lovely 'Itsy Bitsy' girls, Dawn Andrews and Annie Dunkley. They were brilliant dancers and made the whole thing look fabulous. Arlene Phillips did the choreography based on the fashion that year for the dance craze of voguing. After our pop career Annie went on to star in the hugely successful *Thelma and Louise*-style car ads, while Dawn married one of the stars of the next band she danced with – Take That. She is now the happy and lovely Mrs Barlow.

There was something wonderfully manic about each day that summer, and John and my friends reminded me to enjoy every minute because it only happens to a few select people – and the Beatles.

One Friday morning in August, I was at TV-am about to present *Wacaday* when I found myself sitting in the make-up room with Simon le Bon, Nick Rhodes and John Taylor from Duran Duran. 'Congratulations, Timmy,' they said. 'You're going to be number one on Sunday.'

I didn't want to get ahead of myself and played down the chances. 'Suzanne Vega, "Tom's diner", is right up there,' I said.

'But we've seen the mid-week sales and the predictions for the weekend. There's no doubt. No one's going to catch you. Nice one, Timmy on the Tranny!' What a lovely generous thing to say, from a band that knows what it's like to strive for the top spot.

On Sunday afternoon we gathered at Andrew's country home near Newbury to listen to DJ Bruno Brookes running down the Top 40 on Radio 1. And there it was – just a few weeks after that fateful meeting. Number one in the UK, followed in the weeks thereafter by topping the charts around the world in at least a dozen countries in the first few months. On Monday morning, Nobby Nolevel – Chris Evans – arrived at my house very early, in his dressing gown, with a bottle of champagne! Thanks, Nobby. Sales continued to climb through the hundreds of thousands, to the million and more. The icing on the cake came on 8 September as the-about-to-be Mrs Mallett walked down the aisle at our wedding (planned months before, when there'd been no mention of a record). The organist struck up 'Itsy Bitsy' and there we were, together. I may have been number one in the world, but more importantly I was marrying the number one lady in my life – my lovely Mrs Mallett.

I don't imagine there have been many chart toppers getting wed while being number one.

You know what my dad said in his address? 'Marriage is like

a painting. It should inspire and uplift you. It has colour, composition, melody, focus, detail, horizons, brush strokes, texture and a frame. It takes effort. Make it a masterpiece . . .' We also have our song. Guess what it is?!

There'll be a few to choose from. There were 14 on the album, *Huggin' an' a Kissin'*. The next single was 'Seven Little Girls, Sitting In The Back Seat, Huggin an' a Kissin With Fred'; then a reworking of Charlie Drake's hit 'My Boomerang Won't Come Back', and our favourite slow number, 'Down Came the Rain'. After that, the titles got shorter. We had 'Splish Splash', 'Three Bells', and 'Speedy Gonzales' with a high-pitched Pinky Punky voice, which was our special Children's Royal Variety number at the London Palladium in 1991.

One day my mobile rang. It was Gary Barlow.

'It's our tenth wedding anniversary, Timmy, and I want to surprise Dawn,' he said. 'Would you be up for singing "Itsy Bitsy" again with her and Annie?'

And this is how the party panned out. Michael McIntyre, Jason Donovan, Lulu and Take That, Ronan Keating, Alesha Dixon and Peter Kay were all the warm-up acts for the finale to the night. Gary announced a special surprise for, and with, Dawn. The curtains parted to reveal me, Annie, Dawn and two young 'Itsy Bitsy' dancers (who weren't even born when we topped the charts around the world) to a room full of cheering celebrities, Barlow family and friends. Instantly Dawn and Annie and I were back on *Top of the Pops*; we were in front of the stadium at the Diamond Awards in Europe; on the Radio 1 Roadshows . . . We were having fun being on top of the world again singing and dancing: '2,3,4, tell the people what she wore . . .' All together the crowd roared back, 'It was an itsy bitsy, teeny weeny, yellow polka dot bikini, that she wore for the first time today, OH YEAH!'

I'm singing to myself as I come to board the Brittany Ferries flagship, *Pont-Aven* . . . Then suddenly there's another cyclist coming on board. Young Harry, 18 years old, carrying a tent and a look of disappointment. He had bike issues on the first day; he didn't have any maps of his route and the camping was a scary disaster. Harry had come expecting everything to fall into place. Instead it's fallen apart. After less than a week he had to abandon his Camino. The importance of preparation and training is all too obvious. I don't doubt he'll learn from his experience and come back better equipped another time. Good luck, Harry.

My Spanish Camino is complete.

Apart from one final Martin Mallett moment. The ship pulls out into the Bay of Biscay, and I imagine hearing the shipping forecast – that radio equivalent of The World is OK – on Radio 4 FM and Long Wave. It begins way to the north near the arctic circle: south-east Iceland, Faeroes, North Utsire, Tyne, Dogger, German Bight, Thames, Portland, Fitzroy, Biscay . . . Good, wind moderate and the sun starts to dip towards the west. My favourite Australian Impressionist artist, Arthur Streeton, used to say, 'Look to the east at sundown and see the last blush of the eastern sky before the sky turns rose and purple and a shiver runs up your spine . . .'

The sea is *Titanic* still, the last rays of sunlight pick out the white spray above the turquoise wake at the stern of the ship. An everlasting view of the eternity of the sea. I hold the blue glass bottle with the Martin Mallett memorabilia and the little message with my contact details and photos. The same bottle that wouldn't leave me at Finisterre. I hurl it over the stern of the ship into the *Titanic* sea. Martin Mallett, favourite film, message in a bottle, journey almost complete, together in the fun times, the tough times, the family times, the noisy times, the quiet times. Together for ever.

The bottle bobs in the wake, and I wonder . . . will it ever wash up somewhere? In two months? Ten years? Never? It is impossible to answer, but that little bit of human hope inside us all still thinks, 'Wouldn't it be great if it did show up again?!'

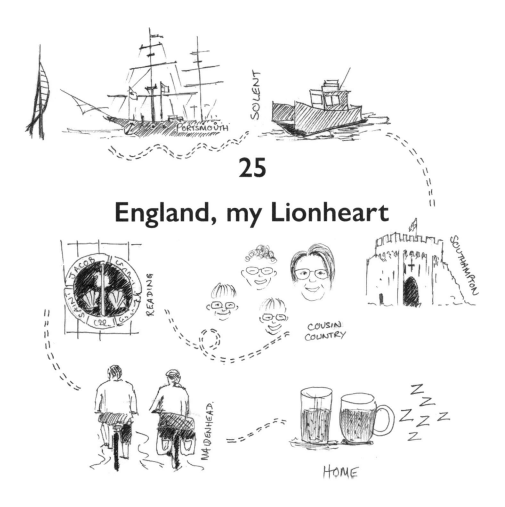

25

England, my Lionheart

Everything has a beginning and an end, so making the most of the happiness in between is always a good plan. Why is it that the lessons we learn from our families can take a lifetime to become clear?

In the back of my road atlas of Britain, there's a whole section of town centre maps. Idly browsing through them, I realise I've been to almost every one of those towns. Some are on the way up, others are in the doldrums – but everywhere has something to commend it. There are still spots I'd like to visit – among them intriguing places like Galashiels, Fermanagh, Cardigan and Shaftesbury. There are lots of reasons to go to these corners. Whether it's for shows and filming reasons, or just to explore on a bike trip. I always enjoy visiting somewhere new and I never like to leave until I've found something of note that impresses me. I'm almost on a pilgrimage to see every town in the country. Two important ones I've visited are Fleetwood, the purpose-built, Lancashire show town, where my mum had connections; and Lewisham, where my dad lived before moving to Marple.

Back in the 1860s my mother's grandparents moved from Penrith to Fleetwood for economic reasons. Here, Wilfred Owen, the First World War poet, lived in Bold Street; a few doors down from his home is the bakery shop where my grandad Will first set eyes on Minnie with her tempting vanilla slices. Their first kiss was behind the mail bags on Preston station as he eagerly went off to fight in the Boer War. They married in Fleetwood on his safe return and were given three kitchen chairs. One each for the couple and one for a friend. We still have those chairs in our kitchen now, if you ever come to visit.

They moved to the Midlands and from a postcard of the street in Orton, Birmingham, I found the house where my mum was born in 1914. The lovely Victorian tiles in the porch were still there and I can imagine Nancy's little bare feet running over them – the same way I can picture my dad, little Michael, with his hands on the banisters of his Lewisham home, in south London. I found that house during panto season one year. I knocked at the door and was surprised how, even though it's now converted to flats, that banister rail instantly connected me with the 1920s.

In 1942 Michael was posted to India for a mundane desk job in the Pay Corps. He spent his war there and it was a life-changing experience. Recently, on a three-day stopover in Delhi, Mrs Mallett and I went in search of the places featured in his tiny photograph album of 27 snaps. Yes, a photo album of all the pictures he took with the little Box Brownie over two and half years on the other side of the world. Those small square photographs revealed the exact places he'd been: the Taj Mahal, the Viceroy's Palace, the Old Mosque in Delhi. I could stand in the same location and wonder what it was that inspired him to take each simple black and white shot. We climbed the steps to the courtyard of the Old Mosque. Like him, we gasped as we reached the top of the stairs. Like him, we reached for our cameras. We all do it: take the photo immediately, in case it goes away!

At the Taj Mahal, visited at full moon August 1943, he'd taken a night time exposure, and the following day had stood by a tree gazing at the world's greatest memorial to love. Those two photos were simple to place. I stood on the same spot as my dad 70 years later and felt his sense of wonder as he penned this sonnet at the age of 24:

Perhaps an artist on a summer's day
Stretched up his arms and plucked from the sky
A silver cloud, flecked by the golden sun
And fashioned it, with gentle soft caress
Until his heart's desire before him lay,
Fragile, a thing of dreams impermanent.
Maybe, whilst yet he worked alone, enrapt,
An angel saw his dream and was much moved
Yet marvelled that a mortal man could plan
Such loveliness. 'Praise be to God,' he sang.
'Grant that this splendour may not pass away.'
God heard the angel's prayer and breathed upon
The tenuous vapours. Straightaway they were stone.
How else do you suppose the Taj was built?

As well as Dad's photos and some letters are the little cartoons he sketched with great observation, for the Pay Corps magazine, on pieces of scrap paper. Michael was based in Meerut, Uttar Pradesh, not far from Delhi – a 27-hour train ran from Bombay where his troop ship docked. Meerut is where the cataclysmic uprising known as the Indian Mutiny began over an army religious dispute in the mid nineteenth century. Rumour had it there was pig's fat in the cartridge casings, and Muslim troops were outraged. The resulting bloodshed across the country was terrible.

We learned of the importance to Dad of the tiny pink Pay Corps church in Meerut, where the pews had little cut-outs in which to prop the army rifle. The rifle he only ever carried once, without any ammunition, and with no training in how to use it. I discovered his confirmation Bible, dated 'March 1943, Meerut'. Without ever expressing it, we became aware that his two years in India had been the catalyst for my dad's exploration of his spirituality. Surrounded by all those of different faiths – Hindus, Muslims, Jews, Buddhists and Christians – he'd used that time to examine what he believed, and his cartoons became a gentle commentary on his fellow countrymen.

Travel broadens the mind, begs us to ask questions about the familiar and the unfamiliar. Some 24 years later, Michael Mallett took the plunge, stuck his head above the parapet and turned his collar around after a long career in advertising. Following theological training at Gladstone's Library, and approaching 50 years of age, he became a clergyman. His faith, gently shared with the family, was offered not as something we were expected to follow but simply what he believed and what fashioned his life. The things we learn from our parents are not always obvious, and can take decades to reveal themselves.

It's a fine, fabulous English afternoon as I dock in Portsmouth and come around to the Historic Dockyard. Last time I was at *HMS Victory* was with the family and brother Martin, and I pretended we were sailors and pirates. It is great to get such a lovely welcome from the enthusiastic team there.

In Lee-on-the-Solent a B&B beckons me, where Susie the landlady recognises the scallop shells on my panniers and the conversation naturally turns to the Camino. Sometimes I think things are just meant to be. My phone rings and my pal Gary welcomes me back to England and shares with me the arrival of his memorable brass Camino scallop shell. I've got a couple of days left. I don't want this adventure to go too fast or to miss a thing.

England has a distinctive and gorgeous aroma, particularly in springtime. It's the smell of the sea as I cycle along the Solent, the scent of Queen Anne's lace, or cow parsley, and the fragrance of vanilla from the bluebells. The pungent whiff of oilseed fields in full bloom and the vintage essence of wild garlic. Everywhere I go today my senses are alive to the country growing greener and more abundant. I never underestimate the power of scent to stir the emotions.

Then there are the colours: the *Wacaday* pink of the Hamble ferry; the matching pink of the Judas tree flowers; purple wisteria around so many doors and windows, with violet aubretia cascading off garden walls.

At Southampton old town I ride through the ancient Bargate that's been here for 900 years. Pilgrims have come and left from here over the centuries: it's where King Henry V's army embarked for Agincourt. Slightly more up to date is the glorious St Mary's Stadium of Premier League Southampton Football Club, who kindly give me a pin for my cycling tie and are breathing a little easier after their win last night. Five leagues below them, Eastleigh Football Club have a lovely new restaurant open every day for lunch. I leave with full stomach and two Spitfire badges on my now-weighty necktie.

I can't ride up to Winchester Cathedral without singing at the top of my voice.

I need to thank Bishop Tim of Winchester and his chaplain Mat for their help with the cathedral at Santiago. 'If ever I can do something for you in return, just ask,' I offer. I also call on a Winchester art gallery to thank them for their support of my art and my Camino. I'm grateful to all the fine art galleries that show my work.

It is fitting to stay with cousin Katy on the first and last nights of my pilgrimage. Her boys are impressed I've made it in one piece and walk me to school in the morning to show me off again to their excited teachers. 'This is our cousin Timmy Mallett. He's just cycled to France and Spain and back and he stayed with us last night with his bike!'

I'm expecting this to be my final day and I pedal Berkshire's Roman roads to Silchester. I've travelled lots of Roman highways on this adventure. I wonder if any infrastructure we put up today will last 2,000 years like these roads. Always straight as a rod and wonderfully unending. I stop to paint the flowering horse chestnut blooms and the bluebells. Half of the varieties of bluebell in the world are native to the British Isles and on my way home today I'll pass Shakespeare's wood, close to where I live, thick with blue and purple and delicate scent. Here the bard met a girlfriend, Lady Lanyon, and wrote:

Shall I compare thee to a summer's day?
Thou art more lovely and more temperate.
Rough winds do shake the darling buds of May,
and summer's lease hath all too short a date . . .

At which point, I imagine, Lady Lanyon said, 'Yes, Will, I'm yours!'

There's a church at Beech Hill in Berkshire with a village shop in it. How unique. Church and shop keeping the village supplied spiritually and materially. Got to stop here for a cuppa and a chat . . . I like the idea of churches being open for more than just religious services. It's so obvious really. More often than not they're the largest buildings in the community, so why not use them more than one day a week?

Along the Kennet and Avon Canal to St James's Church next to Reading's ruined abbey, which is to reopen shortly as the centrepiece of the Abbey Quarter. Here, Father John stamps my pilgrim credential and we discuss the links between Reading, Marlow and Santiago de Compostela. Friends start calling to say 'Well done; you've done it!' which worries me. Strangely, the closer I get to home, the more anxious I become about having an accident. *Be in the moment, Mallett; don't start looking ahead to triumphant finishes.*

'Did you take a drink every 20 minutes?' asks Terry, who joins me for the 20 miles to Maidenhead. Here we meet my son Billy and my bike buddy Andy at the York Road ground of Maidenhead United. It's the oldest football ground in the world, still used by the same side, and it's a joy to watch them play. Look out of the north-side window of any passing train, and you may see my handiwork at the Bell Street end. I helped paint the Maidenhead United name on the back of the stand. You may even spot the 'Billy the Gardener, keep your garden top of the League' sponsorship board. The season ended happily two weeks ago with Maidenhead delighted to be in the top half of the table.

It's lovely to find my Timmy pic still in the window of the phone box, and the Martin Mallett name tag still in place in the village war memorial. The daffodils are over, but there are little white flowers instead.

In Martin's favourite musical, edelweiss covers the Austrian hillsides. Mrs Mallett starts playing the opening bars of *The Sound of Music* on the piano and it's the highlight of Martin's stay with us. Arm around Mrs M's shoulders Martin is loudly singing something close to the tune with the occasional word. On *Wacaday* we recreated *The Sound of Music* in a fabulous barmy moment. We called it 'The hills are alive with the sound of muesli' and I danced over the snowy Alpine hills singing:

Doh a deer, a female deer,
Ray, a name I call myself!
Me, Me Me Me Me Me Me
Blaah, a note to follow so!

'Me work hard,' Martin says as he comes in from mowing the lawn. 'Me stay here!' he announces as we finish the washing-up together. 'My friend,' he says to anyone who comes to the door – Andy the postman, the delivery person or a tradesman. 'Soft lady,' he says to Irene, our neighbour, as he gently touches her cheek with the back of his hand. He's a charmer, our Martin, and what he lacks in language skills he makes up for with a smile, a greeting, an engagement with whoever is here, right now. For 30 years he's been coming down from Aberdeen, where he loved working in the bakery at Newton Dee, to spend some weeks with us at Christmas and during the summer holidays. The first time he came alone by train, travelling from Aberdeen to Edinburgh, where the guard helped him on to the London train. I say 'alone', but when I met him at King's Cross, Martin was like the Pied Piper. He walked down the platform with a group of strangers. He'd made friends with all around him and shown them his piece of paper with his name, our names and other contacts. 'Martin's really made our journey special,' they said. 'You're going to have a wonderful time together.'

Latterly, he'd fly down to Heathrow, on unaccompanied special assistance, making friends with all the crew and check-in staff. Family gatherings, when Martin is here, are always that extra bit special and his face lights up when big brother Paul and wife Pat arrive. We three brothers become the bonkers brother Malletts, playing old childhood games and teasing each other as brothers do. Martin always went back to his home at Newton Dee village with a letter explaining what we'd been doing, so that they could guess the miming he'd provide.

One time, we were visiting Stevie and Lorraine Kelly, who was in painful recovery from being trodden on by a horse. Martin saw her distress and put his hand on her head and blessed her. 'Dear God, make her better . . .' Lorraine burst into tears. He may have had language and learning difficulties, but he knew how to pray for someone, and how to offer a healing hand. What a gift.

When he was younger, life expectancy for someone with Down's syndrome was not very high. Many times people would say, 'He won't make it through his teens'; 'Don't expect him to last beyond his 20s'; '30 is old for someone with Down's' etc. Then people stopped second-guessing Martin's life expectancy and started marvelling at his abilities.

Abilities, though, also have a lifespan. I first noticed this when the vegetable scraps were ready to go to the compost bin. Martin, in his 60s, stood at the door with his finger to his lips, a puzzled expression on his face. He'd forgotten where the compost bin was. Cutlery was put away in the fridge, he'd put his teeth away at night into a drawer. It wasn't the Down's, that extra chromosome, that was affecting him, but the onset of dementia. Martin needed more reassurance. He'd take someone's arm when he walked anywhere. Daily tasks became a bigger chore. He'd get confused. Not at the big things – he still looked forward to Sundays 'churley morley' (church in the morning) and his eyes would sparkle at the thought of being dressed in his robes and carrying a candle as a server.

The day came when he moved into the care home that our big brother Paul had researched and chosen. It was a good choice. In activity sessions Martin lit up the room – singing, dancing in the carers' arms. 'I'm happy,' he said. 'You me.' Wow, that's it. All it takes to be happy is to be together with someone who cares. I took him to the football. The Dons were playing Rangers and we were down at the touchline in the special needs area. The noise was deafening and he covered his ears and laughed. At half-time we shared a hot chocolate and macaroni pie. On the way home he was an animated, stimulated Martin, saying, 'I'm happy!'

But these moments contrasted with putting a cup of tea in front of him when he would mime drinking it, saying, 'Nice tea.' He was forgetting how to feed himself. Then his head would drop and he'd disappear for a while, coming back ever so slightly less each time. We watched Martin's world shrinking and dipping. The priest came to pray with him. Martin recognised the rhythms and breathed, 'Amen.' With a little prompt he'd repeat 'You me', 'ma bubba', and then his life, well lived, far beyond anything that Nancy and Michael could ever have dreamed of, came to a gentle slow finale and finally stopped at 64 years and 7 months.

Mahatma Gandhi said, 'The true measure of any society can be found in how it treats its most vulnerable members.' I believe Martin had the opportunity to make the most of his abilities, and then some. The way Trafford and Aberdeen councils supported and enabled him over more than 37 years at Camphill Trust Newton Dee was impressive. 'You are not your brother's keeper,' our parents had said to Paul and me. 'You each have your own life to live to the fullest that you can.' It was our choice to include Martin in our lives and it was never a chore, always a revelation. We commented when we were younger, 'Martin may be "special", but he's better than us. He doesn't have to try in order to be nice.'

Reaching your potential is what Martin exemplified; and reaching it with a smile. 'You me', because after all, 'he ain't heavy – he's ma bubba.'

I know that he's been with me throughout my Camino and now we ride along the bright yellow Green Way, thick with oilseed rape flowers and smelling sweetly of summer's promise, into the village, with my bike pals Andy, Terry and Billy. 'Want me to ride your bike, Dad?' asks young Mr Mallett, and I feel like saying, 'Next time, son, if you ever want to follow the route . . .' At Holy Trinity Church someone goes in search of Reverend Nick the Vic. 'Where have you been, then?!' he asks with a grin and pats my shoulder. Billy remarks, 'Well done, Dad. I'm proud of you.' Why is my son's commendation so special?

We want to go to the King's Arms for a beer. I lock the bike . . . and pause. I'm exhausted. I feel as though I'll sleep until September. I need to quietly absorb the enormity of what I've done solo on the bike over two months, 3,500 kilometres, 2,250 miles: the equivalent of Land's End to John o' Groats, back to Land's End, turn around and up to Scotland again.

People come up and comment, 'Did you have a nice time?' 'Bet your bum is sore!' 'What was the best bit?' 'Did you get lost?' 'My friend walked some of that once.' 'I've got a new car.'

'Bet it was warm and sunny abroad – where's your tan?' 'How were the beaches?' 'I've been to the Costa del . . .'

It was not a jolly.

It was not a holiday.

It was a much tougher challenge than expected.

It was the biggest thing I've ever done.

Not the biggest thing I'll ever do. These are the golden years and I fully intend to make every hour of every day count and, like my brother Martin, to reach my potential in each and every way I can.

That's the plan, at any rate.

Two days later Mrs Mallett is home after an emotional final visit with Maisie on her big hundredth birthday. The same day I'm on stage at a holiday park, performing 'Itsy Bitsy' and playing Mallett's Mallet with hundreds of happy holidaymakers; a week later, I'm at a stately home, performing in front of thousands of excited festival-goers; in between, there are TV appearances talking about Martin and my Camino, immediately followed by an after dinner speech at a charity event for the Friends and Family of Clergy, where previous speakers have been Prime Minister Theresa May and comedian and actor Hugh Dennis. Phew, busy!

It's not over, is it?

Life continues.

Aim for the stars.

Postscript

Buen Camino

The weather is fierce. Lashing storms come in one after the other – Erik, Freya, Gareth – to mark an anniversary. I'm tense and ratty for a day or two.

'Are you all right, Malley?' asks Mrs Mallett.

'It's just Martin's anniversary coming up and he's on my mind.' First anniversaries are always the hardest and the pain will of course ease as the years roll on. I re-read my diary and recall the stress of his death mixed with the anxious start of my Camino.

I'm still on the big adventure. I wake each morning recalling an image, a moment, and needing to paint it. Not every painting works. It doesn't matter. I keep going. It's not the destination; it's the journey. I'm painting every day. I've been busy creating throughout the autumn and winter. The series is growing larger and the studio is filled with artwork. I want to exhibit the collection, but not until it's ready.

A friend comments, 'You should do the first day again – without the chain issue, if you can!' Stevie agrees he's up for it, and so is my pal Tim. We meet at the church, the vicar gives us a blessing and away we go again. As it was a year ago, there's some rain; but this time we're more comfortable, confident and we stop more. There are interesting people to meet throughout the day, little exchanges that you only get when cycling, and I end up 40 miles later at cousin Katy's, where young Jed welcomes me: 'Timmy, I would talk to you, but today is tablet day and I'm going to play on my tablet.'

I wrote to all those who had sent me letters of encouragement. I told Theresa May of the invitation from Santiago Cathedral and she sent her condolences for Martin. I wonder if the never-ending Brexit saga will impact on Britons making their own Caminos in the future?

At Marlow, the custodian of the Hand of St James, Canon Tony Griffiths, asked his brother-in-law, Alan Todd, to carry out a little research. Alan runs Microscope Services in Oxford, and his colleagues at the university's Archaeology Department agreed to help. As expected, investigations using radiocarbon dating have produced just as many questions as answers. Indeed, the provenance of the mummified hand is as inconclusive as anyone would think. The radiocarbon dating reveals possible ages between 987 and 1047, with a strong likelihood peaking between the years 1020 and 1030. There are other intriguing dates between 1088 and 1150, and questions about the material the hand may have been preserved in to produce mummification. If those early years of the eleventh century are correct, that could add credence to the story of the important gift from the Archbishop of Santiago to the Patriarch of the Orthodox Church. The dates also go some way to coinciding with the gift to Empress Matilda on her wedding day in Mainz. However, they don't do much for the theory that this was the hand of St James the Apostle, brother of Christ, and no DNA was tested. That aside, I still find the idea that this hand has survived all these centuries in almost impossible circumstances an extraordinary story. Where did it come from? How was it collected in the first place? Whose hand was it? And what does it tell us about faith and connections and human yearning?

After the bike is stolen there's an enormous coverage in the media. Far and away more than the theft of a bicycle would ever deserve. I assume it's because of my dear brother and this adventure. The loneliness of the task. The vastness of the distance. There's not a day goes by without someone asking me, 'Did you get your bike back, Timmy?'

A call comes from someone I've never met. James Thompson owns a great bike shop – Spokes of Bagshot – and he's a Wideawaker. 'I loved you on *Wacaday*, Timmy, and after what you did I can't bear you not being on the bike any more. I want to sort you out with a new Timmeee E-bike.'

I'm astonished, and deeply touched. 'But I'm certain I'm going to get the bike back ...'

'In the meantime, use this ...'

And that's how I'm back on a gorgeous new Giant Explore 1 Timmeee E-bike. Similar to the one that went missing, but a new model. It's glorious. James and I have been on expeditions together exploring the Chilterns and the Thames Valley. Chatting, laughing, enjoying each other's company and the great outdoors. At the *Chitty Chitty Bang Bang* pond at Russell Water, James caught a one-clawed freshwater crayfish; at Mapledurham we went in search of Second World War bunkers near where *The Eagle Has Landed*. James has many friends who are cycling adventurers and ambassadors, and he's fascinated by the process and inspiration for my paintings. He knows a number of art collectors and has introduced them to my work. This has been a great new friendship to make – and in such unexpected circumstances.

Then, by chance, I get a call from *Crimewatch Roadshow*. 'Could we do an appeal for your E-bike?'

Of course. I take the train to Cardiff on a stormy night, the dark sleet and rain battering the windows of the hotel. At half past five I'm woken and driven to the studio for a walk through, two rehearsals and a live on-air appeal. 'It was this week a year ago I set off alone, on a bike like this, to see if I could cycle and paint an adventure across three countries . . . I was inspired by my brother Martin to try to reach my potential.' Three minutes later I'm finished and we've moved on . . .

What happened to that bike? Someone struggled out of the pub's car park, cursing the weight of it and the awkwardness of its padlocked bulk. Down a side road, he and his associates got it into the back of a stolen 4x4 and tore off down the High Street towards Slough. The car was found abandoned with no sign of the bike.

Forensics were checked over the next two months. Just before Christmas I had a call about doing a victim statement. Intelligence had led them to the likely suspect.

But no sign of the bike.

Yet.

So where is it? Is it still in a lock-up somewhere? Has it been dumped in the river? Sold abroad? Or is it being ridden by some oblivious happy cyclist? We can speculate and here's my thought.

There are a number of people who know where that bike is. There is an extended group of associates of those who took it. My guess is that they now know what was achieved on that bicycle and how much it meant to all those who heard and connected with the story of my Camino. I'm patient. A lot more patient than I used to be. I'm waiting. There's still a substantial reward on offer for its return and it won't be a surprise when I get the call: 'You know that E-bike of yours . . .'

In the meantime, if someone is riding that bike, I hope they're reaching their potential. Perhaps it was picked up for a bargain at a car boot sale? Sold on for a fix? It would be a shame if it's been dumped in the river. I hope this magical Martin named Timmeee E-bike is continuing to give pleasure and opportunity to the next person.

After all, it's just a bike, and perhaps the easiest way to think of it is that it's someone else's turn.

In the six months I had the bike I cycled over 4,500 E-kilometres, mostly on my Camino, exploring, painting, living. I found that I like making the most of every day. I like meeting people and being absorbed in the moment. I love it when I see a great goal scored. I easily laugh when I know what's going to happen and then it does. I appreciate seeing someone make an effort . . . And I'm thrilled that a smile can make the day go better. I know it's not how far you go, and certainly not how fast . . . It's all about how much fun you have along the way. This is my journey, and so far I'd say that by and large it's been utterly brilliant. Good luck with your story and may you reach your potential.

Have a nice life! See you in heaven!

I'd like to thank St James the Apostle for handing me a little inspiration.

My deepest appreciation to all who offered support and encouragement, and to all those I met along the way who gave me a smile, a cuppa, a warm handshake or just a greeting. Thanks for being part of my adventure.

Buen Camino!

Copyright acknowledgements